I0114422

#METOO AND THE POLITICS OF TRANSNATIONAL FEMINISM

#MeToo and the Politics of Transnational Feminism

An Anthology

Edited by
Chaitanya Lakkimsetti *and* Vanita Reddy

NEW YORK UNIVERSITY PRESS
New York

NEW YORK UNIVERSITY PRESS
New York
www.nyupress.org

© 2025 by New York University
All rights reserved

Please contact the Library of Congress for Cataloging-in-Publication data.

ISBN: 9781479825653 (hardback)
ISBN: 9781479825691 (library ebook)
ISBN: 9781479825660 (consumer ebook)

This book is printed on acid-free paper, and its binding materials are chosen for strength and durability. We strive to use environmentally responsible suppliers and materials to the greatest extent possible in publishing our books.

The manufacturer's authorized representative in the EU for product safety is Mare Nostrum Group B.V., Mauritskade 21D, 1091 GC Amsterdam, The Netherlands. Email: gpsr@mare-nostrum.co.uk.

Manufactured in the United States of America

10 9 8 7 6 5 4 3 2 1

Also available as an ebook

CONTENTS

PART III: RECOGNIZING

Introduction

Routing #MeToo Through Transnational Feminist Thought

CHAITANYA LAKKIMSETTI AND VANITA REDDY

#MeToo is often represented as a social media campaign that generated unprecedented conversation around workplace sexual harassment and changed how we view survivors' testimonies and experiences. Indeed, #MeToo's unparalleled global reach makes it a particularly powerful social movement with which to contend. MeToo was founded by Black feminist activist Tarana Burke in 2006. The movement emerged out of Burke's Brooklyn-based organization Girls for Gender Equity, which worked with sexual assault survivors, mainly young women of color. MeToo's incarnation as a social media hashtag followed immediately after the publication of an October 5, 2017, *New York Times* article that named Hollywood producer Harvey Weinstein as the subject of multiple sexual assault violations spanning the last thirty years (Kantor and Twohey 2017). Immediately after the *New York Times* article, on October 15, 2017, Hollywood actress Alyssa Milano tweeted a request to her followers who have faced sexual violence to tweet "metoo" (Milano 2017). Milano's tweet went viral and was shared on Facebook more than twelve million times within twenty-four hours of her tweet. In Burke's formulation, MeToo was intended to make women and girls of color visible as sexual assault survivors and to facilitate collective healing. However, as a social media hashtag, #MeToo became associated primarily with workplace sexual harassment. Subsequently, #MeToo gained global visibility and emerged as a solidarity-building digital platform that amplified the voices of survivors.

As transnational feminist scholars who have been studying feminist social change for over two decades, we were excited to engage with #MeToo's virality. It offered us an occasion to invite feminist scholars to

1

dialogue about its intellectual and political exigencies. Despite the global uptick of the movement, there are very few feminist accounts of the transnational politics of #MeToo. Rather than frame #MeToo as a global feminist campaign that originated in the United States and spreads outward to the rest of the world, we frame it as a transnational feminist movement with uneven itineraries, goals, and outcomes. This volume takes a transnational and comparative feminist approach to #MeToo, focusing on the multiple ways that feminist activists have pushed the boundaries of what counts as politics, justice, solidarity, violence, precarity, and vulnerability. Our goals in this anthology are thus twofold. The first is to frame #MeToo as a transnational feminist movement that exceeds "the global." The second is to show how an engagement with #MeToo allows us to extend and sharpen the empirical, theoretical, and methodological parameters of transnational feminist thought.

MeToo in a Transnational Feminist Frame: Shared Discourse Versus Shared Experience

Even though the #MeToo movement was started in the United States, its global reach and impact are not assimilable to a Western model of gender justice. The contributions in this anthology demonstrate that MeToo's virality is not a simple celebration of a geographic "scaling up," that is, a socially progressive movement whose virality transcends geographic borders wholly intact and is impervious to local processes. Rather, it is a social movement that has provided us with the opportunity to "critically examine the very practice of scaling up" (Tambe and Thayer 2021, 14). This anthology thus builds on rich feminist scholarship that critically foregrounds the transnational over the global (Grewal and Kaplan 1994; Alexander and Mohanty 1997; Basu 2000; Desai 2005). Transnational feminism emerged in the 1990s in opposition to white second-wave feminists' emphasis on gender as a single axis of analysis and its universalizing discourse of global sisterhood. This was a discourse that elided complex locations and systems of oppression faced by women in the Global South as well as practices of oppositional politics that emerge from these particular locations (Herr 2014). The call for a transnational versus a global framing of feminist politics is a call not only to be attentive to new configurations of power and hegemonies in the context of global capitalism but also to reject a universal concept of patriarchy, which was the foundation of global feminisms (Grewal and Kaplan 1994).

Following transnational feminist genealogies that attend to the global asymmetries of power, we position #MeToo as a shared discourse rather than a shared experience. When conceived of as shared experience (such as in the much-critiqued global sisterhood model of feminist politics), "MeToo" risks naturalizing the category "woman" and binary gender more broadly within legal frameworks and within transnational civil society. As shared experience, "MeToo" thus risks being seen and heard as "I am like you," where the "you" is, however implicitly, the US-based, Anglo (cis-hetero) feminist subject. In contrast, we conceive of #MeToo as a shared discourse—as allowing for an uneven and heterogeneous feminist politics that is irreducible to a shared experience of sexually violable womanhood.

Conceiving of #MeToo as a shared discourse accounts for the way that feminist movements in the Global South have been grappling with sexual violence for several decades and calling for social, cultural, and legal transformations. For instance, feminist struggles against custodial rape galvanized the autonomous women's movement in India in the 1980s. Similarly, beginning in the 1990s, feminist activists in South Korea fought against forced sexual servitude in the context of Japanese colonization. And, more recently, feminist groups in Latin America have used campaigns such as *Ni Una Menos* to fight against femicides and broadened the understanding of gender-based violence to include lack of access to abortions. Hence, we are interested in documenting and understanding how #MeToo movements interact with, complement, or push against existing feminist politics in the countries where we see the uptick of the engagement with #MeToo. This means seriously engaging with how local power structures, institutions, and cultural practices shape normative expectations about how to conceive of and respond to gender-based violence and gender justice, as well as feminist resistance practices.

An emphasis on #MeToo as a shared discourse also allows us to center the politics of #MeToo in the Global South—Argentina, Egypt, India, Pakistan, South Korea (the UK and the US are exceptions to this Global South focus)—rather than rehearse a genealogy of it as a US-based social movement. Certainly, many of the essays in this volume seek to name Burke as MeToo's founder, to recenter Black feminisms, and to critique its glamorous white female celebrity mainstreaming in the United States. However, collectively, their primary focus is on how the heterogeneous and diffuse feminist politics of #MeToo as a transnational social movement transforms the very concepts that are so at risk of being universalized within a US-based genealogy of #MeToo and gender-based violence.

In contrast to the assimilative imperative of shared experience, #MeToo as shared discourse operates as what Michel Foucault (1998) calls "reactivation," or the way that discourse allows for the transformation of knowledge and power rather than their mere replication, which presumes discourse's pure form. By reactivation, Foucault means shifting attention away from questions of origin and authenticity and toward questions such as "What are the modes of existence of this discourse?" and "Where does it come from; how is it circulated; who controls it?" (1998, 222). A Foucauldian understanding of discourse as reactivation allows for the production of new feminist knowledge and practices.[1] This anthology's contribution to feminist knowledge is not merely to decenter the United States in mapping #MeToo's transnational trajectories but also to apprehend its reactivation—as polyvalence, disaggregation, contingency, and inflection point—within and across various national contexts.

In Hae Yeon Choo's essay, for example, the conceptualization of #MeToo as a shared discourse reveals its polyvalence rather than its homogeneity such that the very (linguistic) meaning of MeToo remains unstable and open to multiple translations that determine how gender-based violence is understood and contested. Similarly, disaggregation allows us to attend to the various social antagonisms that constitute the category "woman." For example, Sudeshna Chatterjee, in her contribution to this dossier, addresses the ways that "woman" is overdetermined not only by white Western gender binaries but also by divisions between formal and informal labor, such as sex work. Somewhat differently, Ayesha Khurshid's essay on embracing vulnerability as a spiritual practice decenters concepts of womanhood that are grounded in liberal secular understandings of the subject, such that women's empowerment can also exist beyond liberal notions of rights and state-based recognition. Likewise, the essays in this anthology by Landon Sadler and Barbara Sutton both point to contingencies in our understandings of political solidarities and political outcomes. First, they force a consideration of solidarity as a form of political relationality that one cannot know or name in advance. Sutton's work on Argentina discusses how #MeToo produces unlikely alliances among gossip television channels, actresses' associations, and feminist groups inciting support for abortion rights, which were already part of feminist conversations prior to #MeToo. Second, they point to the radical contingencies of legal and political outcomes of #MeToo (Lakkimsetti and Reddy, this volume; Cossman and Kapur, this volume). As Chaitanya Lakkimsetti and Vanita Reddy show, the legal recognition of sexual assault as violating the dignity of women in Indian journalist Priya Ramani's defamation case not only invokes the feminist language of rights but also draws on Hindu ideals of Indian womanhood. Feminists must thus reckon with the way that dignity as a concept can serve both feminist and conservative political ends. Finally, as an inflection point (Hannaford, this volume), #MeToo reveals political inequalities that remain hidden or obscured within transnational civil society. Dinah Hannaford's essay on developmental aid agencies discloses how gender violence is embedded within the very structure of these agencies, so that a decolonization of aid demands an intersectional critique of the structural violences that have remained underaddressed within aid work.

Transnational Feminist Forms

Transnational feminist movements are, of course, not new; nor are they merely outcomes of more recent digital activism. While transnational feminist movements have roots in nineteenth-century suffragist movements and in international socialist movements, the United Nations Women's Decade that started in 1975 and subsequent global women's conferences provided opportunities for the transnationalization of women's networks. The 1995 Beijing conference was crucial in establishing the feminist discourse of "women's rights as human rights." The much-cited Beijing conference followed the 1993 UN Declaration on the Elimination of Violence Against Women, which for the first time recognized violence against women as a human rights abuse. In doing so, it provided a common discourse that feminist groups could organize around and use to place political demands across the Global North and the Global South (Basu 2000, 73). This form of transnationalism, in which "women" are folded into the discourse of human rights, was seen as more effective in contexts where state repression is strong and "women's movements are weak" and as less effective in contexts where autonomous women's groups are strong and already fighting for their rights in local or national contexts (Basu 2000, 76). At the same time, as Manisha Desai (2005) observes, women's groups in places with histories of robust feminist movements, such as Africa, South Asia, and Latin America, nonetheless mobilized the discourse of women's rights as human rights in ways that emphasized localized understandings of human rights. As forms of "contingent universalism," these discourses are unassimilable to Western formulations of the human and to liberal notions of rights. If seen as a form of contingent universalism, the discourse of women's rights as human rights was an early iteration of what we have called *shared discourse.*

#MeToo as a shared discourse presents us with a new opportunity to conceive of transnationalism, this time within the realm of digital feminisms. While, as we have already mentioned, #MeToo emerged not as a digital movement but as a grassroots women of color feminist movement, its global reach was a direct result of its uptake as a social media hashtag.

Hashtag activisms can certainly produce new universal discourses around sexual violence and women's rights (Baer 2016). Hashtag activisms allow for increased visibility and diffuseness of the multidirectional flows, such as South to North and South to South, of feminist discourses. Though we remain attentive to the way that digital activism can and does traffic in a neoliberal politics of self-promotion, entrepreneurship, and self-motivation that can lead to an "undoing of feminism" (McRobbie 2009), we also attend to the possibilities for digital activism to decentralize feminist movements. Feminist media scholars have observed the way that digital feminist activism has enabled a shift away from rights-based discourses that rely upon the state as a guarantor of those rights to a feminist disaffection with the state and to more creative appeals for gender justice (Jackson and Welles 2015). Hashtag activism, according to feminist media scholars, constitutes a "paradigm shift in feminist protest culture" as it enables networked feminist counterpublics (Baer 2016, 18; Travers 2003; Jackson and Welles 2015).

We also recognize that digital feminisms such as #MeToo to some extent reinforce Amrita Basu's (2000, 82) argument that "transnational networks and activists seem to be most effective when the basis for mobilization is sexual victimization." However, as the chapters here demonstrate, #MeToo's virality cannot be reduced to a narrative of sexual *victimization*—even as it is a movement anchored in sexual *violence*. Even when narratives of victimization are central, they are equally productive of new ways of thinking about sexuality as a dense transfer point for relations of power, such as the way that sexual violence can produce new forms of sexual subjectivity as well as new political alliances and formations (Alcoff 2018).

Where earlier models of transnationalism may have been more likely to mobilize around sexual victimization in ways that assimilate and exceptionalize the victim of gendered violence, digital feminisms can reveal the banality of such forms of violence and the ways in which this banality intersects with other local feminist movements (Baer 2016). For example, #YesAllWomen trended in the United States in May 2014 after the mass shooting undertaken by a white man, Elliot Rodger, which resulted in six deaths. Rodger cited sexual rejection and hatred for women as the reasons for his rampage. This incident triggered a conversation around everyday sexism and misogyny as norms of US culture that in turn normalize gender-based violence. #YesAllWomen also drew connections between the prevalence of gender inequalities and gender-based violence, emphasizing that gender-based violence will be normalized as long as these inequalities, such as the gender wage gap and gender-based health disparities, exist (Jackson, Bailey, and Welles 2020). While these shooting deaths might have otherwise been framed as a result of an individual bad actor—a "sick" man—its social media uptake opened up a larger conversation about the normalization of misogyny and gender inequalities in US culture. #YesAllWomen was picked up and reclaimed by feminists in South Asia and Latin America and is often seen as a precursor to #MeToo (Banerjee and Kankaria 2022).

Other social media hashtags have also emerged out of a recognition of the cultural norm of gender-based violence as well as the need to highlight the intersectional nature of this violence. #FastTailedGirls (2013) and #YouOkSis (2014) have highlighted Black women's everyday lived experiences of hypersexualization and the cultural devaluation of

Black femininity. Similarly, #GirlsLikeUs (2012) forged online intimacies among transfeminine subjects who are disproportionately affected by gender-based violence. #WhyLoiter (2014) and #PinjraTod (2015) in India drew connections between women's exclusion from public spaces, their restricted mobility, and gender-based violence. Together, these hashtags produce a narrative not of exceptional gender-based violence but of the banality of such forms of violence.

In considering digital activisms as a new terrain for transnational feminist politics, we must also reckon with the uneven flows of social media technology, such as cell phones and other smart devices, through which such paradigm shifts emerge. Furthermore, hashtag activism can exclude marginalized women, such as those in rural and non-English-speaking regions or those belonging to marginalized castes, who might not have access to X (formerly Twitter) and other social media platforms. But that does not mean that marginalized women lack digital literacy or lack access to other digital platforms, such as WhatsApp. For example, Gloria González-López and Lydia Cordero Cabrera (2021) discuss how discarded cell phones from the United States are repurposed and recycled in Ciudad Juárez, Mexico. In the context of extreme gender violence that women face in this border city, cheaply available repurposed cell phones, flexible data plans, and no-cost access to social media apps such as WhatsApp have been crucial in promoting activism against gender-based violence. González-López and Cordero Cabrera caution us against a simplistic understanding of a rich-poor divide around access to media technologies. Representations of poor and marginalized groups as categorically not having access to social media reinforce a binary of "digital haves" and "digital have-nots." Instead, we ought to consider how state and market regulations result in these groups having more open access to certain media technologies and much more restricted access to others. Thus while earlier forms of transnationalism characterized the limitations of networked feminism as resulting from an uneven access to technology determined by class divides (Basu 2000), the limitations of digital activisms are now the result of a broader range of factors that have to do with availability of certain media technologies; state censorship of (social) media; the reality of backlash cultures that can and do work to undercut the feminist possibilities of digital activisms; and the introduction of new laws that adjudicate digital spaces, such as the

Prevention of Electronic Crimes Bill (2015) in Pakistan, that can also impact how survivors access social media and narrate their experiences of violence.

Extending Transnational Feminist Thought Through MeToo

We argue that as a form of social media feminism, #MeToo allows us to renew and expand existing transnational feminist frameworks, namely comparing, decentering, and recognizing. These frameworks yield new knowledge about gender-based violence, the changing nature of social movements, and the limitations and possibilities of digital media for inciting feminist social change. Some of the authors in this anthology use these frames to illuminate feminist goals and struggles, while others use them to challenge the conceptual foundations—such as gender, patriarchy, liberal rights, and secularism—on which politics itself is built in order to advance transnational feminist knowledge projects. Next, we expand on each of these frameworks by drawing out resonances, overlaps, and divergences among the essays that follow. We understand comparing, decentering, and recognizing more as heuristic tools for advancing connections among the essays than as discrete frameworks.

Comparing

While transnational feminist thought has implicitly engaged in projects of comparison, comparison has much less often been explicitly claimed as a framework of mapping configurations of power, diagnosing new hegemonies, and documenting and conceiving of new feminist practices of resistance both between and within nations.

Lakkimsetti and Reddy undertake a comparative analysis of the United States and India, the two countries where #MeToo emerged most strongly. We focus on two concurrent events that took place between 2017 and 2018: the resignation of M. J. Akbar from Narendra Modi's cabinet due to allegations of sexual harassment by journalist Priya Ramani, and the Supreme Court confirmation of Brett Kavanaugh despite Christine Blasey Ford's allegations of sexual assault. Through our comparative approach, we find that "patriarchal protectionism" and "toxic masculinity" are the main frames through which these debates are approached in India and the United States, respectively. Both these frames miss important institutional and intersectional analyses of gender-based violence. In the United States, the deployment of "toxic masculinity" reduces gender to an identity rooted in individual choice rather than a social process entrenched in patriarchal structures. In India, an emphasis on patriarchal protectionism frames the solution to workplace sexual violence as a matter of increased state protection of women. We suggest an expansive understanding of patriarchy not as a universal structure of male power and privilege, but as itself an uneven form of gender management across the Global North and South. By expanding understandings of patriarchy to include the regulation of gender, we challenge both teleological and essentialized narratives of gender-based violence. We emphasize the differing legal outcomes of these two high-profile cases: Ramani won a criminal defamation suit that Akbar filed against her while Blasey Ford's serious allegations of sexual violence had no impact on Kavanaugh's confirmation as a Supreme Court justice. Ramani's case resulted in a resounding victory for the Indian #MeToo movement as the court affirmed the dignity of survivors of sexual violence, while Kavanaugh's confirmation as a Supreme Court justice was a major setback for the US #MeToo movement because it failed to dignify Blasey Ford's testimony. Furthermore, Kavanaugh's role as a Supreme Court justice in the *Dobbs v. Jackson Women's Health Organization* ruling that overturned *Roe v. Wade* and denied federal protections for abortion access reveals the need for an institutionalized critique of patriarchy in which Kavanaugh's confirmation and the *Dobbs* decision are connected forms of gender-based violence rooted in the denial of women's bodily autonomy. These starkly different legal outcomes trouble the temporality of the United States as gender progressive and the essentialization of India as gender regressive in mainstream and developmentalist discourses.

While Lakkimsetti and Reddy focus on India and the United States as their project of comparison, Brenda Cossman and Ratna Kapur take up the particular issue of defamation charges and counter charges leveled against prominent women who spoke up against their abusers in Pakistan, India, and the United States: Meesha Shafi, Priya Ramani, and Amber Heard, respectively. These cases challenge what constitutes legitimate speech and expand the boundaries of speech for sexual assault survivors both within courtrooms and beyond, especially in social media. Ramani's defamation case was dismissed; Shafi was able to file a constitutional challenge against defamation law; and Heard lost her defamation case. Despite these uneven legal gains, Cossman and Kapur argue that defamation charges do not always lead to silencing and censorship; they can also be productive of speech. Shafi's case, for example, provided momentum for the Aurut Marches (Women's Marches), leading to public discussion around women's bodies and rights.

Comparative approaches help us to understand how contestations around defamation across national boundaries not only produce speech, but also help to decenter the US #MeToo movement as the default or implicit referent for feminist gains. Ramani and Shafi were able to achieve some legal recognition through their struggles, but Heard could not. As Cossman and Kapur point out, these disparate outcomes can be attributed to the differences between criminal defamation charges (India and Pakistan) and civil defamation charges (US), where different evidentiary practices are deployed. Yet, it is worth asking whether high-profile survivors like Shafi and Ramani received more public support in India and Pakistan than Heard did in the United States.

Like Kavanaugh's confirmation hearings, Heard's case also allows us to see how #MeToo US must contend with a "post-feminist" context that is also "post-patriarchy." It is precisely since the United States is seen as gender progressive that patriarchy seems an unlikely concept through which to engage gender-based violence—it is understood as rearguard and even obsolete because of its association with second-wave feminist concerns with women's access to the workplace and reproductive rights. In contrast, in the Indian and Pakistani cases, where patriarchy as a discourse is entrenched in state and international developmentalist projects, the deployment of patriarchal protectionism ironically results in measurable legal gains as well as mass mobilization in support of survivors.

Lakkimsetti, Reddy, Cossman, and Kapur focus on comparisons across nations. Following other transnational feminist scholars, however, we must also prioritize the national and local within transnational feminist thought (Herr 2014; Lukose 2018; Tambe and Thayer 2021). In this anthology, Zeina Dowidar and Nadeen Shaker's essay performs a comparative analysis of two legal cases of sexual harassment that have served as "anchors" for Egypt's #MeToo movement: the ABZ case (centered on the rape of a university student) and the Fairmont case (centered on a gang rape of a woman from an elite background at an upper-class party). Each case's different mobilizations of *ird*—discourses of sexual morality that tie family honor to women's sexuality—led to two very different legal outcomes. In the ABZ case, the perpetrator was convicted because survivors were seen as sexually innocent "daughters" of the Egyptian state and as in need of paternalistic protectionism. Moreover, this case also led to the passing of an anonymity law that protected survivors' identities when they legally came forward. In contrast, in the Fairmont case, the perpetrators were exonerated because of their elite class status, whereas the victim's attendance at what was perceived as an erotically charged party among elites cast her as sexually immoral.

The outcomes in the Egyptian cases reveal that class has a temporal dimension: elite women who are perceived as sexually promiscuous are seen as adjacent to the "modernity" of the West such that they are outside the "moral time" of the nation and, therefore, outside its protection. In contrast, the university students, who are perceived as sexually innocent, are folded into the moral time of the nation such that it facilitates their inclusion within patriarchal protectionism. Shaker and Dowidar's comparative analysis follows in the transnational feminist tradition of marking the nation as a gendered and classed formation.

Decentering

As the previous section begins to argue, the project of comparison is one that results in the decentering of dominant knowledge about gender, patriarchy, class, and legitimate speech. We see the set of essays in this section as continuing the project of decentering in ways that both include and exceed the decentering of the United States as the epicenter of #MeToo. Collectively, we conceive of decentering as a framework that also demands an engagement with geographic and temporal heterogeneity (Tambe); linguistic polyvalence (Choo); and hemispheric approaches to feminist solidarity (Sutton).

Ashwini Tambe provides us with an analytical framework to understand the geographic and temporal scope of #MeToo. First, she implores us not to celebrate or diminish #MeToo's impact. Instead, she draws on

Nancy Hewitt's ideas of long and short waves to understand its impact and scope. In radio wave theory, short waves travel longer distances but remain fuzzy in their content, while long waves travel shorter distances but contain clearer and sharper content. In this framework, the pithy and unspecific messaging that inheres in the hashtag form "#MeToo" makes it amenable to its transnational reach as a short wave; and these short-wave forms of #MeToo interact with the long waves of existing local struggles and conversations around sexual violence. Tambe's extension of Hewitt's wave framework allows us to conceive of #MeToo's heterogeneity as deeply intertwined with conversations that are concentrated, dense, and specific, rather than as replacing or subsuming past, present, or future struggles around sexual violence in specific locales.

Hae Yeon Choo's contribution exemplifies the short- and long-wave framework that Tambe proposes. In South Korea, "MeToo" coalesces not as "I, too, am a victim" but rather as "I, too, accuse" or "I, too, speak out." Choo discusses how the ambiguity and looseness of the meaning of the phrase "MeToo" lends itself to its different uses, hence its polyvalence. Choo shows how in South Korea, the translation of "MeToo" as "I too accuse" or "I too speak out" is rooted in South Korean feminist genealogies of speaking out against military sexual violence during Japanese colonial rule. The South Korean emphasis on speaking out in public has a different meaning and sensibility than Milano's formulation of #MeToo as standing in solidarity with individual victims of sexual violence. Focusing on the 2018 legal case of Seo Ji-hyun (a public prosecutor who leveled sexual harassment allegations against the prominent law firm Korean Prosecution Service), Choo shows how the rallying cry of "I too accuse" directed attention toward sexual violence in power-laden relationships and allowed for an institutional critique of patriarchal workplaces.

Similar to Choo's analysis of "I too accuse," Barbara Sutton's contribution examines how the collective Actrices Argentinas (Argentine Actresses) challenged the sexist claim "look what you do to me," a phrase actor Juan Darthés reportedly told actress Themla Fardin as he sexually assaulted her. They coined the phrase "look how we get," which refers to the capacity for actresses to pull together and organize against gender-based violence, as a show of collective solidarity and agency. The collective politics of "look how we get," Sutton argues, is rooted in collaborations among Latin American feminists as well as past and present Argentinian feminist struggles, both of which broadened conceptions of gender-based violence. Sutton thus takes a hemispheric viewpoint that counters the North-to-South flow of feminist movements and emphasizes South-to-South and even South-to-North flows. Specifically, she references feminist *encuentros*, or Latin American and Caribbean feminist meetings that were challenging various forms of state-based violence—from state violence under military rule to the lack of abortion access in the region—that have been taking place since 1981. Most recently, in 2015, the killing of fourteen-year-old Chiara Páez by her boyfriend reinvigorated struggles against femicide under the banner *#NiUnaMenos* (not one less woman). *#NiUnaMenos* (*NUM*) found resonance across Latin America and drew connections among the devaluation of women's lives, labor, and bodies in order to confront intertwined injustices of workplace harassment, femicide, and lack of access to abortion (through the Green Tide movement). This robust and geographically widespread understanding of gender-based violence preceded #MeToo in Argentina, and thus, as Sutton argues, forces us to shift our attention away from the "impact" of #MeToo and toward how #MeToo "interacts" with entrenched feminist practices and movements.

Whereas in the United States, #MeToo focused on sexual violence in the workplace, in Argentina, #MeToo provided an unlikely opportunity for actresses and activists to come together to speak about abortion. In this way, #MeToo Argentina popularized a lack of abortion access as a form of gender violence by bringing mainstream media attention to it. As we, too, observe in our contribution, a lack of attention to state patriarchies is precisely what prevents #MeToo in the United States from making connections between abortion access and sexual violence. Centering the Green Tide movement and legal gains for abortion access in Argentina and other parts of Latin America means emphasizing South-North flows rather than the dominance of North-South flows.

Recognizing

If decentering draws attention to polyvalence, hemispheric approaches, and minor transnationalisms, this section, on recognizing, considers the place of marginalized feminist political frames and minoritized subjects within transnational approaches to #MeToo. Dinah Hannaford's essay draws attention to the #AidToo movement to highlight the sexual exploitation of the most precarious workers within the aid industry as well as the recipients of aid. Both Sudeshna Chatterjee and Landon Sadler examine how the legal binaries of consent and coercion and victim and perpetrator relegate minoritized subjects such as sex workers and nonwhite subjects to the margins of #MeToo. And finally, Ayesha Khurshid draws attention to spirituality and nonsecular activism that is often not recognized within the mainstream #MeToo movement.

Hannaford demonstrates that #MeToo lent momentum to publicizing the pervasiveness of sexual exploitation within the transnational aid industry. These practices include sexual assault against female aid workers; the exchange of sex for aid; the subjection of women and nonbinary workers to harassment and mistreatment; and the mishandling of reports of sexual abuse. While the aid industry has acknowledged that these practices need to change, such realization, as Hannaford argues, did not lead to any systemic changes. Aid workers worried that reporting such incidents could potentially result in conservative backlash and reduced funding for development work. #MeToo, however, invigorated a discussion on sexual abuse in the aid industry, with the publication of a front-page article in the *Times of London* in 2018 that detailed abuses perpetrated by employees of Oxfam (a leading international charity) during their earthquake relief work in Haiti in 2011. Hannaford argues that by giving power to individuals who wanted to report the "poorly kept secret of aid agencies," #MeToo became an important reckoning moment for the aid industry.

At the same time, Hannaford highlights the limitations of humanitarian projects such as aid work, in which aid workers are understood as benevolent moral agents bringing much-needed relief and support to subjects in the Global South. The framing of aid work as a transnational moral project contributes to aid agencies' complicity with sexual misconduct. Drawing on María Lugones's concept of the coloniality of gender—in which the sex/gender binary is deployed as a way to discipline and manage racialized subjects under colonialism—Hannaford brings attention to the coloniality of aid. The coloniality of aid refers both to the colonial histories of development work and the absence of an intersectional analysis of race, patriarchy, and colonialism that aids and abets violence against aid workers and recipients. Hannaford argues that as long as we view aid work as a "benign force for good," aid organizations can remain exculpable from sexual predation. Hannaford calls for us to decolonize #MeToo, which would involve recognizing gender violence as integral to past and present colonial projects such as aid work. By calling out the colonial and racialized foundations of aid work, Hannaford's essay demands vigilance around the purported benevolence of other humanitarian projects. Thus, the project of decolonizing #MeToo moves us away from individual grievances of sexual violation (as in the US #MeToo movement) to an emphasis on institutional and collective violence.

Chatterjee's focus on Indian sex workers further reveals how global anti-trafficking discourses, another striking example of benevolent humanitarianism, often conflate sex trafficking and sex work, resulting in a lack of recognition of consenting adult sex workers as deserving fuller rights as workers. The legal precarity that sex workers experience through complete or partial criminalization of their occupations prevents them from reporting sexual harassment for fear of police retaliation and violence. The precarity of sex workers from countries in the Global South like India, whom Chatterjee centers in her essay, is further compounded by anti-trafficking discourses that view non-Western sex workers as quintessential victims who cannot consent to sex as work. When seen as victims of trafficking, sex workers are seen as needing to be rescued and rehabilitated. This is in contrast to sex workers who are viewed to have freely "chosen" and consented to sex work, and therefore as not in need of legal or social protections. The binaries of sex and work and consent and coercion further marginalize sex workers and preclude the possibility of addressing coercion within transactional sex (Tambe 2018; Lakkimsetti 2021). As Chatterjee asserts, as long as sex workers are placed in socially and legally precarious positions, #MeToo cannot claim to be a movement that represents all survivors. Indian sex workers were able to gain the status of informal workers during the pandemic, which allowed them to receive welfare support from the state. However, their legal recognition as informal workers sits uneasily with anti-trafficking discourse, which refuses to recognize sex workers as laboring subjects.[2] The recognition of sex work as legitimate work and of transactional sex as containing both coercive and consensual elements is essential to amplifying the voices and experiences of sex workers within transnational feminist discourses.

Sex workers' experiences of transactional sex show us how work is saturated with sex, rather than "liberated" from it. In this way, sex workers force us to be critical of #MeToo's overemphasis on desexualizing the workplace as the solution to workplace gender-based violence.

Chatterjee's work also helps us to contend with how #MeToo's normative framing of victimhood, whether explicitly or implicitly, is shaped by respectability politics. Respectability politics shapes the ways that sexual and racial minorities are seen as sexually inviolable within both legal and cultural discourses. Indeed, what Shireen Roshanravan (2021) calls the "white feminist detours" of #MeToo detract from MeToo's foundation in Black feminist Tarana Burke's call to center Black women's experiences of routinized sexual violence. For example, the erasure of Black women's experiences within US #MeToo attests to the way that a politics of (sexual) respectability has historically positioned Black women as sexually deviant and failed to recognize them as requiring legal and social protection (Cohen 1997). In lacking an explicit intersectional politics, #MeToo elides an accounting of race in its very conception of sexual violence. Indeed, as Black feminist scholars remind us, rape when directed at Black women is also a form a "racial terror" (Crenshaw 1991).

Heeding this call, Sadler's contribution to this anthology brings racial and sexual minorities into #MeToo's orbit by focusing on cultural representations of Black British immigrants. He analyzes the television show *I May Destroy You* (*IMDY*) as both participating in and challenging the narrative conventions of the consent drama genre, also called "MeToo television." Rather than centering a white cis woman as the universal victim of sexual violence, as is common in consent dramas, *IMDY* centers the Black British Ghanian protagonist Arabella Essiedu's experience of and struggle to recall a drug-induced rape. Her memory of the event unfolds through her interactions with other characters in the show. These characters' own experiences of sexual violence do not fit neatly into the consent drama rape narrative. In addition, in contrast to a binary notion of consent, consent in *IMDY* emerges as what Sadler calls a "constellation." By *constellation*, Sadler refers to the way that power operates in dynamic and shifting ways so that a person can be both victim and perpetrator. Indeed, Kwame, a cisgendered queer man and Arabella's close friend, contends with his own possible sexual violation during a casual sexual encounter with a Black gay man and with whether his lack of transparency about his own sexuality violates consent during sex with a cisgender woman. *IMDY* thus reveals the limitations of legal categories of consent.

Sadler's discussion of *IMDY* also moves us beyond a model of legal redressal of sexual violence and toward individual and collective healing fostered through Arabella's cultivation of an intersectional consciousness. Before she is raped, she thinks of herself primarily as a racialized subject. However, she begins to understand her intersectional identity as a Black woman when she recognizes how histories of racism and colonialism render her Black body as always already violable. Sadler's analysis of the show reveals how healing is not merely limited to neoliberal therapeutic models. Rather, healing is inextricably connected to recognizing one's injury as tied to past and present forms of racialized and gendered violence.

In order to realize the radical potential of #MeToo, it is necessary to cleave healing from its roots in liberal practices. Khurshid draws on Indigenous and women of color feminisms to theorize past the (liberal) secular self in Pakistani singer Meesha Shafi's feminist response to sexual violence in Pakistan. Shafi's name became synonymous with #MeToo Pakistan when she spoke publicly about her experience of sexual violence and because of the ongoing litigation she is pursuing against her abuser, Ali Zafar. Shafi's is a landmark case in that, to date, it is the first case in Pakistan, and one of only a few, in which a public figure accused another public figure of sexual harassment in a public forum. Through her legal activism, Shafi was able to bring attention to a Pakistani law that prevented harassment against women in the workplace but remains vague about definitions of the "workplace." Her case catalyzed the first Aurat March in 2018, and since then, these marches have grown and become an important platform for generating awareness around gender-based violence. While Shafi's role in #MeToo Pakistan has been highlighted by Pakistani feminists, Khurshid argues that the role of her music in her activism has not been recognized and claimed by the feminist movement, even as her spiritual music engages with important feminist issues such as vulnerability, empowerment, and healing. Khurshid shows how Shafi's musical album "Na Tuttaya Ve" takes up feminist thought on vulnerability not as an obstacle to be overcome, but as a condition of possibility for collective healing and empowerment.

Employing Black and Indigenous feminist frameworks, particularly those of Audre Lorde and Gloria Anzaldúa, Khurshid observes that the failure to recognize her music is tied to the separation of Shafi's work into two separate realms—political and spiritual. This political-spiritual split is the result of the colonization of knowledge and the resulting "epistemic violence" that obliterates nonsecular ways of being and knowing. Khurshid's essay is a call to center a decolonial feminist engagement with the spiritual in order to bring about epistemic shifts within transnational feminist thought around concepts such as vulnerability, power, and healing.

Radical Possibilities of Shared Discourse

Together, these chapters demonstrate the usefulness of framing #MeToo as a shared discourse rather than a shared experience. Indeed, it is through an understanding of #MeToo's transnational trajectories as polyvalence, disaggregation, contingency, and inflection point that we shift focus away from #MeToo as shared experience, one in which the movement's elision of and erasure of certain "experiences" would make "the entire movement worthy of condemnation" (Tambe 2021, 356). Rather, our framing of #MeToo as a shared discourse forces a consideration of this social movement's heterogeneity, thus pointing to it as an unfinished political project and, concomitantly, as generating a feminist politics we cannot know or name in advance. In addition, while our focus has been on the #MeToo movement, our framework of shared discourse can be applied broadly to other global feminist movements as well. For example, how might past and present global feminist movements such as Slut Walk, Vagina Monologues, Take Back the Night Campaigns, and #YesAllWomen benefit from the shared discourse framework? Might we look (back) to these movements through the framework of shared discourse not (merely) as universalizing the social identity "woman" or appealing to liberal concepts of "freedom," but rather as pointing to the limits of these very identities and concepts through their radical instabilities and contingencies? Pushing this question even further, might shared discourse offer up the possibility of moving beyond the universal-particular binarisms that have plagued liberal humanist thought, including but not limited to human rights frameworks?

Finally, globally, gender-based human rights are under attack not only because of the ongoing assault on reproductive rights but also because of the rise of right-wing nationalisms that are eroding the gains of feminist movements across the globe. Therefore, it is imperative for feminist scholars to develop frameworks—such as shared discourse—that focus simultaneously on affiliative, uneven, and contingent solidarities. Shared discourse can, we believe, wrench us away from the allure of feeling good in our politics, whether that good feeling is rooted in a feminist righteousness in solving global problems by trafficking in unchecked universalisms or whether it is rooted in our insistence on the particularities of our struggles. Such an allure prevents us both from imagining and creating the political solidarities necessary to challenge global inequities.

NOTES

1 See Butler 1990; Grewal and Kaplan 1994; Brown 1995; Puar 2007.

2 Most recently, the same Supreme Court that recognized sex work as informal work amended its handbook to substitute the term "sex worker" with "trafficked survivor," "women engaged in commercial sexual activity," and "woman forced into commercial sexual exploitation." This was a result of advocacy anti-trafficking groups that frame sex work as force and fraud.

REFERENCES

Alexander, Jacqui, and Chandra Talpade Mohanty, eds. 1997. *Feminist Genealogies, Colonial Legacies, Democratic Futures.* New York: Routledge.

Alcoff, Linda. 2018. *Rape and Resistance.* Hoboken, NJ: John Wiley & Sons.

Baer, Hester. 2016. "Redoing Feminism: Digital Activism, Body Politics, and Neoliberalism." *Feminist Media Studies* 16 (1): 17–34.

Banerjee, Sutanuka, and Lipika Kankaria. 2022. "Networking Voices against Violence: Online Activism and Transnational Feminism in Local-Global Contexts." *Wagadu: A Journal of Transnational Women's & Gender Studies* 24 (1): 81–97.

Basu, Amrita. 2000. "Globalization of the Local/Localization of the Global Mapping Transnational Women's Movements." *Meridians* 1 (1): 68–84. https://doi.org/10.1215/15366936-1.1.68.

Brown, Wendy. 1995. *States of Injury: Power and Freedom in Late Modernity.* Princeton, NJ: Princeton University Press.

Butler, Judith. 1990. *Gender Trouble.* New York: Routledge.

Chakrabarty, Dipesh. 1992. "Provincializing Europe: Postcoloniality and the Critique of History." *Cultural Studies* 6 (3): 337–57.

Cohen, Cathy. 1997. "Punks, Bulldaggers and Welfare Queens: The Radical Potential of Queer Politics?" *GLQ* 3 (4): 437–65.

Crenshaw, Kimberlé. 1991. "Mapping the Margins: Intersectionality, Identity Politics, and Violence against Women of Color." *Stanford Law Review* 43 (6): 1,241–99.

Desai, Manisha. 2005. "Transnationalism: The Face of Feminist Politics Post-Beijing." *International Social Science Journal* 57 (2): 319–30. https://doi.org/10.1111/j.1468-2451.2005.553.x.

Foucault, Michel. 1998. "What Is an Author?" *Aesthetics, Method, and Epistemology*. Edited by James D. Faubion. Translated by Robert Hurley et al. New York: New Press.

Garibotti, María Cecilia, and Cecilia Marcela Hopp. 2019. "Substitution Activism: The Impact of #MeToo in Argentina." In *#MeToo and the Politics of Social Change*, edited by Bianca Fileborn and Rachel Loney-Howes, 185–200. London: Palgrave Macmillan.

Gilson, Erinn Cuniff. 2016. "Vulnerability and Victimization: Rethinking Key Concepts in Feminist Discourses on Sexual Violence." *Signs* 42 (1): 71–98.

González-López, Gloria, and Lydia Cordero Cabrera. 2021. "The Borders of #MeToo: A Conversation about Sexual Violence Against Women in Ciudad Juárez." *Feminist Formations* 33 (3): 333–50.

Grewal, Inderpal, and Caren Kaplan, eds. 1994. *Scattered Hegemonies: Postmodernity and Transnational Feminist Practices*. Minneapolis: University of Minnesota Press.

Herr, Ranjoo. 2014. "Reclaiming Third World Feminism: or Why Transnational Feminism Needs Third World Feminism." *Meridians* 12 (1): 1–30.

Jackson, Sarah J., and Brooke Foucault Welles. 2015. "Hijacking #myNYPD: Social Media Dissent and Networked Counterpublics." *Journal of Communication* 65 (6): 932–35.

Jackson, Sarah J., Moya Bailey, and Brooke Foucault Welles. 2020. *#HasthtagActivism: Networks of Race and Gender Justice*. Cambridge, MA: MIT Press.

Lakkimsetti, Chaitanya. 2021. "Stripping Away at Respectability: #MeToo India and the Politics of Dignity." *Feminist Formations* 33 (3): 303–17.

Lukose, Ritty. 2018. "Decolonizing Feminism in the #MeToo Era." *Cambridge Journal of Anthropology* 36 (2): 34–52.

McRobbie, Angela. 2009. "Post-Feminism and Popular Culture." In *Media and Cultural Theory*, edited by James Curran and David Morley, 350–61. London: Routledge.

Mohan, Megha. 2020. "Coronavirus: Domestic Violence 'Increases Globally during Lockdown.'" *BBC News*, June 12, 2020. www.bbc.com.

Milano, Alyssa. 2017. "If You've Been Sexually Harassed or Assaulted, Write 'Me Too' as a Reply to this Tweet." Twitter, October 15, 2017. https://twitter.com/Alyssa_Milano/status/919659438700202496.

Puar, Jasbir. 2007. *Terrorist Assemblages: Homonationalism in Queer Times*. Durham, NC: Duke University Press.

Kantor, Jodi and Megan Twohey. 2017. "Harvey Weinstein Paid Off Sexual Harassment Accusers for Decades." *New York Times*, October 5, 2017. www.nytimes.com.

Kim, H., and Jyoti Puri. 2005. "Conceptualizing Gender-Sexuality-State-Nation: An Introduction." *Gender & Society* 19 (2): 137–59.

Roshanravan, Shireen. 2021. "On the Limits of Globalizing Black Feminist Commitments: 'Me Too' and Its White Detours." *Feminist Formations* 33 (3): 239–55.

Rubin, Gayle. 2002. "Thinking Sex: Notes for a Radical Theory of the Politics of Sexuality." In *Culture, Society, and Sexuality*, edited by Parker, Richard Guy, and Peter Aggleton, 143–78. New York: Routledge.

Tambe, Ashwini. 2018. "Reckoning with the Silences of #MeToo." *Feminist Studies* 44 (1): 197–202.

———. 2021. "Afterword: Walking Alongside Many #MeToos." *Feminist Formations* 33 (3): 351–59.

Tambe, Ashwini, and Millie Thayer, eds. 2021. *Transnational Feminist Itineraries: Situating Theory and Activist Practice*. Durham, NC: Duke University Press.

Travers, Ann. 2003. "Parallel Subaltern Feminist Counterpublics in Cyberspace." *Sociological Perspectives* 46 (2): 223–37.

PART I

Comparing

1

Patriarchal Protectionism, Toxic Masculinity, and #MeToo

A Comparative Feminist Analysis of Gender-Based Violence in India and the United States

CHAITANYA LAKKIMSETTI AND VANITA REDDY

Introduction

This chapter focuses on two concurrent high-profile cases involving top-ranking US and Indian state officials charged with sexual misconduct in the era of #MeToo: the Senate confirmation hearings of US Supreme Court nominee (now justice) Brett Kavanaugh and the resignation of Indian minister of state for external affairs M. J. Akbar. These cases serve as a useful starting point for a comparative transnational feminist analysis of the #MeToo movement in India and the United States.

We argue that whereas patriarchy remains a powerful explanatory framework of sexual violence in the Akbar case, gender becomes a much more salient framework in the Kavanaugh case. While patriarchy and gender are not mutually exclusive social formations, we distinguish between them in the media coverage of these cases. In India, feminine vulnerability in state institutions, the workplace, and familial patriarchal codes of conduct remain important sites of feminist critique in the #MeToo era. This is distinct from the way gender performance and toxic masculinity—such as in the focus on rape culture, masculine aggression, and bro culture—have emerged in recent years as politically exigent sites of feminist critique in the United States. Our analysis reveals that insufficient attention to social constructions of masculinities in the Indian case, and patriarchy (as structuring relations of gender) in the US case results in a reductive understanding of the machinations of gender-based violence. We conclude by observing that a concern with women's victimization and vulnerability in the Indian case precludes a more sustained discussion of masculine gender norms, while a concern with toxic masculinity in the US case precludes a more sustained discussion of patriarchal institutions such as the family, the workplace, and the state.

Transnational feminist scholars have argued for the need to decenter the US origins of the #MeToo movement and to situate its various itineraries and its place within longer histories of local feminist movements (Tambe 2018, 2021; Choo 2021). We add to this important body of transnational feminist scholarship by calling attention to the persistent discursive framings of sexual violence in order to trouble both teleological understandings of gender progress and essentialized understandings of gender-based violence. Here we are interested in how gender and patriarchy, respectively, circulate as explanatory frameworks for gender-based violence, with gender being seen as a progressive framework and patriarchy as one that is a rearguard and often associated with the Global South. We ask why, in India, patriarchy is the primary optic through which gender-based violence is apprehended and analyzed, while it remains woefully absent in the way gender-based violence is addressed in the United States. We argue that the deployment of a narrow definition of patriarchy and an inattention to gender in India and feminist nonrecognition of patriarchy as a system of violence in the United States limit the transformative potential of #MeToo as a transnational social movement. While gender has been usefully deployed to de-essentialize patriarchy as a singular, universal structure of power (West and Zimmerman 1987; Butler 1990), liberal feminist discourses have also reduced gender to individual performances of identity that fail to consider the larger structures of power that condition such performances in the first place. In other words, a focus on gender (as performance) holds sexism, rather than patriarchy, responsible for gender discrimination and violence, where sexism is understood as individual behavior. Eliding patriarchy in favor of gender as an explanatory framework for gender-based violence not only individualizes violence but has geopolitical implications such that patriarchy's explanatory power is reduced to a "pre-feminist" past and a non-Western elsewhere.

Instead of using patriarchy merely to name a system that naturalizes male dominance and maintains and upholds gender inequality, we draw on postcolonial and Indigenous feminist reexaminations of patriarchy as a concept that reaches beyond familial and social structures to address state and imperialist racialized projects. Such an understanding helps us conceive of patriarchy not just as a kinship structure particular to the "unmodern" Global South but as the structure for the state management of gender across the Global North and South. The concept of patriarchy as an explanatory—or missing—discourse of gender-based violence can make intelligible intersectional relations of power that might otherwise remain obscured.

#MeToo in India and the United States

While #MeToo began as a smaller scale, grassroots movement in both India and the United States, it garnered mainstream attention when actresses in the Bollywood and Hollywood film industries, respectively, came forward with sexual assault charges. In the United States, MeToo was founded by Tarana Burke in 2006 to empower young women of color who were sexual assault survivors. #MeToo's popularity as a social media hashtag followed immediately after the publication of an October 5, 2017, *New York Times* article that named Hollywood producer Harvey Weinstein as the subject of multiple sexual assault violations spanning thirty years. The cases against Weinstein continues to garner public and media attention (including his most recent conviction of rape in December 2022). Meanwhile, another high-profile case involving a US government official played out in public media. Christine Blasey Ford, a California psychologist and professor, accused then Supreme Court nominee Brett Kavanaugh of sexual assault thirty-six years prior, when both Ford and Kavanaugh were attending Georgetown Preparatory School as high school students. The hearings became a public media spectacle that some media outlets called a landmark event for sexual assault survivors in that Ford was praised for her courage in relaying the traumatic details of the assault in front of the Senate and in a live tele-vised broadcast to the nation and for the way her testimony prompted numerous women to come forward with their own sexual assault sto-ries on social media (Edwards 2018). Ford's emotional testimony and the Senate Judiciary Committee's ruling in favor of Kavanaugh evoked memories of an eerily similar case nearly thirty years prior: in 1991, law professor Anita Hill accused then US Supreme Court nominee Clarence Thomas of sexual assault, and the committee ruled in Thomas's favor. Despite Ford's compelling testimony against him, Kavanaugh's nomination was confirmed, due in large part to overwhelming partisan support for his confirmation by Republican lawmakers. Kavanaugh's appointment to the Supreme Court as a conservative justice heightened feminist concerns around the role he would play in the legal battles over abortion access. These concerns were confirmed when Kavanaugh ruled in favor of *Dobbs v. Jackson Women's Health Organization* on June 24, 2022, which overturned the landmark 1973 *Roe v. Wade* decision that granted women access to abortion.

The origins of #MeToo in India can be traced to Raya Sarkar, a US-based Dalit Indian academic who published a crowdsourced list of alleged sexual predators in Indian universities on October 24, 2017. Similar to Tarana Burke's erasure as the originator of the #MeToo movement in the US mainstream media, Sarkar's role in the creation of #MeToo India is often forgotten, and this forgetting further obscures the specifically Dalit feminist origins of the movement. #MeToo caught on in the Indian mainstream in September 2018 when Tanushree Dutta, a young Bollywood actress, spoke openly in Indian media about the molestation and intimidation she faced from a prominent senior Bollywood actor, Nana Patekar, during a film shoot in 2008. Subsequently, the hashtag spread to other arenas including journalism and politics when journalist Priya Ramani named Bharatiya Janata Party (BJP) minister M. J. Akbar as her abuser on October 8, 2018, reporting that the incident occurred twenty-five years prior when she was interviewing for a journalist position for the *Asian Age* newspaper where Akbar was serving as the editor in chief. On October 15, 2018, Akbar filed a criminal defamation lawsuit against Ramani and resigned his post two days later. In February 2021, a New Delhi District Court ruled against Akbar's criminal defamation charge, and the Indian media celebrated the ruling as a major victory for #MeToo and as an important precedent for legitimizing the voices of sexual assault survivors. The court emphatically argued that "the woman cannot be punished for raising voice against the sex-abuse on the pretext of criminal complaint of defamation as the right to reputation

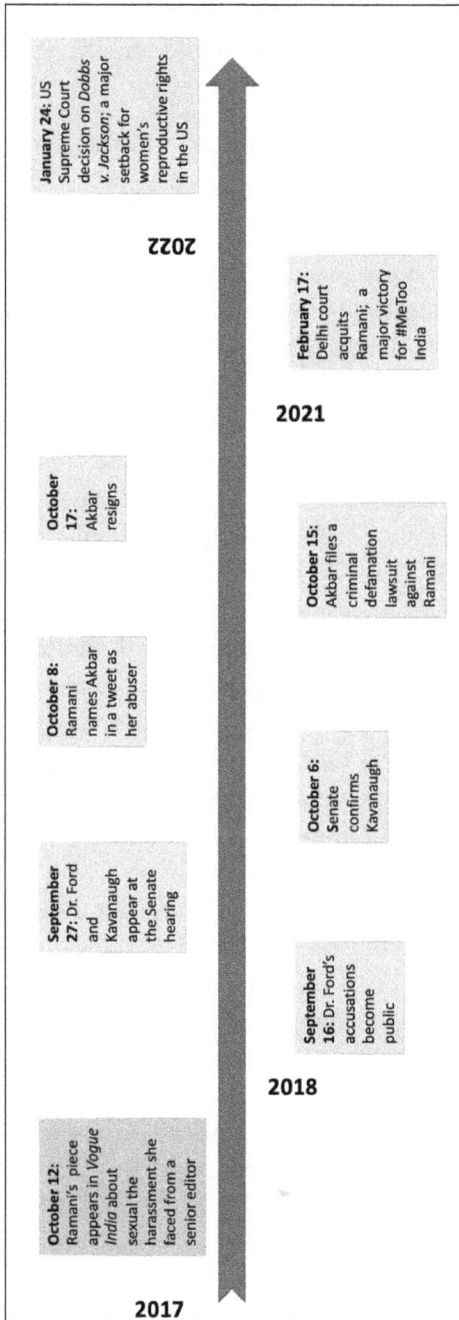

Figure 1.1 Timeline of Major Events in Kavanaugh's and Akbar's Cases

cannot be protected at the cost of the right of life and dignity of woman" (*Mobashar Jawed Akbar v. Priya Ramani* 2021, 90).

Power, Prestige, and Indignity: Akbar and Kavanaugh

Akbar and Kavanaugh both denied the allegations against them by claiming that the allegations discredited and disqualified them as public officials. What is more, a shared sense of indignation, victimization, and self-righteousness became the normative responses to these allegations. Akbar discredited Ramani by accusing her of not naming him in her *Vogue India* article in the first instance and of continuing to collaborate with him even after the alleged assault occurred. He called Ramani's allegations (and those by nineteen other women journalists who came forward with their stories of harassment afterward) "false, baseless, and wild," claiming that they had "caused irreparable damage to [his] reputation and goodwill" (Deepika 2018). Describing the accusations leveled against him "a circus," Kavanaugh similarly claimed that "this grotesque and coordinated character assassination will dissuade confident and good people of all political persuasions from serving our country" (*New York Times* 2018). While Kavanaugh demanded a hearing in order to clear his name as soon as his allegations were made public, Akbar filed a criminal defamation lawsuit against Ramani. Despite these differences, both men expressed an unexamined sense of entitlement that is routinely conferred upon men in positions of power.

Within these familiar performances of male privilege and fragility, the different political outcomes in these two cases speaks to the differential impact of MeToo on Indian and US institutions such as the state and the media. The Kavanaugh case was seen as a partisan issue and as a political vendetta against a Republican Supreme Court nominee, which was reflected in even (Republican) women Senate members supporting Kavanaugh. In contrast, Akbar's case was explicitly *not* cast in politically partisan terms. Members of the BJP—including some women ministers—remained strategically silent or took a clear stand against Akbar's alleged misconduct, rather than backing him. In addition, while both Kavanaugh and Akbar used aggressive speech in countering the accusations leveled against them, Akbar's aggression was never named as part of his overall tone and never discussed as having to do with his gender, whereas Kavanaugh's expressions of rage and indignation were named by both feminists and mass media as part of his masculine aggression. In addition, rather than framing Akbar's subsequent resignation as a political compromise to save his image, it was represented as part of his "personal" decision to pursue a criminal defamation lawsuit against Ramani.

While each case represents different levels of governance and non-equivalent political systems, we highlight the way that the difference in the outcomes of these cases heeds the transnational feminist call to decenter the United States (and other Global North regions) as the site of gender progress and justice. The Indian response suggests a more entrenched critique of patriarchal injustice that cuts across party lines, while the highly polarized US response suggests the ways in which feminist politics are sidelined when it comes to partisan politics. Ford's witness testimony and the subsequent FBI investigation into her allegations against Kavanaugh did not result in him stepping down. In being confirmed, Kavanaugh becomes the metonymy of US law, which is now seen as threatening women's rights and progressive politics (most recently in the *Dobbs* ruling), rather than as protecting them. In contrast, the #MeToo movement in India was successful in pressuring Akbar to step down from his position. Moreover, after Akbar filed defamation charges against Ramani, the Indian news media—the very institution in which Akbar rose to power before becoming a minister—collectively mobilized against him. In addition to the nineteen women journalists who came forward to testify against Akbar, the Editors Guild publicly declared their support for the women and even offered them legal counsel. In what follows, we examine the different ways in which gender-based violence is articulated in both these cases. We observe that patriarchal protectionism emerges as a major discourse in the Akbar case, whereas, in the US, toxic masculinity emerges as a major discourse in the Kavanaugh case.

Patriarchal Protectionism

In India, the media conversation around sexual violence in the context of #MeToo has focused on patriarchal institutions such as the workplace. The workplace has been identified as lacking protections for women who are entering the public sphere in significant numbers due to liberalization and globalization. The wider conversation in India has focused on political change, such as the need for enforcing workplace anti-harassment laws. While legal protections for women at work are crucial for addressing gender inequality, both the state and the populace have tended to fold these protections into a practice of patriarchal protection*ism*. During the infamous 2012 anti-rape campaign in India, for example, both women and men called on the state to protect women from sexual assault by, among other things, demanding the death penalty for rape. This demand characterizes sexual violence as a particularly heinous crime committed by a few "bad men" from which the state will protect women, and therefore silences Indian feminist critiques of gender-based violence as emerging at the intersections of caste, class, regional, and religious hierarchies.

In generating an urgent conversation about sexual harassment in the formal workplace, #MeToo India has implicated men who are in powerful professional and state positions. These men had been largely overlooked until #MeToo, as previous campaigns against rape focused mostly on marginalized men as perpetrators. But rather than providing a sustained critique of masculine power and privilege held by upper-caste and upper-class men, #MeToo discourses frame sexual violence at the workplace as a problem in which women require protection from sexual aggression committed by a few "big shots."

This discourse of protectionism is entrenched within state-sponsored feminism, as well. When Women and Child Development minister Maneka Gandhi called for setting up a special investigation to look into various MeToo allegations of gender-based violence, she declared: "The Prime Minister has always given top priority to the rights of women. The first programme [sic] that he launched was *Beti Bachao, Beti Padhao* [Save the girl child, educate the girl child]. We don't save our daughters by allowing big shots to insult them later in life" (Chandra 2018). Gandhi's comments praise Modi for upholding women's rights by "saving" girls and women. The ministry here participates in the official discourse of women and girls as needing protection by conflating these two groups, effectively infantilizing women—and thereby casting them as vulnerable girl-children—in the process. The discourse of patriarchal protectionism also explains why Modi himself is still considered a champion of women's rights despite the fact that his "manly" leadership style helped explain his rise as a national leader (Srivastava 2015). Protectionist discourse also fails to see patriarchy as a system in which Modi's manly protection of women is in tension with other powerful men who violate women in the workplace. The discourse of patriarchal protectionism thus allows Akbar to emerge as a "bad patriarch," rather than as a subject who is disciplined by a patriarchal system of violent masculinity that creates the conditions for feminine vulnerability to sexual violence in the first place. In keeping its distance from Akbar, the BJP sent a clear message that he essentially failed to uphold the model of a "good patriarch," one who protects, rather than harms, women.

It is worth considering the extent to which Akbar's visibility as a bad patriarch has to do with his identity as a Muslim man: in India, the Hindu right-wing has systematically "othered" and ostracized Muslims and other religious minorities to establish India as a Hindu nation. Before the Ramani case, the BJP—the Hindu right-wing party headed by the current prime minister Narendra Modi—framed Akbar as a "good Muslim," a figure who could be assimilated into Brahmanical (upper caste) ideals. During the Ramani case, the BJP neither explicitly implicated Akbar in nor absolved him of these crimes, raising the possibility that Akbar, as a Muslim politician, is more expendable than other Hindu politicians who are accused of similar crimes. For example, in a recent #MeToo case in which women wrestlers accused the Wrestling Federation of India's (WFI) president Brij Bhushan Sharan Singh (a member of the parliament from the BJP party) of sexual misconduct spanning several years, the Modi government's position was to protect Singh. Despite the months-long protests of women wrestlers to charge Brij Bhushan Singh with a crime, the Modi government kept protecting him. More than this, the women wrestlers and their supporters were handled violently by the police and even arrested for rioting. Singh's protection as an indispensable Hindu subject for the BJP in comparison to Akbar's dispensability as a now "bad," inassimilable Muslim subject reveals the need for an intersectional analysis of #MeToo campaigns in India. Such an analysis would attend to the intersections of religion and gender in order to engage with the extent to which Hindu religious ideologies, masked as nationalist discourses, instrumentalize gender-based violence in order to preserve their dominance.

Akbar's resignation buoyed two main feminist claims about women in the workplace. The first is that most women lack access to, and, in some cases, face cultural barriers that preclude them from accessing, the formal workplace (which is still seen as a masculine domain). The dismally low percentage of women in the Indian workforce—despite a larger enrollment of women in higher and professional education—is often cited as perplexing within media and developmental narratives, even as there is no sustained attention from the state to address this situation (John 2020). The second is that the women who do enter the workforce must still contend with masculine aggression once there. State-sponsored feminist discussions such as those espoused by Gandhi, preclude a fuller discussion of how ideologies of domesticity and a cultural emphasis on middle-class ideologies of sexual purity and respectability for women lead to inequalities in the formal workplace.

In addition to the lack of conversation on systemic inequalities that preclude women from participating in the workplace, another missing piece from MeToo discourse is a discussion of Brahmanical patriarchy—which upholds the status of upper-caste Hindu men—as the norm of Indian masculinity and gender socialization. Dalit feminists in India have been articulating the need for an intersectional approach to gender, particularly in terms of the ways that laws against gender-based violence are applied to protect upper-caste men from charges of sexual violence and to erase women from the marginalized castes as victims or further subject them to disciplinary gender-based violence (Rege 1998; Ponnaih and Tamalapakula 2020; Paik 2021). The latter is evidenced by several instances in which Dalit women were paraded naked as punishment for transgressing caste norms and by the routine trivialization of the sexual violence to which they are consistently subjected. In yet another recent example of institutionalized violence against Dalit women, in 2020, a nineteen-year-old Dalit woman was gang raped and killed by upper-caste men in Hathras, Uttar Pradesh, while collecting fodder with her mother (*The Hindu* 2020). The police hastily cremated the victim's body without the consent of her family in order to erase evidence of the crime, thereby protecting the upper-caste men who raped her. The police's attempt to erase the violence by cremating the victim's body indicates that the state is complicit in upholding caste hierarchies. This example, and others, indicates a need to think of sexual violence beyond the framework of gender victimization and as part of caste-based violence and terror.

Such incidents of caste-based violence currently remain unintelligible within #MeToo India as it is a movement that is framed as "female-as-victim and male-as-perpetrator" and one that focuses on middle-class professional labor and ignores caste hierarchies. A large percentage of Dalit and other marginalized caste women work in the informal sector doing domestic work, construction jobs, street vending, and other day labor where sexual harassment is endemic. A sustained focus on the experiences of women in informal sector jobs, rather than the formal workplace, would require not only conversations around caste hierarchies but also considerations of economic exploitation as central to gender-based violence.

Similar to the need for an intersectional critique of gender-based violence, there is a need to seriously rethink how masculinities are constructed through familial, caste, and state patriarchies (though certainly not limited to these institutions) in the Indian context. The construction of upper-caste male superiority through a discourse of protectionism is tied to the role that family plays as a disciplinary regime of gender. Young men's sexuality is under scrutiny and surveillance by families and educational institutions—even if such practices are not as consequential for men as they are for women—that socialize them into being providers and protectors of patriarchal households. Unlike in the United States, where sexual conquest is frequently an ingredient of men's identity and socialization process, such as in sexually aggressive bro culture, in India, Gandhian ideals of masculinity, such as renunciation and celibacy, have been central to the construction of nationalist and postcolonial masculinity (Srivastava 2004). The de-eroticization and desexualization of Indian masculinity were deemed essential by nationalist projects to counter colonial discourses that represented the native as either oversexed or effeminate (Dasgupta and Gokulsing 2014; Sinha 2017). While upper-caste and Hindu men are expected to uphold these Gandhian ideals of sexual restraint, lower-caste and Muslim men are often scapegoated as sexually deviant aggressors. In particular, migrant men, working-class men, and Muslim men (marked as terrorists) are viewed as a threat to national safety and security, and the (upper-caste) women who are seen by extension to embody the nation deserve the state's protection from these deviant men.

A serious critique of gender socialization in the family and of Indian masculinities must be part of a conversation around sexual assault, even when addressing the workplace. Familial ideologies that privilege men and masculinity also function to silence and undermine women's roles in the public sphere. For example, women who seek advancement in education and career are subjected to everyday violence in the streets, and women's right to public space is still a charged and contentious issue (there are of course class- and caste-based distinctions). This is why, since 2011, India has also witnessed campaigns such as Why Loiter, Pinjra Tod (Break the Cage), and Bekhauf Azadi (Freedom without Fear) that challenged Brahmanical patriarchal standards which confined upper-caste and middle-class women to "private" spaces in the name of "respectability" while branding Dalit and working-class women as morally repugnant because of their participation in "public" life (Anveshi 2019; Lakkimsetti 2021). These campaigns have contested Brahmanical patriarchal control and articulated the fight for public spaces as a struggle not only against sexism but also against caste and class oppression (Lakkimsetti 2021). Despite the history of Dalit feminist articulations of caste discrimination as part of gender-based violence, the #MeToo movement in India has yet to develop an intersectional framing of sexual harassment at the workplace.

We witness this narrow understanding of gender-based violence in the workplace in the 2021 Delhi High Court judgment overruling a case of criminal defamation (itself a colonial-era law) that Akbar filed against Ramani, in which Akbar claimed that Ramani's speaking out against him had ruined his reputation as a public figure. The judgment was hailed as a landmark ruling for survivors of sexual violence, as the court unequivocally stated that the dignity of women who speak out against sexual violence is more important than the reputation of male accusers. However, the language and the media coverage of the ruling reinforce the tenacity of Brahmanical patriarchal ideals on legal decision-making. Even while seemingly moving away from Brahmanical ideas of female respectability by acknowledging women's participation in the workplace, the ruling centers Hindu mythologies that imagine women as in need of rescue and protection. As the ruling states, "It is shameful that the incident [sic] of crime and violence against women are happening in the country where mega epics such as

'*Mahabharata*' and '*Ramayana*' were written around the theme of respect for women." Referencing a different version of the *Ramayana*, the
ruling goes on to note that a "noble tradition of protecting, respecting
and promoting the dignity of women is found" (*Mobashar Jawed Akbar
v. Priya Ramani* 2021, 90). By invoking the patriarchal protectionist
ethos of these Hindu epics, the ruling upholds the idea that women
should be more carefully protected by respectful men who honor the
patriarchal "system of alliance," in which women belong to husbands
and fathers. The ruling importantly moves away from the language of
respectability, which had been the primary discourse of Indian wom-
en's sexuality before #MeToo, and cites the "dignity of women" as an
important constitutional protection. However, the ruling undermines
the radical potential of dignity as a gendered right by situating dignity
within Hindu ideals of patriarchal womanhood rather than in women's
rights to bodily autonomy and sexual agency.

Toxic Masculinity

The media coverage of Brett Kavanaugh's confirmation hearings took
a different approach to gender-based violence than that of Akbar's
case. Rather than engaging with Christine Blasey Ford's victimhood
and vulnerability as the outcome of patriarchal culture of violence, as
the Indian media did with Ramani, the US media emphasized that the
culture of misogynistic violence is part of male gender socialization in
the United States. The media indicated that for young American men,
joining a fraternity is part of a developmental narrative of heteronormative adulthood that is predicated upon cementing bonds between
men through sexual conquest and violence (most often directed toward
women and queer people). Kavanaugh's elite prep school and high
school fraternity were framed as institutions representing larger US cultural norms of toxic hetero-masculinity. For example, a *New York Times*
article described the Kavanaugh hearings as a reminder of "the aggressive, hypersexualized 'bro culture' that has stubbornly persisted on high
school and college campuses across America" (Hartocollis and Goldstein
2018). Within this framing, women are viewed as "collateral damage" of
a larger culture of toxic masculinity (Stoeffel 2018). This is in contrast to
the Akbar case, in which women are constructed as potential victims of

sexual violence who require the protection of "benevolent patriarchs." Both these approaches naturalize male violence, albeit in different ways. The depiction of Indian women as in need of rescue casts men as both protectors and perpetrators of male violence. The depiction of women in the US as collateral damage naturalizes (white) male violence as a prerequisite for social power and status.

The focus on toxic masculinity and feminine fragility in the Kavanaugh hearings was nowhere more apparent than in news coverage that marked the stark differences in the affective dimensions of Ford's and Kavanaugh's testimonies, emphasizing Ford's timidity, docility, and reverence in the face of Kavanaugh's unbridled defensiveness, indignation, and rage. Newspaper headlines referred to a "high-stakes duel of tears and fury" (Baker, Stolberg, and Fandos 2018), and news stories and op-eds described the "shaking" and "soft-spoken" Ford and the "ranting and raving" Kavanaugh (Ali 2018; Freedland 2018). Such affective constructions are of course racialized, as what remains unmarked is the way that public displays of rage are here understood as acceptable when performed by white masculine subjects (and as timidity and fragility are likewise understood as proper performances of white femininity).

Whereas US feminists have argued that #MeToo has been amplifying the voices of survivors, our reading of the Kavanaugh case points to how the focus on male bro culture, toxic masculinity, and gender socialization has directed both media and popular attention to Kavanaugh rather than to Ford. Whether among the voices of conservative women in Congress who supported Kavanaugh's innocence, or among those in the larger US public who accused him of sexual violence, Kavanaugh becomes a protagonist of sorts—whether hero or villain—in the stories that circulated about the Kavanaugh-Ford case.

The attention to Kavanaugh's performance of toxic masculinity may have to do with an entrenched liberal feminist ethos in the United States that understands toxic masculinity as gender performance rather than as rooted in a system of patriarchy. In other words, Kavanaugh is portrayed as having opted into a toxic performance of masculine gender, instead of naming such a performance of masculinity as part of entrenched gender inequalities, which are themselves a result of patriarchy. Here, we can think about the Kavanaugh case and the Akbar case as foregrounding, albeit differently, the ways in which male violence is naturalized. Whereas in India, the discourse of protectionism allows gender-based violence to be reduced to a few bad patriarchs who fail to protect women from sexual violence, in the United States, the discourse of toxic masculinity allows gender-based violence to emerge as men who "opt in" to masculine gender performances based in misogyny.

A focus on toxic masculinity in the Kavanaugh-Ford case may seem like a more advanced critique of patriarchal gender relations, insofar as it demands that we name and recognize male violence. However, by focusing on individual gender performance, #MeToo in the United States misses the opportunity for an institutional critique of patriarchy (Tambe 2018, 2021). Put differently, #MeToo feminism in the United States has not identified (hetero)patriarchy as a system that upholds and reproduces such gendered norms and identities in the first place. Media coverage of US women who supported Kavanaugh's confirmation often took at face value that such women were "gender traitors," instead of understanding that the category "women" is not equivalent to "feminist." Perhaps more importantly, the women interviewed in news media failed to see that a patriarchal system disciplines and manages women as well as men, such that women can be and often are agents of patriarchal norms and values.

The focus on individuals (gender performance) rather than institutions (such as the family, law, etc.) that produce and manage them further lends itself to a partisan framing of gender-based violence. The Kavanaugh confirmation hearings demonstrated the overwhelming way in which partisan politics diverts attention away from an entrenched feminist critique of patriarchal violence. For example, Republican senator Susan Collins (Maine), expressed that she voted for Kavanaugh's confirmation because he privately expressed his support for *Roe v. Wade*, as though such support for women's reproductive rights attests to his incapacity for engaging in gendered violence. Interestingly, Kavanaugh's key role in ruling to strike down *Roe* in the recent *Dobbs* case can be seen as an occasion to revisit what Collins assumed was Kavanaugh's support for women's bodily autonomy.

Within this partisan framing, accusations of gender-based violence, such as those by Ford, are seen as liberal grievances that seek to take down a would-be conservative judge. Here, gendered violence is forcibly inserted into a liberal-versus-conservative political framework rather than viewed as part of an overarching patriarchal system that informs both liberal and conservative political ideals. The entrenched political partisanship informing the discourse on women's bodily autonomy not only glosses over toxic masculinity as a manifestation of male power and privilege, it also precludes a framing of a lack of access to abortion as itself a form of gender-based violence (an argument that has been made elsewhere, most recently in Argentina, where #MeToo has advanced feminist movements for abortion rights). Thus, even as media expressed that Kavanaugh's swift and decisive "desire to overrule *Roe*" and his desire to "greenlight complete bans on all forms of abortion at every stage of pregnancy" were "surprising" (Stern 2021), Kavanaugh's role in the *Dobbs* ruling is in fact consistent with the framing of gender-based violence in the United States as something that occurs along partisan lines. His role in the *Dobbs* ruling is also consistent with a hegemonic masculinity that emerges as identitarian politics rather than as an institutional critique of patriarchy: conservative politicians like Kavanaugh can distance themselves from patriarchy as something relegated to the past and elsewhere, even as they strip away women's rights to bodily autonomy. A framing of patriarchal gender-based violence rather than a narrower focus on toxic masculinity would help us to apprehend #MeToo and the *Dobbs* ruling as deeply connected, rather than mutually exclusive, political issues.

Conclusion: The Here and Now of Patriarchy

The focus on men versus women and workplace harassment in the Akbar case and on toxic masculinity in the Kavanaugh case fails to engage with institutional and intersectional critiques of gender-based violence. This failure, as we have argued, has to do with narrow definitions of patriarchy as a system of male supremacy that is rooted in tradition, a premodern past, and non-Western familial and social structures. In the West, patriarchy is often associated with an "unfree tradition" that is attributed to historically colonized or non-Western women (the Global South) (Patil 2013, 851). Patriarchy is also seen as rearguard and even obsolete in the United States because it is associated with second-wave feminist concerns with women's access to the workplace and state recognition of sexual and reproductive rights. Indeed, the recent *Dobbs* decision has for many liberal feminists signaled a movement backward to a time when patriarchal ideas about women's subordination dominated cultural discourse. The *Dobbs* decision is indeed a major setback for women's rights to abortion access. However, the liberal indignation at the ruling indexes a belief in American exceptionalism of forward political progress, in which patriarchy is relegated to the past and viewed as out of step with a liberal feminist ethos that is centered on choice and consumption as avenues to social change. Meanwhile, the consistent invocation within India of patriarchy as a culture of protection reinforces the idea that patriarchy is essentially non-Western. Stereotypical representations of India as the "rape capital of the world" or the "most unsafe place for women'" justify the construction of Indian women as in need of state protection. Moreover, framing gender-based violence primarily as a form of patriarchal backlash against changing gender norms obscures how colonial and postcolonial politics have reshaped gender norms and institutional practices in contemporary India.

We have sought in this chapter to approach patriarchy not as a universal structure of male power and privilege, but as an uneven form of gender management across the Global North and South. In India, #MeToo's focus on patriarchy as a discourse of protectionism otherwise obscures an intersectional framing of gender-based violence as occurring through caste, class, religious, and other forms of social domination. In contrast, in the United States, patriarchy remains virtually unintelligible within #MeToo's focus on gender identity, which is rooted in liberal ideals of individual expression. We need to attend more carefully to structures of power and inequality that would, for example, make Kavanaugh's brand of misogyny, male privilege, and masculine aggression appear not as exceptional nor as rearguard but as rooted in past *and* present US patriarchal projects, both imperial and humanitarian. Relegating patriarchy to a second-wave-feminist past in the United States enables liberal feminists to redeploy this concept outside the United States as a strategy of othering. The most recent example of this can be found in the antitrafficking debates in which Western feminists construct Third World women as quintessential victims of sex trafficking and therefore as needing rescue and rehabilitation (Bernstein and Shih 2014; Shih 2016). Within these forms of feminist humanitarianism, as Lila Abu-Lughod,

Rema Hammami, and Nadera Shalhoub-Kevorkian (2023, 2) have observed, gender violence can be mobilized as a form of disciplinary power to justify imperialist and militarized interventions, or what they call the "cunning of gender violence."

As women of color and Indigenous feminists have taught us, patriarchal ideals have never been disconnected from the racial projects of colonization and white supremacy and therefore continue to hold explanatory power in the United States. For example, the phrase "white supremacist capitalist patriarchy" names the interconnectedness of these systems of oppression such that they cannot be disaggregated fully from one another. More recently, Vrushali Patil (2013) has argued that insofar as patriarchy has been associated with universalizing and totalizing narratives of "women's oppression" that are premised upon a gender binary system, other analytical frameworks, such as intersectionality, do the necessary work of de-essentializing gender. Like other women of color feminists, however, Patil argues for the central role of patriarchy in shaping colonial and imperial hierarchies such as the gender binary system. This means attending more carefully to the ways patriarchies continue to structure gender relations in the Global North as well as the Global South. Such a rethinking of patriarchies could loosen the hold of liberal ideals of gender as individual expression in the United States and attend more carefully to structures of power and inequality that would, for example, make Kavanaugh's brand of misogyny, male privilege, and masculine aggression appear not as exceptional nor as rearguard but as rooted in past and present US colonial and imperial imperatives.

Similarly, attention to patriarchy as structuring class, gender, and caste dominance will help to decenter an increasingly ascendant version of Indian feminism that is particularly appealing to upper-caste, middle-class men and women for whom liberalization and globalization of the economy have created new opportunities for upward mobility. The uneven flows of discourses and resources in a globalizing context, while appearing to open opportunities for some women's participation in the workforce through increasing jobs in information technology and expanding the service sector, simultaneously foreclose these possibilities for others by trafficking in what are often cast as antiquated class, caste, and gender inequalities. We need a transnational framing of patriarchy that accounts for the phenomenon of "brown women saving their own from brown men," to rephrase Spivak's (1996, 3) famous quote about white men saving brown women from brown men, and that extends gender politics beyond a simple male-female binary.

REFERENCES

Abu-Lughod, Lila, Rema Hammami, and Nadera Shalhoub-Kevorkian. 2023. "Circuits of Power in GBVAW Governance." In *The Cunning of Gender Violence: Geopolitics & Feminism*, edited by Lila Abu-Lughod, Rema Hammami, and Nadera Shalhoub-Kevorkian, 1–54. Durham, NC: Duke University Press.

Anveshi. 2019. "Breaking the Chains: Understanding the 'Pinjra Tod' Campaign." Interview by Rani Rohini Raman. *Anveshi*, no. 14, 15–17. www.anveshi.org.in.

Ali, Lorraine. 2018. "She Said/He Bellowed: The Optics of the Ford/Kavanaugh Hearings Were as Divided as America." *LA Times*, September 27, 2018. www.latimes.com.

Baker, Peter, Sheryl Gay Stolberg, and Nicolas Fandos. 2018. "Christine Blasey Ford Wants F.B.I. to Investigate Kavanaugh before She Testifies." *New York Times*, September 18, 2018. www.nytimes.com.

Barriteau, Eudine. 1998. "Theorizing Gender Systems and the Project of Modernity in the Twentieth-Century Caribbean." *Feminist Review* 59 (1): 186–210.

Bernstein, Elizabeth, and Elena Shih. 2014. "The Erotics of Authenticity: Sex Trafficking and 'Reality Tourism' in Thailand." *Social Politics* 21 (3): 430–60.

Butler, Judith. 1990. *Gender Trouble*. New York: Routledge.

Chandra, Jagriti. 2018. "Maneka Gandhi Proposes Committee of Legal Experts to Look into #MeToo Cases." *The Hindu*, October 12, 2018. www.thehindu.com.

Choo, Hae Yeon. 2021. "From Madwomen to Whistleblowers: MeToo in South Korea as an Institutional Critique." *Feminist Formations* 33 (3): 256–70.

Dasgupta, Rohit, and Moti Gokulsing. 2014. "Introduction: Perceptions of Masculinity and Challenges to the Indian." In *Masculinities and Its Challenges in India: Essays on Changing Perceptions*, edited by Rohit Dasgupta and Moti Gokulsing, 5–26. Jefferson, NC: McFarland.

Deepika, S. 2018. "'False and Fabricated': MJ Akbar's Full Statement on #MeToo Allegations." *Oneindia*, October 14, 2018. www.oneindia.com.

Edwards, Haley Sweetland. 2018. "How Christine Blasey Ford's Testimony Changed America." *TIME*, October 15, 2018. www.time.com.

Freedland, Jonathan. 2018. "Kavanaugh Has Revealed an Insidious Force in Global Politics: Toxic Masculinity." *The Guardian*, September 29, 2018. www.theguardian.com.

Hartocollis, Anemona, and Dana Goldstein. 2018. "Schools Are Tackling 'Bro' Culture. The Kavanaugh Case Shows Why That's Hard to Do." *New York Times*, September 28, 2018. www.nytimes.com.

Lakkimsetti, Chaitanya. 2021. "Stripping Away at Respectability: #Metoo India and the Politics of Dignity." *Feminist Formations* 33 (3): 303–17.

The Hindu. 2020. "Hathras Victim Was Gang-Raped, Murdered: CBI." March 6, 2020. www.thehindu.com.

John, Mary. 2020. "Feminism, Sexual Violence and Time of #MeToo in India." *Asian Journal of Women's Studies* 26 (2): 137–58.

Mobashar Jawed Akbar v. Priya Ramani, Completing Case No. 05/2019, Rouse Avenue District Court, New Delhi, February 17, 2021.

New York Times. 2018. "Brett Kavanaugh's Opening Statement: Full Transcript." September 26, 2018. www.nytimes.com.

Patil, Vrushali. 2013. "From Patriarchy to Intersectionality: A Transnational Feminist Assessment of How Far We've Really Come." *Signs* 38 (4): 847–67.

Paik, Shailaja. 2021. "Dalit Feminist Thought." In *Routledge Handbook of Gender in South Asia*, edited by Leela Fernandes, 55–69. Abingdon: Routledge.

Ponniah, Ujithra, and Sowjanya Tamalapakula. 2020. "Caste-ing Queer Identities." *NUJS Law Review* 13 (3): 1–8.

Ramani, Priya. 2017. "To the Harvey Weinsteins of the World." *Vogue Magazine*, October 12, 2017. www.vogue.in.

Rege, Sharmila. 1998. "Dalit Women Talk Differently: A Critique of 'Difference' and towards a Dalit Feminist Standpoint Position." *Economic and Political Weekly*, 33 (44): WS39–WS46.

Roshanravan, Shireen. 2021. "On the Limits of Globalizing Black Feminist Commitments: 'Me Too' and Its White Detours." *Feminist Formations* 33 (3): 239–55.

Shih, Elena. 2016. "Not in My 'Backyard Abolitionism' Vigilante Rescue against American Sex Trafficking." *Sociological Perspectives* 59 (1): 66–90.

Sinha, Mrinalini. 2017. *Colonial Masculinity: The "Manly Englishman" and the "Effeminate Bengali" in the Late Nineteenth Century*. Manchester, UK: Manchester University Press.

Spivak, Gayatri Chakravorty. 1996. "Woman as Theatre: United Nations Conference on Women, Beijing 1995." *Radical Philosophy* 75:2–4.

Srivastava, Sanjay. 2004. "The Masculinity of Dis-Location: Commodities, the Metropolis, and the Sex-Clinics of Delhi and Mumbai." In *South Asian Masculinities: Change and Continuity*, edited by Radhika Chopra, Caroline Osella, and Filippo Osella, 175–223. New Delhi: Kali for Women.

———. 2015. "Modi-Masculinity: Media, Manhood, and 'Traditions' in a Time of Consumerism." *Television & New Media* 16 (4): 331–38.

Stern, Mark. 2021. "During Arguments Over the Fate of Roe, Kavanaugh and Barrett Finally Showed Their Cards." *SLATE*, December 1, 2021. https://slate.com.

Stoeffel, Kat. 2018. "On Brett Kavanaugh's Path to Power, Women are Collateral Damage." *ELLE*, September 24, 2018. www.elle.com.

Tambe, Ashwini. 2018. "Reckoning with the Silences of #MeToo." *Feminist Studies* 44 (1): 197–202.

———. 2021. "Afterword: Walking Alongside Many# MeToos." *Feminist Formations* 33 (3): 351–59.

West, Candace, and Don H. Zimmerman. 1987. "Doing Gender." *Gender & Society* 1 (2): 125–51.

2

#MeToo, Speech, and Defamation
(India, United States, and Pakistan)

BRENDA COSSMAN AND RATNA KAPUR

Defamation law has in recent years become yet another site of legal contestation around sexual harm. A 2020 report found that in the United
States alone, more than one hundred defamation lawsuits have been
brought to court by people accused of sexual misconduct or abuse against
their alleged victims since 2014. The turn to defamation has only intensified since the emergence of #MeToo in 2017: many women who said
#MeToo and named their harasser were then sued for defamation (John-
son 2018). In other cases, women who said #MeToo have themselves
sued for defamation where their alleged harassers called them liars. Defamation law has emerged as both a sword and a shield—on both sides
of the allegations—and as a new contested site of the tenacious she said,
he said struggles (Jacobs 2020). This turn to defamation, like #MeToo
itself, is global in scope (Lakkimsetti and Reddy 2021). In this chapter,
we look at three high-profile #MeToo defamation cases following public allegations of sexual harassment: Meesha Shafi's allegations against
Ali Zafar in Pakistan; Priya Ramani's allegations against M. J. Akbar in
India; and Amber Heard's (unnamed) allegations of domestic violence
against Johnny Depp in the United States. In each, a woman's MeToo
declaration ignited a firestorm of litigation, including civil defamation
and sometimes criminal defamation cases, alongside counter defamation actions. Social media played a key role in influencing the ways in
which narratives were presented and, in the process, produced sexual
speech. The role of social media has reshaped and complicated the ways
in which #MeToo cases and defamation are understood in the courtroom, beyond the binary of free expression and censorship.

Many have now called defamation law the new silencer, with defamation actions by alleged harassers creating a massive chilling effect and

seeking a return to the culture of silence surrounding sexual violence against women (Dugan 2022). While there is no doubt truth in this claim, we argue that the framework of silencing does not adequately capture the nature and impact of the turn to defamation. We argue that defamation in the #MeToo context operates as a site to contest and constitute legitimate speech about sexual harm. We examine these cases through the lens of #MeToo and defamation as speech challenging and reconstituting the boundaries of what can and cannot be said. Building on critical censorship scholarship, we argue that these defamation cases are not simply about silencing: as speech acts, they are constitutive of the legal, political, and cultural terrain within which sexual harm is given meaning. We then examine the three defamation cases, exploring them as contestations of silencing, with uneven and contradictory effects, interacting in unpredictable ways with social media. In each case, the MeToo narratives of the women were reproduced and engaged with via social media, thus augmenting speech rather than stifling it or simply sending a "chilling effect."

Defamation Beyond Silencing

Many commentators have argued that the wave of defamation cases against women who have spoken out against their sexual abusers has emerged as a legal tactic of silencing. Moira Donegan writes, for example, that "defamation suits are becoming a routine tool of retaliation and revenge for men accused of sexual and domestic abuse" (Donegan 2022). It is, she argues, part of the current antifeminist backlash aimed at "silencing women, or punishing the women who won't shut up" (Donegan 2022). A 2021 *Report of the UN Special Rapporteur on the Right to Freedom of Opinion and Expression*, which explored the important relationship between gender and freedom of expression, similarly observed the silencing of defamation suits: "In a perverse twist of fate in the MeToo age, women who publicly denounce alleged perpetrators of sexual violence online are increasingly subject to defamation suits or charged with criminal libel or the false reporting of crimes. Weaponizing the justice system to silence women feeds impunity while undermining free speech" (Khan 2021, para. 22).[1] Some have argued that

the retaliatory use of defamation claims "has the effect of deterring survivors from reporting, therefore chilling the free exercise of their First
Amendment rights" and that these retaliatory defamation actions "are
being used to silence survivors from reporting acts of sexual misconduct" (Chandra 2021; Nagaraj 2021; Oppenheimer 2020; Toppa 2020;
Whynot 2022, 24, 11).[2]

We have no doubt that defamation lawsuits by those accused of sexual misconduct may be intended to silence the individual accusers, and
that one of their effects is to make other potential accusers think twice
before speaking out. Indeed, when Moira Donegan speaks of defamation
suits as a tool of retaliation and revenge, she knows of what she speaks:
she has been sued for defamation by Stephen Elliot for $1.5 million for
being the creator of the Shitty Media Men list (Donegan 2018). But, in
our view, silencing is not a sufficient analytic framework for understanding the way that these defamation lawsuits are operating.

Defamation is a form of censorship; there has long been a concern
about the potential chilling effect of censoring speech through defamation law (Townend 2017). As a form of censorship, it is insightful
to consider defamation through the lens of critical censorship scholarship. Rather than simply viewing censorship in terms of repressive
state power, new censorship studies have sought to focus on the productive nature of censorship, seeing it as more diffuse and quotidian
(Burt 1994; Freshwater 2003; Holquist 1994; Jansen 1991; O'Leary 2016;
Post 1998; Rosenfield 2001). Michael Holquist (1994, 16) has argued that
censorship is everywhere: "To be for or against censorship as such is to
assume a freedom no one has. Censorship is." Influenced by the work
of Michel Foucault, this scholarship reframes censorship as productive
and constitutive rather than prohibitive (Foucault 1978; Freshwater 2003;
Post 1998). It draws attention to how censorial techniques such as social
norms and the self-censorship they foster are both regulatory and productive (Foucault 1978; Cossman 2013).[3]

While this scholarship tends to direct attention away from juridical
forms of censorship (Butler 1997),[4] we need not abandon interrogations
of state-based censorship. Robert Post (1998, 4) invites us to consider
how these insights may supplement traditional accounts of state censorship, asking that we consider "recognizing always the pervasive,

inescapable and productive silencing of expression." He asks whether we might still say things "distinctive about the particular province of what used to define the study of censorship: the 'direct control' of expression by the state." For Post, we should not create an opposition between these differing visions but explore instead the opportunities that a more expansive interpretation of censorship creates (Butler 1998; Freshwater 2009).[5] Juridical and state censorship does not become irrelevant but serves as one of the many different techniques of silencing as well as a distinct mode of power and method for constructing the speaking subject, though not the only one.[6]

This expansive vision of censorship can help reframe censorship laws—including defamation—as productive and constitutive rather than simply repressive. Censorship laws and challenges to them constitute the very terrain of public contestation over legitimate and illegitimate speech (Heath 2010). For Judith Butler (1997, 131), censorship is "formative of subjects and the legitimate boundaries of speech." She uses the example of the US military policy of Don't Ask, Don't Tell. While prohibiting members of the military from coming out, it did not constrain reference to "homosexuality" (Butler 1997, 130) but further brought it into public discourse and further produced the norms whereby the masculine military subject was constituted. While she is speaking to censorship's more ubiquitous modalities, it is an insight that can be brought to bear on juridical censorship. State censorship produces the space—legal and otherwise—where speech can be contested. In so doing, it can refocus attention to the multiple and contradictory effects of censorship. Holquist (1994, 17) highlights the paradoxical nature of censorship in which each act "is riven in its heart by a fatal division: the prohibition that separates what is banned from what is permitted also fuses them." Butler similarly argues in relation to juridical censorship that "such regulations introduce the censored speech into public discourse, thereby establishing it as a site of contestation, that is, as the scene of public utterance that it sought to pre-empt" (Heath 2010, 130). In other words, censorship performs its own contradictions: it utters the very words or images that it seeks to conceal. At the same time, this expansive vision of censorship can guard against the myopia of focusing only on the legal outcomes, expanding the analysis to some of the broader cultural and social effects of censorship actions, including for example, the ripples created through social media.

The silencing critique of defamation is one that aligns with conceptions of censorship as repressive power. Criminal defamation operates as a form of state censorship, whereas in civil defamation, the state provides the background rules and enforcement for private actions. Both implicate the power of the state, and both can have the effect of punishing speech. Instead of censoring, defamation is an act of self-sabotage as it both constitutes and breaks the silences through the repetition of the particular speech that it targets. Instead of silencing, it harbors speech. At the same time, the speech produced is released into unemancipatory propensities of dominant norms and regulatory discourses and remains tethered to an epistemological framework. These propensities constitute implicit censorship that can more effectively constrain "speakability" than explicit bans. As Wendy Brown (2005, 84) argues, breaking the silence does not escape these constraints and may in turn carry its own possibilities of subjugation and further regulation: "In short, it may feed the powers it meant to starve." Nevertheless, it holds out the possibility of reshaping and disrupting these arrangements when understood outside a repressive and expressive framing of censorship.

Many have written of the potential chilling effect of defamation laws on speech, criminal and civil alike. The silencing critique—that defamation lawsuits over allegations of sexual abuse or misconduct have the intention and effect of warning women against making these allegations—fits within this chilling effect concern. It is an entirely legitimate concern. However, a more expansive vision of censorship can broaden the lens to further consider the contradictory, constitutive, and contested outcomes and reverberations of defamation actions. In the sections that follow, we consider some of the ways in which these high-profile defamation cases have constituted and contested the boundaries between legitimate and illegitimate speech and have had ripple effects beyond the law in social media.

Women Accused of Defamation

Meesha Shafi Versus Ali Zafar

In April 2018, Meesha Shafi, a well-known Pakistani actress and singer, accused musician Ali Zafar of sexual harassment on Twitter: "I have been subjected, on more than one occasion, to sexual harassment of a physical nature at the hands of a colleague from my industry: Ali Zafar . . . This happened to me even though I am an empowered, accomplished woman who is known for speaking her mind! This happened to me as a mother of two children." Shafi framed her accusation in the language of breaking silence: "[I am] sharing this because I believe that by speaking out about my experience of sexual harassment, I will break the culture of silence that permeates through our society. It is not easy to speak out . . . but it is harder to stay silent. My conscience will not allow it anymore. #MeToo" (Shafi 2018). Other women then came forward with similar accusations against Zafar.

The allegations would span multiple cases of complex litigation. First, Shafi filed a sexual harassment case against Zafar under the Protection Against Harassment of Women in the Workplace Act (PAHWW) of 2010. Her complaint was initially dismissed because she and Zafar were not in an employment relationship. But, on appeal, the Pakistan Supreme Court admitted her petition, allowing it to move forward.[7]

Ali Zafar not only vehemently denied Shafi's allegations but brought a civil action for defamation against her.[8] Shafi was subjected to a gag order by the court and prevented from making any negative remarks against Zafar. Zafar continued to be allowed to speak to media, online and in the larger public space. Zafar also reported Shafi's and others' "social media campaign" against him to the Federal Investigation Agency, which then charged Shafi and eight other women with criminal defamation under the Pakistan Electronic Crimes Act (PECA).[9] PECA is a draconian cybercrime law enacted ostensibly to protect women from online harassment. Following derogatory remarks made by Zafar about Shafi, she then brought a civil defamation suit. A lower court dismissed her civil defamation suit, but in January 2022, the Lahore High Court allowed Shafi's action to proceed. Shafi further brought a constitutional challenge to the defamation law under PECA. The Lahore High Court dismissed it, but in June 2022, the Supreme Court of Pakistan gave leave to appeal and issued a stay against the criminal defamation proceedings (*Meera Shafi [Meesha Shafi] v. Ali Zafar* 2022). The court is currently considering the constitutional validity of specific provisions of PECA and if it is being used as a weapon against sexual harassment complaints. At the time of this writing, Shafi's defamation case, her sexual harassment case, and her constitutional challenge are pending. Zafar's criminal defamation action has been stayed, but his civil defamation action is pending.

It is too early in the proceedings to declare winners or losers. For the moment, it is fair to say that although Shafi herself has not been silenced, many others might not be as tenacious as she has been; the time, energy, and resources to engage in these legal wranglings would elude many. But her case(s) have also become a site of contestation of legitimate speech about sexual harm in Pakistan, about what can and cannot be said about the sexual misconduct of others. Shafi's case mobilized the women's movement, becoming "a rallying cry" for the Aurat Marches (Women Marches), first held in 2018. "Shafi's case has become a lightning rod as the organizers and participants have frequently cited her case as an example of what women have to endure for speaking up against sexual harassment. Shafi's case has shaped not only the #MeToo movement but also the public, legal and feminist discourse about women's bodies and rights in Pakistan" (Khurshid 2021, 325).

Public protests, social media, and press coverage before and during the proceedings have shaped the discourse on sexual harms, although the full extent of their impact is difficult to assess given that the case is ongoing. These campaigns reproduced the very speech that Zafar sought to conceal through defamation law. Each legal proceeding, including the ones initiated by Zafar, resulted in more speech about the very claims that Zafar was attempting to deny and shut down. Shafi received support from the global #MeToo survivors, including Hollywood actress Rose McGowan, one of the first "silence breakers" in the sexual assault and harassment allegations against Harvey Weinstein. At the same time, reproducing the speech enabled a fierce backlash. For example, protesters marching in support of Shafi were pelted with stones by religious right-wing groups, and the women were accused of promoting a Western agenda and being immoral and un-Islamic. Calls were made for their arrests. In social media, #MeToo backers who posted on Twitter and Facebook to mobilize support and build a movement were attacked and threatened with rape and violence. Women were mocked and bullied for daring to speak on matters of sexual violence and harm. Despite these taunts and threats, women continued to speak out in all formats and file cases. "People are still speaking out" said Nighat Dad, Shafi's lawyer. "It seems they're not scared anymore. They know the justice system's flaws and that it is inherently rigged against women in Pakistan. Even still, they're speaking up" (Toppa 2020). Dad was also one of the organizers of the Aurat Marches that saw thousands of women, together with men and sexual and religious minorities, on the streets to support #MeToo, among other demands. The Aurat Marches and support from #MeToo supporters helped to reconstitute Shafi's accusations as legitimate speech, beyond the exclusive purview of the law. The constant reiterations of the claims and denials, of support and backlash, reverberated through media and social media, producing more speech. Shafi's ongoing case illustrates some of the ways that defamation actions need to be considered more broadly than simply through their silencing effects: they need to be considered through their contestations of the boundaries of legitimate speech.

#MeToo—as a global movement and shared discourse—provided an important backdrop for Shafi's case. It was not simply that Shafi herself said "MeToo," but that the globally visible social movement provided the discursive context in which not only her utterance could be heard but also the defamation claim could be at least partially defeated and her constitutional challenge could proceed. #MeToo, as a shared global discourse, constituted and shifted the boundaries of legitimate speech; in so doing, it has begun to influence the lines being drawn by the courts. Law and social media are mutually constituting these boundaries against the backdrop of the social movement.

Priya Ramani Versus M. J. Akbar

In 2018, journalist Priya Ramini accused M. J. Akbar, a government minister, of sexual misconduct during his earlier career as a newspaper editor. The harassment occurred when she was twenty-three, during a job interview for the then-new *Asian Age*, a newspaper founded by Akbar. Her public allegations began on October 12, 2017, when Priya Ramani (2017) published an article in *Vogue* magazine entitled "To the Harvey Weinsteins of the World." The article opens with a story about her job interview with her first male boss at his hotel room, and his inappropriate behavior: "Turns out you were as talented a predator as you were a writer. It was more date, less interview" (Ramani 2017). She wrote of the ongoing harassing behavior that women faced at work:

"You're an expert on obscene phone calls, texts, inappropriate compliments and not taking no for an answer. You know how to pinch, pat, rub, grab and assault." She did not name her harasser at the time. But, a year later on October 8, 2018, she named her boss in a tweet: "I began this piece with my MJ Akbar story. Never named him because he didn't 'do' anything. Lots of women have worse stories about this predator—maybe they'll share. #ulti" (Ramani 2018a). A few days later she tweeted that other women had come forward painting "a clear portrait of the media's biggest sexual predator. How many more stories do you need to hear? #MJAkbar" (Ramani 2018b). Within days, twenty women came forward to sign a letter with similar accusations of sexual harassment at the *Asian Age*.

M. J. Akbar immediately denied the allegations, resigned from his cabinet post, and filed a criminal defamation case against Ramani accusing her of "wilfully, deliberately, intentionally and maliciously" defaming him over "completely false, frivolous, unjustifiable, and scandalous grounds" (*India Today* 2018). Akbar sought Ramani's prosecution under Section 499 (defamation) and punishment under Section 500 of the Indian Penal Code, with imprisonment of two years or a fine or each (Cole 1995; Sethi 2019).[10] After months of trial, delays, attempts at changing courts, and a change in the presiding judge, in February 2021, Ramani was acquitted (*Mobashar Jawed Akbar v. Priya Ramani*). The court held that Akbar had failed to prove his case, and that the disclosure was in the interest of preventing sexual harassment in the workplace. This case too is ongoing: Akbar appealed the ruling, and in January 2022, the Delhi High Court admitted his appeal (*Times of India* 2022).

The court decision offers an extensive review of the evidence of the witnesses. The substance of the judgment recognizes the harm of sexual harassment and the importance of being able to speak about it. The court held that "the woman cannot be punished for raising voice against the sex abuse on the pretext of criminal complaint of defamation as the right of reputation cannot be protected at the cost of the right of life and dignity of woman as guaranteed in Indian Constitution under Article 21 and right of equality before law and equal protection of law as guaranteed under Article 14 of the Constitution. The woman has a right to put her grievance at any platform of her choice and even after decades" (*Mobashar Jawed Akbar v. Priya Ramani* 2021). The reasoning of the court is complex, deploying the language of both rights alongside nationalist rhetoric and the respect for and place of women in Indian culture. It recognizes the importance of upholding respect for the dignity and self-confidence of women while it uses a protectionist discourse. The reasoning at times is embedded in sexual and gender stereotypes and identifies the central harm as that of shame or social stigma. At the same time, the court states that it is time for society to understand the implications of sexual abuse and sexual harassment for the victim. Women's economic empowerment and increased and safe participation in the workforce are also highlighted by the court.

In dismissing the case, the district court sided with the "victim" and the right of a woman to complain about sexual harassment and abuse. It pushed the boundaries of legitimate speech and recognized Ramani's defense as writing about her experience in the public interest. The decision ultimately illustrates how defamation law—in its rulings and in the broader public discourse around the ruling—can be productive of speech rather than working only to reinforce and reproduce a culture of silence around sexual harm. The court further recognizes that while the complaint of sexual harassment and abuse may harm the reputation of the abuser, it was nevertheless legitimate speech. It was speech that should be enabled, not punished, in the name of women's rights and dignity and that was therefore in the public interest. Once again, the broader context of the global discourse of #MeToo articulated in and through social media can be seen as shaping the boundaries of legitimate speech within the courtroom. Yet, it was also speech that was protected through partially protectionist rather than progressive narratives of gender.

The burden of proof for criminal defamation is higher than in a civil suit and, in the Ramani case, the complainant failed to meet this threshold.[11] At the same time, perpetrators resort to criminal defamation lawsuits because they are more intimidating than a civil suit given its punitive dimension, which includes the possibility of imprisonment. It can have a chilling effect and discourage victims from complaining. Despite these constraints and threats, Ramani was able to use the defense of defamation and push it in a direction that opens space for women to move the dial in favor of speech that includes speaking about sexual harms.

There was a large social media and press campaign around the case from the outset—both supportive as well as oppositional, including "slut shaming" comments on all forums. From the outset, Ramani used these spaces to assert her decision to fight the complaint of criminal defamation (*Times of India* 2018; Mittal 2018; *Al Jazeera* 2018). After the verdict, Ramani declared through Twitter, "This case was not about me. It was about women's experience in the workplace. My victory belongs to all who said #MeToo" and that "this is what it feels like to smash the patriarchy" (The Quint 2021). There was an outpouring of media support for the decision globally and the case was hailed as India's #MeToo moment (Murthy 2021; Schmall 2021; Ellis-Petersen 2021a). While at one level, the media focused on Ramani's defense of truth and public interest, the case was generative of speech—including debate and discussion on issues pertinent to #MeToo. As one feminist lawyer speaking on the significance of the decision, stated, "This victory is significant because it preserves women's right to speak and have published their true #MeToo accounts of sexual assault and harassment, even if they choose not to file cases against their harassers" (Ellis-Petersen 2021a). However, the content of this speech that gives visibility to sexual harms remains partially framed within the pervasive disciplinary norms and regulatory discourses that govern sex and sexuality, including sexual speech. The speech is taken up within an existing normative structure where the line between sexual speech and sexual harm is invariably blurred. Indeed, few aspects of sexual speech are exempt from some form of regulation, including cultural, legal, and social.

Johnny Depp Versus Amber Heard

The Johnny Depp versus Amber Heard defamation lawsuits are only the most recent and perhaps most high-profile of a growing list of cases in which men in the United States have brought defamation claims against those who have accused them of sexual harassment, violence, or misconduct. In December 2018, Amber Heard wrote an op-ed in the *Washington Post* entitled "I Spoke Up against Sexual Violence—and Faced Our Culture's Wrath. That Has to Change" (2018). The article spoke out against sexual violence against women and the cost that women face for speaking out. The title was more than a little prescient—Heard would come to face unprecedented wrath as the legal machinations unfolded. Heard did not mention Depp by name. But she did refer to having become "a public figure representing domestic abuse" two years earlier. It was a veiled reference to the abuse allegations she had brought against Depp in their divorce.

In 2018, Depp brought a defamation action in the UK against News Group Newspapers, after *The Sun* referred to him as a "wife beater." In the UK, defamation law requires the party accused of defamation to prove their claims. In July 2020, his claim was dismissed, with the court holding that *The Sun*'s article was "substantially true" and that twelve of the fourteen alleged incidents of domestic violence had occurred. But, in the interim, Depp had initiated the defamation action against Heard in the United States in 2019 in relation to the *Washington Post* op-ed. Heard then countersued for defamation in relation to comments made by Depp's lawyer. After a highly publicized, celebrity-studded trial, with accusations of violence and abuse abounding on both sides, in June 2022, a jury ultimately found Heard liable of three counts and ordered her to pay.[12] Depp was found liable on one count. Both Heard and Depp have since appealed. On December 19, 2022, Heard and Depp reached a settlement (Jacobs 2022).

During the course of the trial, social media played a significant role. Yet unlike in the Pakistani and Indian cases, in which social media sided with the victim of gendered violence, the social media outpouring was *overwhelmingly* against Heard (Bot Sentinel Inc. 2022).[13] Indeed, women who expressed their support on Twitter for Heard were also subject to massive online harassment: "Twitter trolls regularly swarmed the tweets of women who supported Amber Heard, and abuse and targeted harassment were commonplace. Tweeting in support of Amber Heard without being swarmed by trolls was difficult at best" (Bot Sentinel Inc. 2022). The Bot Sentinel Inc. (2022) report concluded that it was one of the worst cases "of cyberbullying and cyberstalking by a group of Twitter accounts that we've ever seen."[14] While there was similar trolling in social media against Shafi supporters, the extent of the anti-Heard speech was exponentially greater, perhaps partly owing to the global celebrity status of the parties involved.

The anti-Heard campaign did not go unnoticed in mainstream media. Some called it out for its sexism and misogyny and as part of a backlash against #MeToo (Scott 2022; Donegan 2022, Grady 2022; Goldberg 2022). Others opined on the myth of the perfect victim, and the attack on Heard's credibility for failing to live up to the impossible standard (Dockterman 2022; Tuerkheimer 2022). And many expressed concerns about the potential silencing effect on victims of domestic abuse (Turkos 2022; Donegan 2022). While the weight of popular opinion was against Heard, she was not without her supporters. After the verdict, an open letter in support of Heard signed by the National Organization for Women, the National Women's Law Center, Equality Now, and the Women's March Foundation denounced the verdict and the "rising misuse" of defamation lawsuits to silence victims of violence. It read, "We condemn the public shaming of Amber Heard and join in support of her. We support the ability of all to report intimate partner and sexual violence free of harassment and intimidation" (Amber Heard Open Letter 2022). Of the three cases, the defamation suit against Heard was the most successful to date and the unprecedented harassment online raises the strongest concern about the silencing effect of defamation. But we would caution against only seeing it as silencing; the defamation case has also produced speech about speech, about the speech of survivors of domestic violence, and the feminist advocacy needed to protect it.

Comparative Contestations

There are obvious points of comparison and contrast across these very different cases. Women's allegations of sexual violence against powerful men were met not only with denials, but with defamation actions—both civil and criminal. The women themselves in each case were powerful, elite, or famous celebrities. In all three cases, they were partly heard because of their privileged positions. All three cases were litigated both inside and outside the courtroom, with social media campaigns and hashtag activism. Two of the three women accused of defamation—Shafi and Heard—countersued for defamation. The legal outcomes were mixed. Ramani (for the moment at least) successfully defended against the criminal defamation cases. Shafi's victories have come only in the sense of her cases being allowed to continue. Heard was at best partially successful in her counterdefamation case, but unsuccessful in defending against Depp's. All are ongoing: the "he said, she said" continues.

The mixed results suggest to us that more is at play here than silencing. These women were not themselves silenced, even if that may have been the intention of their accusers.

Social media played a powerful role in relaying the words and actions of the perpetrators that were replayed countless times. The defamation cases in each instance resulted in more speech and more visibility of the issues with which #MeToo has been concerned. Regardless of whether there was a loss or victory in the courtroom, in social media, where #MeToo has continuously had the most traction, the speech and accounts of the victims remained alive and fully visible. In India, social media served as the first place where accusations were made against predators; this is in contrast to the United States, where the reports were initially made in a national publication (Shrivastava, Altstedter, and Chaudhary 2018). The cases demonstrated the power social media has to transcend the limits of defamation as a censorship tool by reiterating and reproducing the searing accounts of sexual harassment presented by the women in the courtroom. The prolific discussion on sexual harassment that these cases have generated on social media has continued to inform the ways in which defamation law has played out in the courtroom in each of the contexts discussed and elsewhere.

Building on critical censorship studies that reject the view that power only operates repressively, and instead argues that it is both constitutive and productive, our analysis rejects the dichotomy between speech and silence. Instead, as we have argued, defamation needs to be understood as a continuous, active and contested arena of speech. The speech of Ramani is not unequivocally liberated by the victory nor is that of Heard silenced by what is perceived as a loss in court. Comparatively, while both India and Pakistan have prosecution-friendly defamation laws in contrast to the United States, where cases of defamation tend to favor the complainant, Ramani and Shafi have so far been more successful than Heard in the courtroom. Part of the explanation for this difference in outcomes lies in the fact that criminal prosecutions require a higher standard of proof. In addition, in both India and Pakistan, these outcomes were tied to a vibrant social media presence that is linked to countering the pervasive climate of threats of sexual violence. Social media offers a platform for contesting dominant sexual norms, as opposed to the law that tends to restrict and curtail sexual speech and discussion of sexual rights. This platform becomes extremely significant where there is the lack of an absolute right to free speech, which is true of both the constitutions in India and Pakistan, and where even progressive groups, including some strands of feminism, have tended to invoke the reasonable restriction clauses to speech rather than the actual right to free speech. All the cases created a larger ripple in the understanding of defamation as contested, where the testimonials, legal outcomes, and social media presence served to challenge the boundaries of what constitutes legitimate speech. Drawing on Foucault's (1978) formulations of the microtechniques by which people are made into subjects, the defamation cases and online responses partly constituted women as subjects whose voices and experiences about sexual harms were heard. They were heard both inside the courtroom and outside of it in the larger public space and online. While sexual speech remains contained within the universal moralizing norms of respectability, shame, and stigma, in all three jurisdictions discussed, defamation has emerged as generative of a speech that offers resistance to these norms. Navigating the treacherous waters of defamation, these cases are producing the fragments of a #MeToo archive of speech and resistance.

We should also take note of Brown's (2005, 91–92) caution of how the speech that gains traction may in turn silence the possibilities of "overcoming it, of living beyond it, as identifying as something other than it." She argues that the very breaking of silence may metamorphose into new techniques of domination rather than being emancipating. In the Ramani case, for example, the speech that gained traction is coded by the court within both a protectionist and neoliberal discourse. Women's dignity is located within a sexually conservative discourse and sexual and gender stereotypes, while the court simultaneously recognizes the importance of a safe working environment as essential to women's role in the labor market and, more significantly, the nation's aggressive neoliberal market pursuits. In this holding, the idea of sexual speech being a part of the rights to bodily integrity or sexual autonomy is occluded, silenced, or simply not engaged. In the cases discussed, Brown's caution impels us to bring out the paradox of defamation as censorious through a more nuanced and reflective analytical engagement with it. We have illustrated how the proliferation of speech through online support for women operates alongside a deep hostility expressed against them. It is this delicate navigation of defamation that cannot be captured in claims that defamation is exclusively silencing; instead, this discourse holds out the possibility of enabling and distributing expression that is disruptive of this claim.

NOTES

1 See also Equality Now 2021.

2 See also Jackson 2018. Jackson says, "Even the threat of a lawsuit can chill an alleged victim's plans to speak out."

3 On the idea of self-censorship and how market conditions affect speech before it is even spoken, see Bourdieu 1991. In the context of gay and lesbian sexual representation, Cossman has explored, for example, how censorship struggles with the state-produced gay and lesbian resistance became battles not only over the legitimacy of the gay or lesbian citizen but also over the legitimacy of the explicitly sexual gay and lesbian citizen. Cossman 2013.

4 Judith Butler has argued that if we see censorship as "a way of producing speech, constraining in advance what will and will not become acceptable speech, then it cannot be understood exclusively in terms of juridical power" (Butler 1997, 128).

5 Butler (1998, 250) has suggested that these various forms of censorship exist on a continuum "in which the middle region consists of forms of censorship that are not rigorously distinguishable in this way"; Freshwater (2009, 11) similarly argues that censorship can be viewed as a continuum "with the brutal extremes of incarceration and murder at one end and the constitutive operation of self-censorship at the other."

6 See Heath 2019. Heath's work reflects concern that has been expressed over the flattening of the meaning of censorship in the new censorship scholarship.

7 Shafi's complaint to the Ombudsman was dismissed. She appealed to the Punjab governor, who dismissed the complaint on the same basis. In August 2018, she appealed to the Lahore High Court to initiate proceedings against Zafar for harassment. The case was again dismissed in October 2019, with the court endorsing the ombudsman's ruling. On January 11, 2021, the Supreme Court admitted her petition against the Lahore High Court order and issued notices to the respondents Ali Zafar and Advocate General Punjab.

8 Zafar instituted a civil suit against Shafi under the Defamation Ordinance of 2002 on June 23, 2018.

9 On August 8, 2018, Zafar made a complaint to the director of the Federal Investigation Agency, requesting action be taken against the social media accounts that were "vilifying" him. The Federal Investigation Agency took cognizance and instituted an enquiry on November 11, 2018. On July 20, 2019, Zafar made two more complaints, accusing Shafi and others of posting defamatory materials against him, and requested an action under PECA. On September 25, 2020, a First Information Report was filed, and cases registered against nine individuals, five women

and four men, who had posted comments about him on Twitter, Instagram, and Facebook. Most were well known. Along with Meesha Shafi, some of the others named in the FIR included Leena Ghani, a celebrity make-up artist; Maham Javaid, a *New York Times* reporter and famous journalist; Ali Gul, a rapper and voice actor; Haseem uz zaman Khan, a wellness entrepreneur; Iffat Omar, a web TV talk show host; Humna Raza, a blogger; and Syed Farzan Raza, an internet celebrity. Humna Raza, who had accused Zafar of inappropriately touching her, subsequently retracted her allegations and apologised to Zafar, stating it was a misunderstanding. For more details, see Ellis-Petersen 2021b. Proceedings against several of these individuals were allowed to continue. See *State v. Meera.*

10 The criminal defamation provisions were introduced by the British in 1837 by Lord Macaulay. These colonial-era censorship laws were among those used to target popular social movements, criminalize dissent, and inoculate the ruling colonial power from criticism, rather than to protect reputations. Social movements were cast as anti-European and threatening colonial rule. See Cole 1995. Free speech was hierarchical, where the speech of the "backward native other" was cast as seditious, mutinous, unreliable, and anarchic and to be censored. This logic continued into the postcolonial period, with criminal defamation being used to ward off criticism and dissent. See Sethi 2019. The constitutional validity of the criminal defamation provision in India has been upheld: *R. Rajagopal v. State of Tamil Nadu*, 1994 Supreme Court Cases (6) 632; *Subramanian Swamy v. Union of India*, 2016 Supreme Court Cases (7) 221. The Indian Supreme Court held that sections 499 and 500 of the Indian Penal Code fell within the "reasonable restrictions" clause of free speech under the constitution.

11 Civil defamation law in India is judge-made. In a civil case, the onus is on the claimant to prove that the statements injured the person's reputation and were published. Thereafter, the onus shifts to the defendant to prove that the imputations or words were either true or amounted to fair comment or were stated in situations that offered absolute or qualified privilege as in the case of parliamentary or judicial proceedings. In a criminal action, the onus is on the prosecution to prove beyond reasonable doubt that there was an offense of defamation that was committed and there was an intention to commit the offense. There are ten exceptions to defamation, and it is for the accused to prove that they fall into one or more of these exceptions by way of defense to the charge.

12 They found the following statements to be false and defamatory: (1) "I spoke up against sexual violence—and faced our culture's wrath. That has to change." (2) "Then two years ago, I became a public figure representing domestic abuse, and I felt the full force of our culture's wrath for women who speak out." (3) "I had the rare vantage point of seeing, in real time, how institutions protect men accused of abuse" (Heard 2018).

13 The platform, tracking bot use and false Twitter accounts, observed anti-Heard hashtags frequently trending on Twitter. Their study found that the anti-Heard tweets were overwhelmingly not the result of organic activity, but platform

manipulation by Twitter trolls. The report concluded: "A group of Twitter trolls repeatedly used platform manipulation tactics to trend anti-Amber Heard hashtags. The trolls encouraged hashtag spamming and openly boasted when they were successful. Trolls frequently used copy paste techniques to amplify pro-Johnny Depp content while spamming negative Amber Heard propaganda." Bot Sentinel Inc. 2022.

14 See also Hess 2022.

REFERENCES

AbbTakk. 2018. "Rose McGowan Supports Meesha Shafi." April 23, 2018. http://abbtakk.tv.

Al Jazeera. 2018. "Minister M.J. Akbar accused in India's growing #MeToo storm." October 9, 2018. http://aljazeera.com.

Amber Heard Open Letter. 2022. "Experts Support Amber Heard." Last accessed October 26, 2024. http://amberopenletter.com.

Bourdieu, Pierre. 1991. *Language and Symbolic Power*. Cambridge, MA: Harvard University Press.

Bot Sentinel Inc. 2022. *Targeted Trolling and Trend Manipulation: How Organized Attacks on Amber Heard and Other Women Thrive on Twitter; Report*. July 18, 2022. http://botsentinel.com.

Brown, Wendy. 2005. "Freedom's Silences." In *Edgework: Critical Essays on Knowledge and Politics*, 83–97. Princeton, NJ: Princeton University Press.

Burt, Richard. 1994. "Introduction: The New Censorship." In *The Administration of Aesthetics: Censorship, Political Criticism and the Public Sphere*, xi–xxx. Minneapolis: University of Minnesota Press.

Butler, Judith. 1997. *Excitable Speech: A Politics of the Performative*. London: Routledge.

———. 1998. "Ruled Out: Vocabularies of the Censor." In *Censorship and Silencing: Practices of Cultural Regulation*, edited by Robert Post, 249–50. Los Angeles: The Getty Research Institute for the History of Art and the Humanities.

Chandra, Rajshree. 2021. "Defamation: The Weapon of Choice to Stifle Pursuit of Justice and Free Speech." *The Wire*, March 11, 2021. http://thewire.in.

Cole, Juan R. I. 1995. "Colonialism and Censorship." In *The Man on the Spot: Essays on British Empire History*, edited by Roger D. Long, 45–62. Westport, CT: Praeger.

Cossman, Brenda. 2013. "Censor, Resist, Repeat: A History of Censorship of Gay and Lesbian Sexual Representations in Canada." *Duke Journal of Gender, Law and Policy* 21 (45): 45–66.

Dockterman, Eliana. 2022. "The Depp-Heard Trial Perpetrates the Myth of the Perfect Victim." *Time Magazine*, June 2, 2022. http://time.com.

Donegan, Moira. 2018. "I Started the Media Men List." *The Cut*, January 10, 2018. http://thecut.com.

———. 2022. "There's an Antifeminist Backlash Silencing Women—More and More Literally." *The Guardian*, July 7, 2022. http://www.theguardian.com.

Dugan, Jorie. 2022. "Defamation Lawsuit: Another Tactic to Silence Survivors." *Ms. Magazine*, January 18, 2022. http://msmagazine.com.

Ellis-Petersen, Hannah. 2021a. "Indian Ex-minister Loses #MeToo Defamation Case." *The Guardian*, February 17, 2021. http://theguardian.com.

———. 2021b. "Pakistan's #MeToo Movement Hangs in the Balance over Celebrity Case." *The Guardian*, January 1, 2021. http://theguardian.com.

Equality Now. 2021. "Weaponizing Defamation Lawsuits Against Survivors Violates International Human Rights." *Equality Now*, November 29, 2021. http://equalitynow.org.

Foucault, Michel. 1978. *History of Sexuality: Volume 1, An Introduction*. Translated by Robert Hurley. New York: Pantheon Books.

Freshwater, Helen. 2003. "Towards a Redefinition of Censorship." In *Critical Studies: Censorship & Cultural Revolution in the Modern Age*, edited by Beate Muller, 225–45. Amsterdam: Rodopi.

———. 2009. *Theatre Censorship in Britain: Silencing, Censure and Suppression*. Houndsmills: Palgrave Macmillan.

Goldberg, Michelle. 2022. "Amber Heard and the Death of #MeToo." *New York Times*, May 18, 2022. http://nytimes.com.

Grady, Constance. 2022. "The MeToo Backlash is Her." *Vox*, June 2, 2022. http://vox.com.

Heard, Amber. 2018. "Amber Heard: I Spoke Up against Sexual Violence—and Faced Our Culture's Wrath. That Has to Change." *Washington Post*, December 18, 2018. http://washingtonpost.com.

Heath, Deana. 2010. *Purifying Empire: Obscenity and Politics of Moral Regulation in Britain, India and Australia*. Cambridge: Cambridge University Press.

———. 2019. "Obscenity, Modernity and Censorship." In *A Companion to the History of the Book*, edited by Simon Eliot and Jonathan Rose, 801–19. Oxford: Blackwell Publishing.

Hess, Amanda. 2022. "TikTok's Amber Heard Hate Machine." *New York Times*, May 26, 2022. http://nytimes.com.

Holquist, Michael. 1994. "Corrupt Originals: The Paradox of Censorship." *PMLA* 109 (1): 14–25. https://www.jstor.org/stable/463008.

India Today. 2018. "MJ Akbar Files Defamation Case against Priya Ramani over #MeToo Charges." October 15, 2018. https://www.indiatoday.in.

Jackson, Daniel. 2018. "Sex-Assault Accusers Turn to Defamation Lawsuits in #MeToo Era." *Courthouse News Service*, January 25, 2018. http://courthousenews.com.

Jacobs, Julia. 2020. "#MeToo Cases' New Legal Battleground: Defamation Lawsuit." *New York Times*, January 12, 2020. http://nytimes.com.

———. 2022. "Amber Heard Says She Has Decided to Settle her Johnny Depp Defamation Case." *New York Times*, December 19, 2022.www.nytimes.com.

Jansen, Sue Curry. 1991. *Censorship: The Knot That Binds Power and Knowledge*. Oxford: Oxford University Press.

Johnson, Bruce. 2018. "Worried About Getting Sued for Reporting Sexual Abuse? Here Are Some Tips." *ACLU*, January 22, 2018. http://aclu.org.

Khan, Irene. 2021. *Report of the Special Rapporteur on the Promotion and Protection of the Right to Freedom of Opinion and Expression: A/76/258*. N.p.: UN Office of the High Commissioner for Human Rights.

Khurshid, Ayesha. 2021. "Na Tuttiya Ve: Spiritual Activism and the #MeToo Movement in Pakistan." *Feminist Formations* 33 (3): 318–32. https://doi.org/10.1353/ff.2021.0053.

Lakkimsetti, Chaitanya, and Vanita Reddy. 2021. "#MeToo and Transnational Gender Justice: An Introduction." *Feminist Formations* 33 (3): 224–38. https://dx.doi.org/10.1353/ff.2021.0046.

Murthy, Laxmi. 2021. "A Vindication for India's #MeToo Moment." International Federation of Journalists. February 26, 2021. http://ifj.org.

Meera Shafi [Meesha Shafi] v. Ali Zafar, Supreme Court of Pakistan, Civil Petition Leave to Appeal 1795/2022.

Mittal, Priyanka. 2018. "M.J. Akbar Files Criminal Defamation Case against Priya Ramani." *Mint*, October 15, 2018. http://livemint.com.

Mobashar Jawed Akbar v. Priya Ramani, Completing Case No. 05/2019, Rouse Avenue District Court, New Delhi, February 17, 2021.

Nagaraj, Anuradha. 2021. "Lawsuits Seen Having a 'Chilling Effect' on #MeToo Movements in South Asia." *Reuters*, February 19, 2021. http://reuters.com.

O'Leary, Catherine. 2016. "Introduction: Censorship and Creative Freedom." In *Global Insights on Theatre Censorship*, edited by Catherine O'Leary, Michael Thompson, and Diego Sanchez, 1–23. New York: Routledge.

Oppenheimer, David B. 2020. "Defamation Law is Being Weaponised to Destroy the Global #MeToo Movement: Can Free Speech Protections Help to Counter the Impact?" In *The Global #MeToo Movement*, edited by Ann M. Noel and David B. Oppenheimer, 497–507. Englewood Cliffs, NJ: Full Court Press.

Pauly, Madison. 2020. "She Said, He Sued." *Mother Jones*, March/April 2020. http://motherjones.com.

Post, Robert. 1998. Censorship and Silencing *Censorship and Silencing: Practices of Cultural Regulation*. 1–12. Los Angeles: Getty Research Institute.

The Quint. 2021. "This case was not about me. It was about women's experience . . ." Twitter, February 17, 2021, 7:01 a.m. https://x.com/TheQuint/status/1362009212927111169.

Ramani, Priya. 2017. "To the Weinsteins of the World." *Vogue Magazine*, October 12, 2017. http://vogue.in.

——— (@priyaramani). 2018a. "I began this piece with my MJ Akbar story. Never named him because he didn't 'do' anything . . ." Twitter, October 8, 2018. https://twitter.com/priyaramani/status/1049279608263245824.

——— (@priyaramani). 2018b. "Ten of us have painted you a clear portrait of the media's biggest sexual predator. How many more stories . . ." Twitter, October 11, 2018. https://x.com/priyaramani/status/1050217581808775168.

R. Rajagopal v. State of Tamil Nadu, 1994 Supreme Court Cases (6).

Rosenfeld, Sophie. 2001. "Writing the History of Censorship in the Age of Enlightenment." In *Postmodernism and Enlightenment: New Perspectives on 18th Century French Intellectual History*, edited by Daniel Gordon, 117–45. New York: Routledge.

Schmall, Emily. 2021. "Journalist Cleared of Defamation Charge Revives India's #MeToo." *New York Times*, March 28, 2021. http://nytimes.com.

Scott, A. O. 2022. "The Actual Malice of the Johnny Depp Trial." *New York Times*, June 2, 2022. http://nytimes.com.

Sethi, Devika. 2019. *War Over Words: Censorship in India 1930–1960*. Cambridge: Cambridge University Press.

Shafi, Meesha (@itsmeeshashafi). 2018. "Sharing this because I believe that by speaking out about my own experience of sexual harassment, I will . . ." Twitter, April 19, 2018, 6:45 a.m. https://twitter.com/itsmeeshashafi/status/986918710991519744.

Shapiro, Lila. 2022. "Moira Donegan Created the 'Shitty Media Men' List to Address a Moral Injustice. Stephen Elliott Says He's Suing Her for the Same Reason." *New York Magazine*, October 25, 2022. http://nymag.com.

Shrivastava, Bhuma, Ari Altstedter, and Archana Chaudhary. 2018. "How India's #MeToo Campaign is Different from the Trailblazer in the US." *The Print*, October 23, 2018. http://dev1.theprint.in.

Stone, Meighan. 2019. "Five Questions on #MeToo in Pakistan: Nightat Dad." *Council on Foreign Relations*, July 15, 2019. http://cfr.org.

The State v. Meera alias Meesha Shafi etc., Criminal Revision 72/2020, February 19, 2022 (Court of the Judicial Magistrate, Lahore).

The State v. Meesha Shafi and Others, 2022 Supreme Court Monthly Review 1267, order dated June 8, 2022.

Subramanian Swamy v. Union of India, 2016 Supreme Court Cases (7).

Times of India. 2018. "#MeToo: Ready to Fight Says Ramani, on Case Filed by MJ Akbar." October 15, 2018. http://timesofindia.indiatimes.com.

———. 2022. "Delhi HC Admits MJ Akbar's Appeal Against Acquittal of Priya Ramani in Defamation Case." January 13, 2022. http://timesofindia.indiatimes.com.

Toppa, Sabrina. 2020. "They Accused a Pakistani Megastar of Sexual Harassment. Then They Were Sued for Defamation." *TIME*, October 20, 2020. http://time.com.

Townend, Judith. 2017. "Freedom of Expression and the Chilling Effect." In *The Routledge Companion to Media and Human Rights*, edited by Howard Tumber, Silvio Waisbord, 73–82. London: Routledge.

Tuerkheimer, Deborah. 2022. "This Was Never About Amber Heard." *Ms. Magazine*, June 2, 2022. http://msmagazine.com.

Turkos, Alison. 2022. "The Amber Heard Verdict Could Silence a Generation of Women." *InStyle Magazine*, June 6, 2022. http://instyle.com.

Whynot, Chelsey. 2020. "Retaliatory Defamation Suits: The Legal Silencing of the #MeToo Movement." *Tulane Law Review Online* 94 (1): 1–28.

3

Egypt's #MeToo

Sexual Morality, Class, and Gender Politics Across
Two Critical Cases

ZEINA DOWIDAR AND NADEEN SHAKER

In the summer of 2020, Egyptian university student Nadine Abdel Hamid made the difficult decision to call out her harasser on social media. As Abdel Hamid's post went viral, social media flooded with stories and testimonies of other women implicating her harasser, Ahmed Bassam Zaki, for sexual harassment, blackmail, and rape. Several young women launched online pages to not only mobilize against Zaki and locate other victims assaulted by Abdel Hamid's serial harasser but also share anonymous testimonies about their experiences with sexual assault and harassment (SAH) in Egypt. This latest wave of uprisings against SAH in Egypt, inspired by the global #MeToo movement, allowed the women involved—activists, whistleblowers, and campaigners—to organize around shared pain and victimization. They refocused the conversation to a larger one on endemic sexual violence and harassment while fighting what would become one of the most prominent and widely watched legal cases against SAH in the country.

While Zaki's case resulted in a rare conviction against him, another story unfolded on social networks: an even higher-profile case implicating seven members of Egypt's upper crust in an alleged gang rape. The Fairmont case, as it would become known in the media, would take disastrous turns, leading to the defamation of the victim and other witnesses by the media and the state and the escape of the alleged rapists from justice.

How has the Egyptian #MeToo movement, anchored by these two critical cases, ended with such oppositional outcomes? While the Zaki case saw significant social and institutional support for the survivors and a prosecution that ruled against Zaki, the Fairmont case failed, which sidetracked substantial strides in creating systematic institutional support against SAH in Egypt and highlighted the critical role sexual morality plays in the state's paternalistic protectionism.

Drawing on published and unpublished interviews from our two-part miniseries with *Kerning Cultures*, a Middle East documentary podcast, this chapter investigates the intersection between three key concepts which reflect these differential outcomes: Egypt's institutional family values, the double-edged online nature of Egypt's #MeToo movement, and the interlocking institutional power of sexual morality with the law and social class.

Chronology of the #MeToo Movement in Egypt

The trajectory of the #MeToo movement in Egypt is encapsulated by two cases that gained widespread attention in the summer of 2020: the Ahmed Bassam Zaki (ABZ) case and the Fairmont (Hotel) case. The ABZ case, as it became known in the media, began with Nadine Abdel Hamid, a twenty-two-year-old university student at the American University in Cairo (AUC), an elite university in Egypt. Abdel Hamid blew the whistle on Zaki when she decided to expose him as a serial stalker, assaulter, and abuser on her social media accounts. He and his family were known to be wealthy. Zaki attended several prestigious schools and universities; he attended the AUC from 2016 to 2018 and was enrolled in the EU Business School Barcelona when charges were brought against him.

Egyptian feminists, including Sabah Khodir, an online activist with a notable following, picked up Abdel Hamid's post. Khodir shared it widely with her networks and encouraged other women whom Zaki might have harassed to step forward. This drew the attention of an Instagram account by the name of @AssaultPolice, which was created only a few days after Abdel Hamid wrote her post. Assault Police would quickly rise to fame and become unequivocally tied to Egypt's #MeToo movement and pivotal in helping build the case against Zaki. Assault Police was created anonymously by Nadeen Ashraf, a twenty-two-year-old AUC student, who later revealed her identity on social media.

Within twenty-four hours of publishing the first post on Zaki, Assault Police received more than fifty direct messages via Instagram containing other allegations against Zaki that dated back to 2016, when he was just in high school. Some of these women shared screenshots of messages between themselves and Zaki, often with texts and voice notes detailing threats, threatening blackmail, gloating about assault, and more. Assault Police began publishing testimonies of women who reported being harassed, assaulted, raped, or blackmailed by Zaki, often sharing proof alongside the testimonies. Assault Police's second post, which shared explicit voice notes of Zaki blackmailing a victim if she did not perform sexual acts with him, gained widespread attention on social media and in traditional media.

Assault Police's work concurrently led to an outpouring of online testimonies: thousands of women came out against their own assaulters and harassers on their personal accounts or through anonymous social media accounts like Assault Police. Many online pages were created in the aftermath of the Zaki case, posting dozens of testimonies and offering legal and psychological aid to victims, which many specialists began providing free of charge. Celebrities spoke up against SAH for the first time and joined a media campaign. The Zaki case united the public and gathered momentum against SAH nationally.

Perhaps the most significant feature of the ABZ case is how it quickly and effectively catalyzed legal action. On July 2, 2020, the National Council of Women (NCW), a semi-independent government women's entity, released a statement pleading with victims to file reports against the serial harasser to initiate a civil suit against him (El-Gundy 2020). However, Abdel Hamid voiced her fear to authorities that victims might not come forward for fear that they might not have enough legal protection. Quickly, the NCW urged the Ministry of Justice to draft a new law that would protect victims' anonymity when they legally come forward to report the assault. The anonymity law, Article 113 of Law 177/2020, was then submitted to the Egyptian parliament and approved by both the cabinet and parliament in July 2020 (Farouk 2020). The article stipulates that "it is not permissible for the police officers or the investigation authorities to disclose a victim's information in any of the crimes mentioned in the Penal Code and the Child Law and promulgated by Law No. 12 of 1996"; these include crimes of rape, indecent assault, corruption of morals, exposure to others, and harassment, alongside any actions that affect a victim's reputation (Radwan 2020). In the aftermath of this law's approval, six girls, including the whistle-blower Abdel Hamid, felt protected enough to press charges, and on July 6, 2020, Zaki was brought into custody (*Egypt Today* Staff 2020). The anonymity law allowed survivors to take their experiences of sexual violation and assault to the public domain and circumvent restrictions on social morality.

After a six-month legal battle, on December 29, 2020, Zaki was sentenced to three years for sexually harassing two women using social media. The court that tried him specialized in cybercrimes and found Zaki guilty of sending pornographic photographs and texts to the women's phones and extorting them for sexual favors (*BBC News* 2020). In April 2021, Zaki was further found guilty of assault and blackmail of three underage girls and received an additional eight years in prison (*Ahram Online* 2021). Although the final convictions were for crimes significantly less eggregious than women claimed against him online, and despite few women coming forward to legally press charges, the ABZ case was considered a rare victory, mainly because its unfolding was closely watched nationally and became a matter of public interest. Zaki appealed the first decision, and his appeal was accepted in September 2022 (*Ahram Online* 2022). He remains in prison until the decision of the appeals court.

As Zaki's prosecution was moving forward, on July 26, 2020, Assault Police began publicizing another case that would gain international infamy. The Fairmont case, which occurred six years prior in 2014, involved the alleged drugging and gang raping of a woman by seven men from Egypt's superelite in the upscale Fairmont Hotel overlooking the Nile. The seven men were sons of some of Egypt's most prominent tycoons. The men included Amr El Komy, son of a steel magnate; Ahmed Helmy Toulan, son of a famous soccer coach and ex-soccer player; and Amr El Sedawy, the son of a big pharmacy franchise—El Sedawy was the victim's friend who appears to have been filming the gang rape. The incident occurred at a private party at the Fairmont, where the victim was drugged with a date rape drug and carried to a room. The seven men took turns raping her, marking their initials on her body with a Sharpie pen. They videotaped the entire incident and shared it like a trophy in their circles. The survivor, who remained anonymous throughout the case, was allegedly from the perpetrators' same elite social circle. She filed a complaint with the NCW after seeing the success of Zaki's case (Abuzaid and Sultan 2022). She allegedly looked to submit a joint case alongside other women who had been similarly gang raped by the group of men, who were known to allegedly repeat this gang rape often and always shared videos of them with their friends. Still, she submitted a case alone as no other victims were ready to come forward (*Mada Masr* 2021). Activists such as Khodir and Ashraf quickly started campaigning for the arrest of the suspects, several of whom fled the country as soon as the case began being publicized.

There was initial progress on the case, with the arrest of five suspects on August 24, 2020, three of whom were extradited from Lebanon (*Egyptian Streets* 2020b). However, three key witnesses who voluntarily came forward to support the victim were also arrested and held for months in pretrial detention on charges of inciting debauchery, drug use, and working to damage the image of the Egyptian state (*Mada Masr* 2021). A source speaking to Egyptian media claimed that one of the female witnesses was also held on additional charges of managing a social media account that damaged the image of Egypt in collaboration with foreign stakeholders (*Mada Masr* 2021). The same source claimed that the witnesses were interrogated, intimidated, and ultimately tortured in detention. Moreover, this arrest shifted the traditional media's attention from the suspects to the witnesses. A smear campaign in the Egyptian press launched against the witnesses to discredit them, especially against the sole female witness—Nazli Karim—whose sex videos and nude pictures were leaked to the press (Somensi 2021). The press framed Karim as the Fairmont victim and claimed the gang rape was consensual. Moreover, interviews with the activists and organizers revealed that those working on the case began receiving death threats from detractors of the #MeToo movement, and many were forced to stop their campaigning (Amr 2020; Khodir 2020). Ashraf, the woman behind Assault Police, was similarly intimidated and temporarily deactivated her platform at the end of July 2020 before revealing her identity to gain protection from the international community (*Egyptian Streets* 2020a).

The arrest of the witnesses and its aftermath resulted in the eventual dissolution of the case. In a statement, the case's public prosecutor stated, "We have done everything possible to seek out the truth. We have concluded that the accused had intercourse with the victim without her consent while unconscious in a hotel room during a private party she attended in 2014. But the evidence was insufficient to refer the accused to criminal trial" (*Egyptian Streets* 2021a). In March 2021, a court ruling ordered two of the suspects to be released on bail. The court also reportedly ordered the release of the other suspects in the case pending investigation (*Egyptian Streets* 2021b). By May 2021, Egypt's attorney general moved to close the case, citing a lack of evidence (*Egypt Independent* 2021). None of the investigators or activists could find video evidence of the gang rape, which many claimed to have seen and have copies of but, somehow, no one could submit it as evidence. The suspects allegedly buried it. After the closing of the case, the witnesses were also released. However, in a fortunate turn of events, on November 9, 2021, an Egyptian court sentenced three of the men acquitted in the Fairmont Case to fifteen years and life imprisonment. They were convicted in a similar case involving the almost identical rape of a young woman along Egypt's North Coast in 2015, for which video evidence was found. The sentencing was seen as having brought some justice to the Fairmont case and its survivor (*Egyptian Streets* 2021c).

While the two cases (ABZ and Fairmont) took place in the same year, the handling of these cases by the public and the justice system tells the story of two different versions of Egypt. In one version, the public and the system work hand in hand to bring down a serial harasser. In a classical mark of "paternalistic protectionism," the prosecution and the state officials held themselves responsible for bringing Zaki to justice—ironically, his social status could not protect him from public or legal vilification. They adopted a narrative of "paternalistic state protection" whereby they were protecting Zaki's victim—their "daughters"—from his grasp and gave the case much due attention (Abuzaid and Sultan 2022). In the other version, the public and the state ultimately exonerated the suspects by casting doubt on the sexual morality of the victim and the witnesses. To comparatively analyze how sexual morality played a decisive role in both convicting Zaki and discrediting the witnesses in the Fairmont case, it is critical to investigate the roots of SAH faced by women in Egypt as well as SAH's intersections with culturally endemic manifestations and beliefs around sexual morality and chastity.

Family Honor, Class, and Morality

As Neil Sadler (2019) suggests, Egypt struggles with a proliferation of "rape myths" surrounding SAH in Egypt, which Kimberly A. Lonsway, Lilia M. Cortina, and Vicki J. Magley (2008, 600) describe as "attitudes and beliefs that are generally false but are widely and persistently held, and that serve to deny and justify male sexual aggression against women." These myths serve to delegitimize assault victims by considering whether the actions can be regarded as "genuine" instances of assault rather than "perceived" instances of assault. These myths, which all center on blaming the victim for misconstruing and denying her experience of harassment or for inviting assault through perceived action or behavior, all justify a woman's rape or assault.

The continuous compounding of rape myths within Egyptian society is supported by a culture that upholds female honor and virtue. The historical-cultural context within Egypt and the broader region has led to specific terminology, *ird*, being used to describe honor—not in the Western sense of dignity, but rather a form of family honor that attains its value from the chastity and morality of its female members.

The conceptualization of honor or *ird* "can only be lost or redeemed and is mostly connected with a woman's body" (Baron 2006, 1). This notion of family honor resting upon the chastity of its women leads to prohibitive demands on the girl's actions and behaviors to reduce the temptation of any sexual activity before marriage, for example. Not only does this create an environment in which "to be an Arab woman is to engage in daily practices, an important part of which is to be a virgin," a process that Lama Abu Odeh (2010, 918) describes as the "hymenization of women," but this also plays out in the policing and self-policing of women's public affect of virginity through the scrutiny of their clothing, posture, behavior, speech, movement, and whereabouts. It becomes a community's responsibility to police women, ensuring they remain pure.

Such public exhibitions of chastity encourage and foster silence around SAH and assault cases, even within one's own family. As one interviewee said, "I remember growing up my parents were always like 'if anything happens, you have to tell us. You have to tell us.' And then whenever anything happens, I never end up telling them" (Amr 2020). The construction of shame through the simultaneous hymenization of women and the perpetuation of rape myths leads to a cultural environment that protects aggressors. Thus, while victims of the movement might have felt empowered to speak out, the idea of ruining their family's reputation significantly limited the number of women who stepped forward to testify. While the movement reached an incredible milestone by working with the NCW to encourage the Egyptian cabinet to pass a law that grants anonymity to victims of SAH in July 2020 (*New Arab* Staff 2020), victims still felt nervous about coming forward and risking family reputation and legal status.

Egypt's morality laws often incite hatred toward advocates and witnesses; *ird* is strictly reinforced through these laws. The Egyptian judicial system criminalizes acts that go against family values and public morals, and the vague wording of these laws has led to many arrests of women for everything from making TikTok dances to waving LGBT flags (El-Dabh 2020; Bernstein 2017). The laws, coupled with the public's outrage against any acts or behaviors by women seen to go against Egyptian family values—particularly any vaguely illicit sexual acts—make it extremely difficult for advocates to win over public support for their cause. As mentioned, the law and the state also carry on the role of paternalistic protectionism, in which sexual morality is held to the highest standard in determining the credibility of actors, whether witnesses, victims, or even aggressors. This has been a critical factor in the success of the Zaki case and the unfortunate failure of the Fairmont case. Wesam M. A. Ibrahim's (2022) corpus-assisted analysis of sixty-nine personal accounts of SAH inflicted by Zaki shows how victims often tried to justify their innocence and deflect blame by using a sexual morality framing themselves. They explained how Zaki was seen as friendly and a "decent man" when they first met him before they suffered abuse at his hands. In doing so, the victims worked to shift the blame which they could receive from the public for getting involved with Zaki in the first place. Still, Farah Desouky, an activist and journalist, describes how many people posted on Facebook during the case, blaming victims for putting themselves in situations where they could be assaulted (Desouky 2020). Zeina Amr of

Cat Calls of Cairo described how there was even a nuance to the victim blaming by the public in either of the cases, stating how while sympathy was afforded to Zaki's young victims, the victim of the Fairmont case, on the other hand, was blame-worthy for her actions due to the influence of the public's perception of her: people "explicitly said that the girls were young with the Zaki case, so maybe they were [sexually] inexperienced, but [the Fairmont victim] is old, and she was at a party. So we saw this difference, and I think it hit many people that, okay, this will not always work" (Amr 2020). The culture of sexual morality was used by the alleged rapists in the Fairmont case as a weapon to undermine the victim's credibility by painting her as an immoral woman in the eyes of the public. While the case was on trial, the media quickly framed the Fairmont party as an "erotic party" or an upper-class group sex party, implying that the rape was simply an unfortunate (but not unexpected) consequence of the victim's attendance at this party. In situating the victim as a frequenter of such seemingly illicit events, the media successfully buried "the seeds of sympathy with the victim." They alienated her from ordinary Egyptian families, who judged and even condemned these parties as proof of the extravagant lifestyles led by the rich (El Ammar 2020). The media and judicial system pounced on this narrative of the Fairmont rape being a case not of rape but rather of morality, which led to the arrest of witnesses. During their detention, they were accused of promoting debauchery, indecency, and homosexual practices (some of the witnesses were painted in the media as "gay," and authorities had uncovered "the biggest network of homosexuality"), which was critical in turning the public against them and the case more broadly (Belal 2020). Further, the Egyptian press leaked nude pictures and videos of one of the critical witnesses mentioned earlier, Nazli Karim. The media campaign aimed to discredit Karim as a witness, arguing that she could not be taken seriously because she betrayed Egyptian values of modesty.

Karim was the ex-wife of one of the alleged perpetrators of the Fairmont rape and had been given assurances that her testimony would be sealed. However, when her identity was revealed, her mother said that her ex-husband threatened to leak these explicit photos and videos if she testified against him (*Egyptian Streets* 2021a). The perpetrators relied on Egypt's conceptualization of sexual morality to turn the tide of public support away from Nazli by vilifying her as an immoral woman and releasing her nudes on the internet. They also tried to frame her in the media as the actual victim of the Fairmont case, thus posing that the gang rape could not have been nonconsensual if it was with such an illicit woman. As Jihan Zakarriya (2019, 144) highlights, this form of sexual violence specifically "aims at pushing women and opposition to hide or go underground." The Fairmont alleged rapists hoped that releasing the nudes—an act of sexual violence—would cause the victim and witnesses to rescind their statements of violence against them.

When the perpetrators seemed to be working toward confusing the public about who the Fairmont victim was—spreading rumors that Karim was the Fairmont victim—women nationally and internationally came to the victim's defense by circulating the hashtag "I am the Fairmont Victim." As hundreds of women posted the same image in which they named themselves the Fairmont victim, this created intentional confusion around who the real victim was and ultimately worked to protect her identity. Moments such as this proved singularly crucial to the survival of the Fairmont case and overall bore out the effectiveness of the online nature of the movement.

While young activists were able to use social media and online spaces as possibly the only outlet perceived as "safe" enough to move Egypt's #MeToo movement forward, they also were confronted with its limitations and how it catapulted them to the center of another type of backlash from the guardians of Egypt's sexual morality gatekeepers—the public, society, and parents.

Social Media: A Liberal but Contested and Dangerous Space

The nature of the online movement was characterized by a particular brand of rawness and boldness that stemmed from how #MeToo actors saw themselves and the role of social media in driving their activism. For example, victims and advocates strategically employed and reproduced the same language used against them by their harassers, whether by sharing screenshots of the original assault or using the same terminology in the retellings of their stories. In doing so, the victims reproduce the feeling of assault first-hand for the reader and bystander, ensuring the gravity and vulgarity of the SAH are received. This is a tool used by many cyberactivists in combating sexual harassment—Loubna Hanna

Skalli (2014, 253) reports that a young Moroccan activist wrote "But how can we change a reality, if it is imaginary? Telling sexual harassment in all its details, its vulgarity, and describing the consequences it has on us, we make visible and real this epidemic."

Social media was arguably the only tool of resistance young Gen-Z actors could use to fight patriarchal family values and SAH in 2020. It is essential to acknowledge the flurry of anti-SAH initiatives and groups that have operated in Egypt since 2005, during Hosni Mubarak's reign, and that have especially flourished in the five years after the 2011 uprising, which has made the movement's rise possible; it is also essential to note the political environment in which the 2020 movement emerged. In 2015–16, the state severely repressed street-level activism and grassroots initiatives after the "NGOization" and breakdown of civil society. According to Abdelmonem, feminist digital media remained one of the "last spaces and tools through which activists may try to keep movements alive in periods of forced demobilization when state repression limits political opportunities for mobilization, framing, and contention" (Abdelmonem 2023, 129). While #MeToo actors escaped the perceived repression temporarily, it eventually caught up with them, and some of the same issues of sexual morality policing were reproduced on social media.

The #MeToo movement began faltering under the many pressures it came under, including the Fairmont case taking a rogue legal course and activists starting to feel the backlash from the negative publicity of the case framed through crude attacks on sexual morality. Perpetrators of SAH equally used social media to attack and denigrate advocates and their work. As Mohamed Lotfy, the executive director of the Egyptian Commission for Rights and Freedoms, explained, "Social media, and especially Facebook, has become the 'media battlefront' in Egypt where winning over or losing the population and support of public opinion happens" (*EuroMed Rights* 2020, 2).

Personal safety was something every advocate struggled with in the Fairmont case. Ashraf posted anonymously since the start of the movement; however, when she started receiving significant threats to herself and her family while sharing information on the Fairmont case, she went offline for a considerable period (*Egyptian Streets* 2020a). Once she returned online, she revealed her identity to be protected by the public

(Khairat 2020). Many in the movement faced significant physical and reputational damage for speaking against SAH.

Social reputations also affected activists from an indirect standpoint; for younger activists, their fight was with their parents, with the state's potential perception of them, and even with the public, especially as state authorities began spreading statements "urging parents to pay attention to the moral upbringing of their children and youth to beware of internet influence" (Abuzaid and Sultan 2022). Unsurprisingly, the #MeToo actors were leveled with accusations of going against Egyptian family values concerning their activism, significantly as the Fairmont case intensified and the state's perception of it became known. Smear campaigns were a constant fear of everyone involved in the movement, from activists to survivors and claimants. These attacks ranged from publishing fake testimony, spreading rumors about victims' and advocates' morality, questioning the reliability of their characters, and more (Abuzaid and Sultan 2022).

This reality not only reflected the struggle of young women in enacting social change, especially on the topic of harassment, but also highlighted how they perceive their personal safety to be at risk vis-à-vis the state's construction of morality and control over the limitations imposed on them and the redlines they draw for themselves. These limitations are significantly influenced by the moral authority extended to their parents indirectly through state control and the values it imposes. Going against nation and state, and risking national and personal reputation, is a big one.

Class Rules: How Class Tipped the Scales

Sexual morality alone does not play a singular role in determining how SAH cases will play out, particularly in the context of these two cases. The interlocking institutional power of sexual morality with class and the legal system can also propel different outcomes and redirect the course of the movement. In this instance, while class played a significant role in popularizing the #MeToo movement in Egypt, it also worked to shield perpetrators in the Fairmont case from receiving justice.

Most activists and organizers behind the latest #MeToo wave in Egypt came from the middle- and upper-middle classes (Fayed 2021). Ashraf, credited for sparking the movement and later named one of the BBC's 100 Women of 2020, spoke fluent English and went to an elite private university in Egypt that most Egyptians could not afford. When Assault Police first appeared, its posts targeted the AUC community. Amr Marzouk and Gabry Vanderveen (2022, 2,234) analyze how Assault Police utilized its privileged beginnings and expanded into a fully fledged accessible platform for all women by translating posts into Arabic: "This was crucial for the spread of the account since English is considered to be an elitist language in a society where Arabic is the main language. This step transformed a singular rally against 'abz' into wider activism against sexual harassment in Egypt and prevented labelling of sexual harassment as 'rich people's' or 'AUCian problem.'"

Ashraf and other organizers' English-language skills helped propel the movement internationally. "This gave her the advantage of being able to effortlessly sit for interviews with international media outlets," Nadia El Sayed (2022) writes, adding that the same applied to other founders of pages that popped up in support of the movement: "The strong English-language skills of the founders of the pages, or the women, allowed them to communicate their messages and ideas well, thus gaining press attention locally and internationally and expanding their reach." While #MeToo activists could leverage their social class to enact meaningful change toward their cause, especially through bringing justice in the Zaki case, the alleged perpetrators in the Fairmont case could also use their social positioning to co-opt and undermine the case. Several of the six alleged rapists were from families that "wield pervasive influence within the Egyptian state administrations and reach those most sheltered in the pillars of the ruling system, both politically and economically" (El Ammar 2020). Compared to Zaki's social class, they were of a much higher social standing, and they possessed excessive wealth. Khodir (2020), seen as one of the leading activists in the movement, describes how their class and wealth foreshadowed the outcome of the case: "And as we know, money influences everything, including politics. So all of these boys came from really powerful families, and very famous, powerful fathers. And it was a really terrifying situation because when the girls came forward to speak to me, I did not know what I was getting into; actually, no matter how many times somebody tried to explain to me how vulgar, insane, and psychotic and violent these people are, that there are no limits" (Khodir 2020). A physical manifestation of this influence can be seen in how the prosecution dragged its feet in issuing arrest warrants for the alleged rapists even after the complaint was filed and the case was making the rounds on social media, allowing several of them to flee the country. Azza Soliman, a prominent feminist lawyer in Egypt, told Reem Awny Abuzaid and Yosra Sultan (2022, 307) how state agents treated the Fairmont case with apprehension and used it as an "opportunity to condemn the lifestyles of a group of young, upper-class Egyptians who had dressed, partied, and socialized according to a set of social rules that differed from the state's conservative morality." In contrast, in Zaki's case, the power of the activists' class in publicizing the case coupled with sympathetic public opinion for the survivors, who were depicted in the public imagination as victims baited by a sexual predator, worked in the victims' favor.

Conclusion

The #MeToo movement in Egypt was a landmark event in the history of Egyptian women's subversive and resistance movements. Egyptian cultural values of chastity and purity for women have long silenced victims of SAH, who become fearful of the familial and social repercussions of speaking out against their abusers. This is further perpetuated by the severe infestation of rape myths in Egyptian public thinking that places the burden of responsibility on the victim, often blaming her appearance or behavior for the assault. Two cases represented the rise and fall of the #MeToo movement in Egypt: the Zaki case, in which a university student serially harassed and abused young women for over eight years, and the Fairmont case, in which a group of friends filmed their gang raping of a young woman at an upscale party at the Fairmont Hotel in Cairo (*Kerning Cultures* 2022). These two cases showcased the interplay of sexual morality, social media, age, and class in their results. In the former, social media and the state worked hand in hand to bring down Zaki, where his upper-middle-class status could not save him from his brazen sexual immorality according to Egyptian family values. In the latter, the Fairmont perpetrators' upper-class status saved them from a swift prosecution, while the public's admonition fell not on their actions but on the victim's sexuality. Traditional media pointed the sexual morality gun at the victim and supporting witnesses, and social media alone could not save the witnesses from detention. While the movement was able to push back against these values to an extent and saw significant wins, such as introducing a law to anonymize the identities of victims of SAH within the judicial system, the institutionally embedded nature of these sexual morality values ensured limited progress. The conceptualizations of family values that underpin these morality laws also contributed to activists receiving significant pushback online, in their social circles, and even from their own families, inevitably affecting the movement's momentum.

The online nature of the movement played a critical role in providing a safe space for women to speak up, naming and shaming the perpetrators of SAH through online accounts such as Assault Police, Cat Calls of Cairo, and more. This provided the movement with legitimacy internationally while ensuring the safety and presence of the advocates within Egypt. However, these online platforms became a media battlefield as the movement progressed from Zaki's to the Fairmont case. Sympathizers of the alleged perpetrators in the Fairmont case used social media to defame witnesses and the victim, compounding rape myths to establish the "sex party" as a situation where rape should be an expected consequence and the victim does not deserve any sympathy.

Many vital persons within the movement belonged to the upper class, from the activists to the victims to Zaki and the Fairmont perpetrators. Activists and victims used their class and status to leverage the movement, further pulling it into the spotlight and exercising positive relationships with state bodies to exact progress. However, this same class status was also used by the alleged perpetrators in the Fairmont case to push the prosecution to delay issuing an arrest warrant, defame a key witness, escape the country, and thereby escape justice. The interplay of class and state in the justice process in these cases cannot be understated and further reflects the intricacies of SAH advocacy in Egypt.

While the #MeToo movement of 2020 has lost momentum, the progress and pitfalls that activists and victims saw offer a unique perspective of SAH advocacy in the Egyptian context. Just as some activists found inspiration from global cyberactivists, we hope that future movements worldwide can draw inspiration and best practices from Egypt.

REFERENCES

Abdelmonem, Angie. 2023. "Egypt's #MeToo in the Shadow of Revolution: Digital Activism and the Demobilization of the Sexual Harassment Movement." In *The Palgrave Handbook of Gender, Media and Communication in the Middle East and North Africa*, edited by Loubna H. Skalli and Nahed Eltanawy, 175–95. Cham, Switzerland: Palgrave Macmillan.

Abu Odeh, Lama. 2010. "Honor Killings and the Construction of Gender in Arab Societies." *American Journal of Comparative Law* 58 (4): 911–52. https://doi.org/10.5131/ajcl.2010.0007.

Abuzaid, Reem Awny, and Yosra Sultan. 2022. "On Social Networks, Anonymous Testimonies, and Other Tools of Feminist Activism against Sexual Violence in Egypt." *Journal of Middle East Women's Studies* 18 (2): 301–10. https://doi.org/10.1215/15525864-9767968.

Ahram Online. "Egyptian Court Jails Former Student for 8 Years over Sexual Assault Charges—Politics—Egypt." April 11, 2021. http://english.ahram.org.eg.

———. "Egyptian Court Acquits Ahmed Bassam Zaki from Charges of Sexually Assaulting Three Minor Girls—Courts & Law—Egypt." *Ahram Online*, September 12, 2022. http://english.ahram.org.eg.

Amr, Zeina. 2020. Personal interview by Zeina Dowidar and Nadeen Shaker, July 11, 2021, Cairo, Egypt, in person.

Baron, Beth. 2006. "Women, Honour, and the State: Evidence from Egypt." *Middle Eastern Studies* 42 (1): 1–20. https://doi.org/10.1080/00263200500399512.

BBC News. "Ahmed Bassam Zaki: Egypt Jails Harassing Student Who Sparked MeToo Campaign." December 29, 2020. www.bbc.com.

Belal, Shaaban. 2020. "حفل جنس جماعي نظمه مصاب بالإيدز لممارسة الشذوذ ومحامٍ".جريمة الفيرمونت ["Fairmont Case" . . . an (شهير ينقذ ابنة ممثلة معروفة ونجل مرشح رئاسي سابق) تفاصيل صادمة orgy organized by an AIDS patient to practice homosexuality, and a famous lawyer saves the daughter of a famous actress and the son of a former presidential candidate (shocking details)]. *Cairo24*, August 31, 2020. http://cairo24.com.

Bernstein, Alyssa. 2017. "Sexuality- and Gender-Based Crackdowns under Egyptian Law." *Lawfare*, December 28, 2017. www.lawfareblog.com.

Desouky, Farah. 2020. Personal interview by Zeina Dowidar and Nadeen Shaker, July 11, 2021, Cairo, Egypt, in person.

Egyptian Streets. 2020a. "Anti-Harassment Egyptian Instagram Account Assault Police Forced into Silence Due to Threats." July 29, 2020. http://egyptianstreets.com.

———. 2020b. "Interpol Extradites Three Egyptians Implicated in 'Fairmont Gang Rape' from Lebanon to Egypt." *Egyptian Streets*, September 24, 2020. http://egyptianstreets.com.

———. 2021a. "Egypt's Public Prosecution Orders Release of Seif Bedour and Nazli Karim." *Egyptian Streets*, January 6, 2021. http://egyptianstreets.com.

————. 2021b. "Public Prosecution to Appeal Court Ruling to Release 4 Accused Fairmont Rapists." *Egyptian Streets*, March 30, 2021. http://egyptianstreets.com.

————. 2021c. "Two Egyptian Men Sentenced to Life Imprisonment for North Coast Gang Rape." *Egyptian Streets*, November 9, 2021. http://egyptianstreets.com.

Egypt Independent. 2021. "Suspects in Fairmont Gang Rape Case Released Due to Lack of Evidence." May 12, 2021. http://egyptindependent.com.

Egypt Today Staff. 2020. "Egypt's Public Prosecution Releases Statement on Sexual Predator Ahmed Bassam Zaki." *Egypt Today*, July 7, 2020. www.egypttoday.com.

El Ammar, Maya. 2020. "The 'Fairmont' Case: Sexual Violence and Class Immunity." *Daraj*, September 22, 2020. http://daraj.media.

El-Dabh, Basil. 2020. "Egypt's TikTok Crackdown and 'Family Values.'" *The Tahrir Institute for Middle East Policy*, August 13, 2020. http://timep.org.

El-Gundy, Zeinab. 2020. "Egypt's National Council for Women Calls on Victims to Make Official Reports after Rape Allegations against Man Go Viral." *Ahram Online*, July 3, 2020. http://english.ahram.org.eg.

El Sayed, Nadia. 2022. "Social Change Will Be Tweeted—by a Select Few." *Cairo Review of Global Affairs*, September 12, 2022. www.thecairoreview.com.

EuroMed Rights. 2020. "Dangerous Liaisons: Social Media as a (Flawed) Tool of Resistance in Egypt." September 15, 2020. https://emhrf.org/euromed-rights.

Farouk, Menna A. 2020. "Egypt Approves Law to Protect Identities of Women Reporting Sex Abuse." *Reuters*, August 16, 2020. www.reuters.com.

Fayed, Ismail. 2021. "Mada's Feminist Roundtables 01 | Justice Now: A Feminist Moment of Reckoning." *Mada Masr*, January 20, 2021. http://madamasr.com.

Ibrahim, Wesam M. A. 2022. "Breaking the Silence: A Corpus-Assisted Analysis of Narratives of the Victims of an Egyptian Sexual Predator." *Open Linguistics* 8 (1): 158–88. https://doi.org/10.1515/opli-2022-0188.

Jaber, May Abu. 2010. "Murder with Impunity: The Construction of Arab Masculinities and Honor Crimes." *Al-Raida Journal*, no. 131–132, 38–45.

Kerning Cultures. "The Rise and Fall of #MeToo in Egypt: Part 1." March 25, 2022. http://kerningcultures.com.

Khairat, Farah. 2020. "Meet Assault Police's Nadeen Ashraf: The Student Behind Egypt's Anti-harassment Revolution." *Egyptian Streets*, September 20, 2020. http://egyptianstreets.com.

Khodir, Sabah. 2020. Personal interview by Zeina Dowidar and Nadeen Shaker, October 15, 2021, Cairo, Egypt, over Zoom.

Lonsway, Kimberly A., Lilia M. Cortina, and Vicki J. Magley. 2008. "Sexual Harassment Mythology: Definition, Conceptualization, and Measurement." *Sex Roles* 58 (9): 599–615. http://dx.doi.org/10.1007/s11199-007-9367-1.

Mada Masr. 2021. "Witnesses Arrested and Intimidated: How the Fairmont Rape Case Fell Apart." September 2, 2021. www.madamasr.com.

Marzouk, Amr, and Gabry Vanderveen. 2022. "Fighting Sexual Violence in Egypt on Social Media: A Visual Essay on Assault Police." *Global Public Health* 17 (10): 2,329–41. https://doi.org/10.1080/17441692.2021.1991972.

New Arab Staff. "Egypt Bill Protects Identity of Sexual Assault Victims." *New Arab*, July 11, 2020. www.newarab.com.

Radsch, Courtney C., and Sahar Khamis. 2013. "In Their Own Voice: Technologically Mediated Empowerment and Transformation among Young Arab Women." *Feminist Media Studies*, 13 (5): 881–90. https://doi.org/10.1080/14680777.2013.838378.

Radwan, Alaa. 2020. "المشرع ..كيف تصدى القانون لجرائم من شأنها تشويه سمعة العائلات والأفراد؟. وضع التشريع 177 لسنة 2020 بشأن الحفاظ على سرية بيانات المجنى عليه فى الجرائم الجنسية.. وأسئلة مشروعة لتجنب البلاغات الكيدية من خربى الذمم" [How does the law address crimes whose nature could tarnish the reputations of families and individuals? The legislation has enacted legislation no. 177 of 2020 targeting maintaining the confidentiality of a victim's identity in sexual crimes and raises legitimate questions about how to avoid falsified reports from those with corrupted morals]. *Youm7*, November 17, 2020.

Sadler, Neil. 2019. "Myths, Masterplots and Sexual Harassment in Egypt." *Journal of North African Studies* 24 (2): 247–70. https://doi.org/10.1080/13629387.2017.1419872.

Skalli, Loubna Hanna. 2014. "Young Women and Social Media against Sexual Harassment in North Africa." *Journal of North African Studies* 19 (2): 244–58. https://doi.org/10.1080/13629387.2013.858034.

Somensi, Mariana. 2021. "Exclusive: Feminist Icon Nazli Karim Shakes up Egypt." *Italian Insider*, January 27, 2021. www.italianinsider.it.

Zakarriya, Jihan. 2019. "Public Feminism, Female Shame, and Sexual Violence in Modern Egypt." *Journal of International Women's Studies* 20 (7): 113–28.

PART II

Decentering

4

Theorizing the Temporal and Geographic Scope of #MeToo

ASHWINI TAMBE

For a while now, I have been struck by the flexible temporal coordinates of #MeToo. As soon as the Twitter hashtag took off in 2017, the rejoinder that the phrase "Me Too" dated back to earlier antiviolence activism by Tarana Burke in 2006 lengthened the temporal scope of the movement. As several feminist academics also pointed out, other digitally driven antiviolence campaigns such as #YesAllWomen, which immediately preceded #MeToo, needed to be viewed in tandem with it. And if we were to consider #MeToo at its core to be the public sharing of experiences of sexual harm, then surely the public speak-outs following Take Back the Night rallies, which started in 1975 and continued for decades, needed to be kept in view as antecedents. Given that feminist efforts to reveal the extent of sexual violence through personal testimony have taken varied forms over several decades, it may be useful, for analytical purposes, to more carefully parse the distinct elements of #MeToo.

The spirit of the hashtag, which could be described as an effort to mark the wide prevalence of sexual violence and harassment via personal testimony, has a much larger scope than its modality, of survivors using digital means to name themselves. If we understand #MeToo as primarily a digitally driven campaign against sexual harm, its temporal and geographic coordinates are marked in one way; if we consider its spirit, we can take a longer and broader view. In this chapter, I offer a case for both widening the temporal and geographic scope of #MeToo while recognizing the distinctness of the digital environment and the specificity of #MeToo's various iterations around the globe. I articulate a transnational conceptual framing that allows for a simultaneous consideration of its multiple temporalities and geographic formations.

The Geography of #MeToo

Much writing about #MeToo has narrated it as originating in response to US actor Alyssa Milano's 2017 tweet calling on those who "have been sexually harassed or assaulted" to reply "me too" to her tweet. When other countries are included in the framing, #MeToo is narrated as a global conflagration emerging from a US hashtag that incited change around the world. The idea of a movement spreading like wildfire from a single spark is certainly appealing. However, this approach risks denying important antecedents in digital feminist organizing against sexual harassment and violence in multiple parts of the world. When we look closely at it from a transnational angle, #MeToo can be seen not so much as a progenitor of an upheaval in multiple parts of the globe but rather as an intensification of an ongoing strain of digitally driven activism about sexual violence in several countries.

Many news articles about #MeToo note the almost immediate and widespread uptake of the hashtag in social media feeds around the globe in mid-October 2017. The hashtag certainly spread in hitherto unprecedented ways, with a highly dense global network appearing almost overnight. Social media researcher Erin Gallagher (2017) notes that there were over ten thousand distinct digital communities formed using the hashtag between October 16 and 18, 2017—more than any she had ever seen—and "over 12 million posts, comments, and reactions on Facebook in less than 24 hours." Gallagher's analysis of digital communities using the hashtag finds that the community centering on Milano's tweet was only one among several and not even the densest community. The hashtag did not just spread in English-speaking parts of the world: nodes appeared in Japan, Argentina, Sweden, Egypt, Portugal, and Korea within the first twelve hours, in addition to the more Anglophone contexts of India, South Africa, Australia, and the United Kingdom (Burke 2018). What explains its instantaneous virality in multiple sites?

I suggest that the ready receptivity to the hashtag could be attributed to prior activism in those locations. If we were to ask where in the world has sexual violence and harassment in public spaces been a focus of digital activism in the past decade, we would name many of the same places where the hashtag took off. In Buenos Aires, Argentina, in May 2015, there was a mass demonstration of twenty-thousand people organized under the hashtag *NiUnaMenos* (Not one more) in the wake of the murder of Chiara Páez, a fourteen-year-old pregnant girl, that then ignited protests against sexual violence also in Uruguay, Peru, and Chile; in 2016, there was a mass strike organized in Buenos Aires under this same hashtag in the wake of the rape and murder of sixteen-year-old Lucia Perez (Lenta 2017). In 2016 in South Africa, students who were part of a campaign to lower university fees initiated the hashtag #EndRapeCulture, with a campaign that included naked demonstrations as a means to counter body-shaming (MacLeod and Barker 2016). In 2015 in Beijing, China, the Chinese government arrested Li Maizi and four other activists of a group called the Feminist Five for their planned campaign against sexual harassment in public spaces. The Twitter response to their arrests, #FreetheFive, led to protests in the streets led by women and global pressure on the Chinese government to release the Five (Zheng 2015). In 2015, Japanese journalist Shiori Ito filed a report of sexual violence against a high-profile colleague affiliated with the Japanese prime minister, then dropped the charges after police pressure, and then came forward on social media in May 2017 with public allegations, generating a historic level of visibility for the issue of sexual violence in Japan (Dwyer 2020). In Delhi, India, the 2012 gang rape and murder of Jyoti Singh Pande led to national-level protests and was followed by several social media-based campaigns such as Why Loiter?, Pinjra Tod, and Bekhauf Azadi, which focused on everyday forms of sexual harassment and violence (Lakkimsetti 2021). In Egypt, the incidence of sexual violence alongside the digitally driven Tahrir Square demonstrations in 2011 led to much more visible feminist agitation around the issue (Naber 2021). The 2010s, in other words, may be characterized globally as a decade of digital mobilization around sexual violence and harassment. The US MeToo hashtag, then, appeared amid such activism. It did not inaugurate anti-sexual-violence activism so much as provide an inflection point in ongoing activism.

Importantly, when #MeToo arrived on the scene in many places, it intensified extant efforts to counter sexual harm. In Sweden, according to Caitlin Carroll (2021), there had been concerted feminist activism since 2013 that focused on changing the sex crimes law to stress lack of consent, rather than victim vulnerability, as the key criterion for defining rape. Although there had been opposition to this consent-oriented law from multiple quarters, the October 2017 upsurge of attention to sexual violence in response to #MeToo led to the swift passage of the law, with no opposition, soon after in May 2018 (Carroll 2021). In other words, in Sweden, the collective disclosure of the prevalence of violence via #MeToo hastened legal reforms that were already under consideration.

In Ciudad Juárez, Mexico, the problem of *feminicidio* (violent crimes against women) has a long and disturbing history: much feminist activist attention has focused since the early 1990s on the disappearances of women, especially factory workers. *Feminicidio* was officially established as a crime in the Federal Penal Code in 2012. #MeToo created a qualitative shift in discourses of *feminicidio* as young women in Ciudad Juárez came forward in greater numbers to expose their experiences of harassment and publicly denounce their harassers through a WhatsApp spreadsheet that circulated on their phones. As Gloria González-López and Lydia Cordero Cabrera (2021) explain, local activists noticed a boldness they had not seen in previous years, with young women's social media access aided by the easy availability of repurposed phones discarded from the global North and resold in small stores in Ciudad Juárez.

In South Korea, where feminists have worked since the 1990s to redress the effects of military sexual violence against "comfort women," there is a history of examining the institutionalized silencing of victims of sexual coercion. Public speak-outs against violence have been led by organizations such as the Korea Sexual Violence Relief Center (KSVRC). In the early 2000s, the Hundred Member Committee collectively named abusers within social movements, according to Hae Yeon Choo (2021). These actions point to a longer tradition of feminists breaking silence about sexual violence. Given this context, then, #MeToo took a distinctly collective turn: the Korean translation of the hashtag changed an individually voiced "Me Too" (which centers on the experience of victimization) to a collective "I Too Accuse," echoing this longer feminist tradition of speak-outs.

In Namibia, #MeToo arrived in a context where sexual and gender-based violence was a long-standing recognizable activist and academic focus, particularly given the problem of wartime rape in the 1990s. The primary difference in activism that #MeToo in Namibia engendered was the sex-positive approach it mobilized—one focused on celebrating sexual pleasure while also denouncing sexual predation. Unusually, such activism also received support from sources affiliated with the state, particularly the Namibian president's wife, lawyer Monica Geingos (Currier, Winchester, and Chien 2021).

These examples each show that #MeToo articulated with preestablished genealogies of feminist activism in each location, taking disparate trajectories that could not have been predetermined. As Chaitanya Lakkimsetti and Vanita Reddy (2021) put it, these trajectories are a reminder of the importance of adopting a vision of politics that we cannot predict in advance, where the outcomes are not preordained. Unlike a diffusionist framing of the 2017 #MeToo hashtag that envisions only US feminism igniting good things around the globe, we can situate US #MeToo feminism *alongside* ongoing impressive activism in other sites.

Why is such an approach important? Why rewrite the narrative—a technically correct one, no less—of a single US-based tweet giving rise to a chorus of retweets around the globe? It is not simply because there is virtue in adopting a more reciprocal and egalitarian account of feminist networks. This approach actually offers the benefits of a more expansive and certainly a less blindered view of feminist activism of #MeToo. The dominant direction of media flows is from the United States to other parts of the world, because of Anglocentrism, media production and distribution infrastructures, and tastes shaped by colonial legacies. Stories of activist successes in the Global South, for example, are not a part of the staple media diet offered to US readers, while stories about US activist successes are widely consumed in other locations. When not required to engage with challenges faced elsewhere, US-based feminisms can fold into themselves, preoccupied with their own fissures. The task of devising effective responses to the presidency of Donald Trump made US feminism's inward turn particularly pronounced. This narrowing of perspective, although understandable and even necessary, can nevertheless be countered by a deliberate seeking out of accounts from elsewhere. There are lessons to be absorbed from #MeToo in other parts of the world: lessons of a collective (rather than individual) refusal of staying silent, of brave refusals of sexual respectability, of creative repurposing of "trash" from the Global North to generate new feminist futures. There is much to be gained by feminists in the Global North staying open to being impressed rather than focusing on exporting inspiration.

A Transnational Analytic

The approach to #MeToo I describe derives from a transnational feminist framing of circulation. In a conventional understanding of circulation, people, goods, and ideas are presumed to travel across borders in intact and unchanged ways. However, a transnational feminist approach to circulation, I argue, considers how these very entities mutate across borders. Holding dear a cultural studies emphasis on the politics of reception, transnational feminist approaches center how goods mean different things in different locations, how people change or have shifting identities across borders, and how ideas gain new resonance. Ideas, in particular, are "responsive to different histories, and they accrue new meanings and generate new solidarities all the time" (Tambe 2020, 472). In this vein, I would argue that slogans such as #MeToo must be understood in geographically contingent ways. Even if the hashtag #MeToo moved across borders with viral speed, it had different meanings in each iteration.

Widening our geographic angle also changes how we discuss the political backlash to #MeToo. As the hashtag's effects have unfolded, scholars of various leanings have expressed negative responses to this movement. A deep unease within feminist circles was felt early on among US women of color who questioned the depth and scope of the upheaval, noting that it denies antecedents in Black feminist antiviolence organizing and primarily centers vulnerable white women's pain (Tambe 2018; Roshanravan 2021). I've argued that shaming perpetrators via digital means works primarily in professional settings where perpetrators' reputations matter. Such settings were not the primary focus of Tarana Burke's efforts, which centered on community-building among Black girls and women to resist sexual violence across a range of contexts. Almost as soon as the #MeToo hashtag took off in 2017, its class- and race-skewed focus in the US became clear, and this focus was troubling because of its claims to universal appeal. The "too" in "#MeToo," as Lakkimsetti and Reddy (2021) note, has an assimilative imperative, hailing its users as a digital community based on a shared experience of violation.

As Heather Berg (2020) also asks, if only some kinds of workplaces, violations, and bodies are being discussed, then who is being established as the normative member of this community?

There have also been detractors within anticarceral sex-positive feminist camps who have depicted #MeToo as overly punitive in its calls for arrests and the lack of accountability for those who name and shame. Many have sought to situate #MeToo as following problematic legacies of antiviolence US feminism. Brenda Cossman's (2021) compelling account describes #MeToo as echoing an earlier generation of radical feminism from the 1980s, because #MeToo activists focus on sexual harms and see them as "pervasive." Cossman frames the debates about #MeToo as a new iteration of the "sex wars" that have beset US feminism, where the divide is primarily about whether to see sex as a source of pleasure or danger. She frames the detractors of #MeToo as the intellectual inheritors of sex-positive activists who warn against carceral solutions to sexual problems and who emphasize women's sexual agency.

Much #MeToo activism certainly continues the work of other important forms of antiviolence activism, particularly those focused on campus sexual violence and Title IX.[1] However, the heterogeneous global range of #MeToo activism cannot be theorized with references to abstractions drawn only from US-specific events and details. For example, US feminist sex wars were triggered by, among other things, city-level antipornography ordinances, power dynamics in BDSM practices, or the apparent overreach of Title IX proceedings in the 2010s. Each of these details sparked particular positions in the US debate that were labeled either sex-positive or radical. In Namibia and India, though, interestingly, #MeToo spurred *more* sex-positive activist actions. Prominent spokespersons were sex workers and a Telugu actress who stripped in public (Currier, Winchester, and Chien 2021; Lakkimsetti 2021). This is a reminder that, as we conceptualize the transnational scope of #MeToo, we must find ways to avoid the intellectual overreach of using only US-specific epistemological framings when describing its stakes, fissures, and drawbacks. The sex wars may definitely be a relevant backdrop for describing the debate about #MeToo in North American feminism, but what of other contexts where the call to publicize sexual violence occurs against a different historical backdrop, in a different register? This remains an open question.

My caution is not a call to reject all US feminist theorizations out of hand. Several concepts that have a US provenance, such as intersectionality and coloniality of gender, are useful in analyzing problems in #MeToo's trajectory. Shireen Roshanravan (2021) invokes María Lugones's critique of the "coloniality of gender" to argue that #MeToo in both India and the United States reinscribes highly limited understandings of the concept of "women." When Dalit or lower-caste women are targets of violence in India, it is not as "women" alone, but as members of an oppressed caste group. The universal "woman" invoked in #MeToo activism, then, works to flatten the range not only of experiences of womanhood but of actual forms of violence. "Women," then, ends up being less meaningful as a category in isolation—a point about intersectionality made with painstaking depth by Black feminist theory.

These critiques are certainly well worth engaging, and I share them (Tambe 2018). The key analytical question, though, is whether to treat examples of #MeToo's skewed focus as earning the condemnation of all things #MeToo. Could we instead treat #MeToo activists' call to speak out against violence and harassment as a salutary impulse that remains an unfinished project? Given how crucially gendered violence can deny people access to livelihoods, education, public spaces, and private safety, it seems unwise to reject the spirit of antiviolence activism.

Several scholars have treated #MeToo's erasures as constitutive, dooming the movement to failure. They see in the story of #MeToo a symptom of what is wrong with dominant forms of feminism today—a liberal individualist focus on personal grievance, a white as well as upper-caste coding of femininity as vulnerability, and a carceral approach to correcting social problems. But there is also a second strain of analysis possible, one that illustrates the polyvalence of #MeToo. In some parts of the world, retweeting the hashtag may not be just a matter of personal grievance—in an authoritarian China, retweeting it can be an act of courage amid the high government surveillance of social media. #MeToo-related activism has also likely increased the fluency of adolescents, who are prime users of digital technology, in addressing abuse by teachers and employers compared to previous generations. In Sweden, it facilitated legal change via a broader recognition of the scale of the problem of sexual violence in a country that otherwise treated its gender policies as a point of pride. In Pakistan, it generated vocal street protests and expanded conversations about what counts as a workplace (Khurshid 2021). In Namibia and India, it offered greater expressive opportunities for marginalized activists with sex-positive orientations who have patently refused sexual respectability as their goal (Currier, Winchester, and Chien 2021; Lakkimsetti 2021). In many of these contexts, #MeToo was supplanted by translations or prior terms that stress collective action (such as voicing externally directed accusations rather than the experience of victimhood), or that stress political positions, such as "Not One Less (Woman)" of *Ni Una Menos* or #EndRapeCulture. These examples cannot be easily dismissed as reproducing a liberal individualist emphasis on membership in an injured category.

The point, then, is that #MeToo has meant, and was, many things to many people. While a critique of its erasures is welcome and important, such a critique should also account for, or at least not discount, the movement's heterogeneity. In the abstractive process of critique, we must guard against the contraction of #MeToo to *only* one type of activism or to a single upheaval. So much critique of #MeToo seems driven by the impulse to reduce the upheaval to something that can be dismissed as "nothing but . . ." This dismissiveness also coincides easily with the logic of an attention-driven social media environment that thrives on generating new trends at ever-smaller time intervals while putting old trends to bed in quick succession. Placing #MeToo in the rearview mirror as something that we've "moved beyond" is really only possible if we are viewing a single problematic feature synecdochally as standing in for *all* of it.

#MeToo's Temporalities

How can we use a process of abstraction that preserves the heterogeneity of the upheavals conducted in #MeToo's name? How can we conceptualize #MeToo in a way that allows its varied forms and trajectories to mean different things? Doing so would, first of all, require acknowledging that perhaps #MeToo is not "over" and that it might have multiple temporalities. For instance, there continue be high-profile trials in the US referencing #MeToo. The legal victory that E. Jean Carroll achieved in her sexual abuse case against Donald Trump was seen by many as a triumphant moment for #MeToo (Goldberg 2023). It is a sign of the greater credence given to victims' voices that she convincingly claimed justice for an event that took place in the mid-1990s. The 2022 films *She Said* and *Tar* engage #MeToo as a theme: the semidocumentary *She Said* renarrates *New York Times* journalists' 2017 exposé of Harvey Weinstein in urgent ways, while the fictional feature *Tar* depicts a woman orchestra conductor accused of sexual misconduct. Many of these US treatments of the topic, however, assume that the movement can be defined by its eruption in US digital settings.

I have been searching for ways to theorize the complex temporal coordinates of #MeToo that accompany its geographic scale. One possibility I find useful for framing #MeToo's geography in nonlinear temporal ways is Nancy Hewitt's (2012) metaphor of short-wave and long-wave radio neighborhoods, which she uses to distinguish between forms of early US feminism.[2] This metaphor requires some familiarity with the physics of radio signals: long-wave radio involves higher quality signals that transmit over small geographic spaces, usually line-of-sight distances; short-wave radio travels very long distances, thousands of miles and sometimes even around the globe, but the signal quality is less sharp. (It is important to note the "long" and "short" here refer neither to distance nor time, but rather to the length of the wave on the radio spectrum.) Hewitt uses the metaphor of these two kinds of radio communities to depict the first wave of US feminism as composed simultaneously of a short-wave community of internationalist antislavery abolitionists and a long-wave community of more geographically circumscribed suffragists. While her analysis is focused on describing early US feminism in a more complex and plural register, the same metaphor of radio waves could be extended to imagine #MeToo's core concerns as both spurring activism over a long continuum of time, and also erupting occasionally in social media settings in a dramatic way.

Here is how the metaphor can be illuminating. We could consider the 2017 hashtag #MeToo's ripple effect as akin to a short-wave radio signal where a diverse range of people across a wide geographic area picked up and echoed a common amorphous principle. The hashtag could be considered a signal that several geographically dispersed audiences could hear. Such short-wave radio listener communities were distinct from long-wave radio neighborhoods already in place, where related antiviolence messages were more sharply defined and restricted to a smaller geographic space. The North American debates about #MeToo's place in the sex wars and the Swedish effort to change sex crimes law might each be classified as examples of long-wave #MeToo conversations confined to specific sites and focused on sharply defined messages. The debates over the racial politics of #MeToo in the United States could also be treated as a long-wave radio conversation since they make sense in the United States, but can't be heard (or don't translate as well) in areas with different racial formations.

Short-wave and long-wave versions of the same movement can coexist temporally. As Hewitt (2012, 669) notes, the value of the radio wave trope is in underscoring how radio signals "do not supersede each other" they "coexist, overlap, and intersect." Even as the short-wave version of the #MeToo hashtag produced a burst of activity across oceans in the many sites where it proliferated, it also merged with preexisting long-wave conversations in each site that shared the same spirit of addressing sexual harm. It is precisely because a short-wave radio signal itself is not sharply delineated that its meaning is amorphous and can appeal to multiple audiences across wider areas—and can also potentially resonate longer across time. In the same way that short-wave radio wave signals often lack clarity and definition, #MeToo works across transnational contexts as a short-wave radio signal precisely because the hashtag is short and multivalent. Since the hashtag is also being translated and morphing, #MeToo around the globe is a short-wave signal with far more potential for different kinds of reception and interpretation.

As short-wave and long-wave versions of #MeToo occur simultaneously, how do their temporal horizons differ? In her discussion of nineteenth-century US social movements, Hewitt (2012, 668) stresses how the use of the radio wave metaphor allows us to conceptualize intellectual heterogeneity and "competing versions of feminism in the same time period." While Hewitt does not posit any necessary temporal coordinates for long or short waves, I argue that short-wave versions of activism against sexual harm can actually have a longer temporal horizon than long-wave activism. A good example for exploring this question of temporality is the activism in India against caste-based sexual violence. A key moment in #MeToo activism in India was an intensely sharp long-wave conversation about the list called LoSHA (List of Sexual Harassment Accused), a Dalit student's Google doc allowing the anonymous naming of upper-caste predatory professors. It generated a loud debate in Indian academic circles, about whether upper-caste Indian feminists were protecting upper-caste male professors in the name of due process. However, the wider movement to bring caste-based violence against Dalit women to the foreground does not rest on just a single historical visible episode. Caste-based violence is routine, mundane, and pervasive—and precisely for this reason, it does not easily rise to the level of an explosive, attention-grabbing flashpoint. While feminists in India have protested against specific instances of egregious caste-and-gender-based violence, from the 1972 Mathura rape case involving the police assault of a tribal girl to the 2020 gang rape and murder of a Dalit girl in Hathras, too many such episodes do not rise to an intense level of visibility. The widespread and "slow burn" nature of the problem merits treating feminist activism against caste-based violence as a short-wave conversation across multiple sectors beyond university workplaces. Such activism has been taking place over a long period.[3] It is a movement whose short-wave signal, amorphous and widespread, has persisted across decades. To loop back to the distinction I opened with, if we separate the spirit of the #MeToo hashtag—an effort to reveal the extent of hidden sexual harm—from the digitally driven upsurge, then we immediately see an even longer history that extends over a broad range of contexts.

Looking Ahead

As I have argued, widening the geographic coordinates of the discussion of #MeToo leads us to also recast its temporal coordinates. My goal has been to lift the analysis of #MeToo out of temporal logic of entertainment and spectacular news. Treating #MeToo as a single US social media driven conflagration empties it of several important resonances. While its distinct feature is its digital context, it is also much more, as I have argued.

Using the analogy of radio wave to analyze #MeToo allows us to hold a number of its complex features together in view. The hashtag #MeToo worked like a short-wave signal that bounced rapidly across landscapes with a fuzzy meaning, allowing much variation in how it was heard.

Indeed, it was heard easily across wide geographic space because the spirit of activism against sexual harm itself had longer histories in each context, histories that were deeply rooted in specific social formations. To examine those histories, we need to understand with greater attunement to the sharp long-wave signals about what forms of sexual violence are widespread in each context, who the most and least visible victims are, and why.

We must also name what #MeToo is not. It was not a completely flexible signifier, even if it was fuzzy. #MeToo addressed a range of problems, but sexually charged workplace harassment came into view as the most common element brought up in activism across multiple locations, whether experienced by lawyers, performers, sex workers, or media personalities. This focus begged two questions: why was sex so heavily emphasized, and which workplaces counted? In my 2018 piece, I noted that the focus on sex coincided with the commercial priorities of advertising-driven social and broadcast news media. Workplaces in sectors such as the restaurant industry and the environments of domestic, factory, and agricultural work see endemic levels of sexual abuse—but these spaces did not garner the same intense attention; #MeToo seemed to be mostly focused on contexts where prominent perpetrators' reputations were at stake. Most troublingly, domestic partner violence, of which we have seen a soaring incidence since the COVID-19 pandemic (Evans, Lindauer, and Farrell 2020), seemed overlooked in #MeToo activism; unwanted sexual advances were the focus.

With the hindsight offered by a global pandemic, we must seek to expand how we understand the problems emphasized by #MeToo. If a good deal of activism was focused on safe access to workplaces and public spaces, then we have to examine how the very meanings of workplaces and public spaces have changed in this intervening period. During the pandemic, there was a collective retreat into homes for those privileged enough to remain workers and consumers within the bounds of their home. Their retreat was facilitated by those whose work supported a transformed consumption and health infrastructure—those deemed "essential workers." For several stark months early in the pandemic, a rift was clear between the dwellers and the fetchers, with the fetchers forcibly exposed to health risks by virtue of their economic need. Given the transformed relationship between work and home for many, the issue of workplace sexual harassment has receded in importance. However, the collective retreat from, or lessening use of, public spaces (including public transportation) has possibly rendered them *less* safe for those who have no choice but to use them. Several sociologists have also noted the exodus of women, especially women of color, from the formal workforce because of the pressures of caregiving during the pandemic (Sun 2021). Thus, at this time when notions of work, public, and home are being revised and transformed, we must stay vigilant about the enormous rise in household violence, compounded by the pressures of confinement, economic precarity, and strained conditions at shelters (Quinlan and Singh 2020), as well as the possibility of greater vulnerability in public spaces that are in decline. Queer people and those without recourse to a home, let alone a safe home, have faced intense challenges. If #MeToo, in one sense, was all about declaring one's vulnerability, each of these depressing turns makes clear that we need new thinking on the mutating forms of gendered vulnerability. As Lakkimsetti and Reddy (2021, 236) urge, we should imagine vulnerability as a defining human condition and highlight the "creative modes of activism and resilience" that people forge daily by working with, through, and alongside their vulnerability. Adopting a sense of #MeToo as having a broad, short-wave-like reach underscores, in a transnational feminist mode, the commonalities across geography related to gendered harm. A simultaneous awareness of the sharp, long-wave-like specificity of each context also allows us, in a transnational feminist spirit, to not draw overreaching unitary conclusions about what #MeToo is.

NOTES

1   The #MeToo hashtag came in the wake of new Title IX protocols in the 2010s addressing interpersonal sexual harm on US college campuses that gave more weight to accusers' voices. An argument could be made that experiencing these college-level changes intensified the disorientation that recent graduates experienced in workplaces as new employees and drove the anger they felt. On college campuses, administrators had been compelled to protect female students who were, in effect, customers. Workplace hierarchies, on the other hand, increased the vulnerability of female employees to predation, despite regulations in place.

2   Hewitt acknowledges the influence of Ednie Kaeh Garrison and Steven Lawson in shaping her thinking on radio waves as a metaphor.

3 Such activism includes scholarship over the past three decades about the intricate routine violence of caste by, among others, Uma Chakravarti (1993), Shailaja Paik (2022), Anupama Rao (2005), and Sharmila Rege (2006).

REFERENCES

Berg, Heather. 2020. "Left of #MeToo." *Feminist Studies* 46 (2): 259–86.

Burke, Louise. 2018. "The #MeToo Shockwave: How the Movement Has Reverberated around the World." *The Telegraph*, March 9, 2018. www.telegraph.co.uk.

Carroll, Caitlin. 2021. "The #MeToo Movement, Sexual Violence, and the Law in Sweden." *Feminist Formations* 33 (3): 281–90.

Chakravarti, Uma. 1993. "Conceptualizing Brahmanical Patriarchy in Early India: Gender, Caste, Class, and State." *Economic and Political Weekly* 28 (14) 579–85.

Choo, Hae Yeon. 2021. "From Madwomen to Whistleblowers: MeToo in South Korea as an Institutional Critique." *Feminist Formations* 33 (3): 256–70.

Cossman, Brenda. 2021. *The New Sex Wars: Sexual Harm in the #MeToo Era*. New York: New York University Press.

Currier, Ashley, Erin Winchester, and Emily Chien. 2021. "#MeToo Activism in Namibia: Sex-Positive Feminism and State Cooperation in the Fight to Stop Rape." *Feminist Formations* 33 (3): 271–80.

Dutta, Debolina, and Oishik Sircar. 2013. "India's Winter of Discontent: Some Feminist Dilemmas in the Wake of a Rape." *Feminist Studies* 39 (1): 293–306.

Dwyer, Shaun. 2020. "What Lies Behind Shiori Ito's Lonely #MeToo Struggle." *Japan Times*, January 26, 2020. www.japantimes.co.jp.

Evans, Megan, Margo Lindauer, and Maureen Farrell. 2020. "A Pandemic within a Pandemic—Intimate Partner Violence during Covid-19." *New England Journal of Medicine* 383 (24): 2302–4. https://doi.org/10.1056/nejmp2024046.

Gallagher, Erin. 2017. "#MeToo Hashtag Network Visualization." *Medium*, October 20, 2017. https://erin-gallagher.medium.com.

Goldberg, Michelle. 2023. "The Fury of MeToo Finally Comes for the Man Who Inspired It." *New York Times*, May 9, 2023. www.nytimes.com.

González-López, Gloria, and Lydia Cordero Cabrera. 2021. "The Borders of #MeToo: A Conversation about Sexual Violence Against Women in Ciudad Juárez." *Feminist Formations* 33 (3): 333–50.

Hewitt, Nancy. 2012. "Feminist Frequencies: Regenerating the Wave Metaphor." *Feminist Studies* 38 (3): 658–80.

Human Rights Watch. "Egypt: Epidemic of Sexual Violence." July 3, 2013. www.hrw.org.

Khurshid, Ayesha. 2021. "*Na Tuttiya Ve*: Spiritual Activism and the #MeToo Movement in Pakistan." *Feminist Formations* 33 (3): 318–32.

Lakkimsetti, Chaitanya. 2021. "Stripping Away at Respectability: #MeToo India and the Politics of Dignity." *Feminist Formations* 33 (3): 303–17.

Lakkimsetti, Chaitanya, and Vanita Reddy. 2021. "#MeToo and Transnational Gender Justice: An Introduction." *Feminist Formations* 33 (3): 224–38. https://doi.org/10.1353/ff.2021.0046.

Lenta, Malena. 2017. "From Feminism in Argentina: From the #NiUnaMenos Protests to the International Women's Strike." *Novara Media*, March 7, 2017. https://novaramedia.com.

MacLeod, Catriona, and Kim Barker. 2016. "Angry Student Protests Have Put Rape Back on South Africa's Agenda." *The Conversation*, April 26, 2016. https://theconversation.com.

Naber, Nadine. 2021. "The Radical Potential of Mothering During the Egyptian Revolution." *Feminist Studies* 47 (1): 62–93.

Paik, Shailaja. 2022. *The Vulgarity of Caste: Dalits, Sexuality, and Humanity in Modern India*. Palo Alto, CA: Stanford University Press.

Quinlan, Andrea, and Rashmee Singh. 2020. "COVID-19 and the Paradox of Visibility: Domestic Violence and Feminist Caring Labor in Canadian Shelters." Special issue, *Feminist Studies* 46 (3): 572–82.

Rao, Anupama, ed. 2005. *Gender and Caste*. New Delhi: Zed Books.

Rege, Sharmila. 2006. *Writing Caste/Writing Gender: Reading Dalit Women's Testimony*. New Delhi: Zubaan.

Roshanravan, Shireen. 2021. "On the Limits of Globalizing Black Feminist Commitments: 'Me Too' and its White Detours." *Feminist Formations* 33 (3): 239–55.

Sun, Shengwei. 2021. "Young Women in the 'She-cession': Centering the Experience of Young Women of Color." *Institute for Women's Policy Research*, April 6, 2021. https://iwpr.org.

Tambe, Ashwini. 2018. "Reckoning with the Silences of #MeToo." *Feminist Studies* 44 (1): 197–202.

———. 2020. "Indian Americans in the Trump Era: A Transnational Feminist Analysis." In *Feminist and Queer Theory: An Intersectional and Transnational Reader*, edited by L. Ayu Saraswati and Barbara Shaw, 468–74. New York: Oxford University Press.

———. 2021. "Afterword: 'Walking Alongside Many #MeToos.'" *Feminist Formations* 33 (3): 351–59.

Zheng, Wang. 2015. "Detention of the Feminist Five in China." *Feminist Studies* 41 (2): 476–82.

5

From Madwomen to Whistleblowers*

#MeToo South Korea as an Institutional Critique

HAE YEON CHOO

MeToo and Its Global Travels: Challenging the False Universality of the United States

What does it mean when we say "MeToo?" Consisting of only two words, this statement, along with the movement based on it, has become a transnational phenomenon, providing a way to reveal and speak out against sexual and gender-based violence. Crossing the national borders of the United States, the form that #MeToo has taken and what it has come to signify have diverged further, depending on local and national contexts. In some places, #MeToo has emerged as a campaign against sexual harassment in the workplace, while in others, it has become a call for women's autonomy and the free expression of sexuality. While the dominant means of transmission for #MeToo has undoubtedly been social media, mainstream media such as television and even sticky notes have played important roles in its spread as well (Kim 2021).

What enabled such heterogeneity in the way that #MeToo traversed national borders are its ambiguity and openness. As a colloquial and mundane expression, MeToo simply states that the speaker affirms the listener based on a shared experience, without specifying what the experience is or on what basis the affirmation is taking place. When Alyssa Milano on Twitter in 2017 called on women collectively to share their experiences of being "sexually harassed or assaulted," it enabled many women to share a broad range of experiences of victimization. Yet, in the

* Previously published in *Feminist Formations*.

context of Hollywood actresses speaking out against Harvey Weinstein, #MeToo in the United States has since been narrowly interpreted as calling out sexual harassment in the workplace as well as publicly naming abusers. This is a different version of MeToo from the one initiated by Tarana Burke, for whom the utterance of "metoo" was an affirmation of a shared experience of sexual victimhood, particularly among marginalized women of color (Burke and Adetiba 2018). As such, the polyvocality within #MeToo is salient in that it can operate simultaneously in multiple senses. In one sense, it is a call to solidarity for women victims, placing it within the legacy of radical feminism. In the other, it is a means of affirmation and solidarity among women of color deriving from intersectional feminism, even within the national borders of the United States. This opens the analytic and political possibilities of #MeToo, which reveal the social and cultural conditions of its travels.

While acknowledging the significance of the momentum that #MeToo brings to feminist mobilizations, feminist scholars have engaged in a cautionary critique, which identifies #MeToo's limitations as arising from a central focus of white women's pain (Tambe 2018), an inability to address workplace abuse as a structural issue along with class politics (Berg 2020), and a narrow focus on individual perpetrators rather than the social relations of power and systemic change (Gill and Orgad 2018). Often, these discussions are framed and understood as a universal discourse on #MeToo despite their empirical basis being limited to the case of the United States and, to a lesser extent, Europe without considering how #MeToo took place in most parts of the world in heterogeneous ways. A critical yet nuanced discussion of #MeToo, which examines its significance and limitations, needs to challenge the false presumption of universality based on a few national cases. Such a discussion should instead seriously consider how #MeToo has been shaped in the social and political contexts of its global travels, where gender is situated in different entanglements with race, class, and other structures of inequality.

In this chapter, I draw on the case of South Korea, where #MeToo has come to signify women's collective attempts to speak out publicly against sexual violence as a systemic abuse of power and authority. Articulations of #MeToo South Korea thus run counter to its dominant form in the US case since it goes beyond individual perpetrators to instead address structures of power within social institutions that enable such abuse.

I delve into the tension over how to translate the English expression "MeToo" into Korean as a contested site where feminists reckoned with the polyvocality of #MeToo to situate it within the legacy of South Korean feminist activism. By examining the landmark case of the prosecutor Seo Ji-hyun and other key cases, I show how #MeToo South Korea emerged as an institutional critique, as the women who came forward articulated the link between sexual violence and gender-based discrimination within male-dominated organizations, becoming whistleblowers instead of mobilizing based on shared pain and sexual victimization. Within such a formation, the scope of #MeToo was limited to sexual violence perpetrated by men in positions of power, embedded in formal institutional structures, such as the workplaces, universities, and schools. While this focus broadly mobilized alliances that transcend gender as a language of power and injustice, it also left out the problem of how gendered oppression not formally inscribed within institutions nonetheless operates across all realms of the public and private divide. Through the #MeToo movement, women have emerged as a collective subject demanding equal recognition in the public sphere. But the movement's swift turn toward gender politics with an emphasis on gender discrimination, away from sexual politics, has yet to foster a nuanced discussion on the interplay between sexuality, agency, and violence.

Feminist Politics of Translation: Tensions Between Sexual Victimhood and Agency in South Korea

When the term "MeToo" was first reported in South Korean media following the 2017 Twitter campaign begun by Milano, South Korean journalists, scholars, and activists had divergent opinions about how to translate it. Although simple English expressions like "me too" are commonly understood in South Korea, especially among those with a formal education, it took a process of translation to provide #MeToo's meaning and context to the South Korean public, until it gained enough familiarity to enter the South Korean lexicon as a loan word in transliterated form: 미투. In this early phase during the first several months, MeToo (as a transliterated word) was often accompanied by a Korean translation in parentheses, and this was where the polyvocality of #MeToo became salient. In late 2017 and early 2018, media outlets translated

MeToo as 나도 당했다 (I too was victimized), largely retaining the meaning of the original. However, feminist organizations and scholars voiced concerns about this translation, stating that it focused on the act of violence and rendered the victim-speaker passive and helpless, rather than an active agent participating in a social movement. Instead, they recommended the use of 나도 고발한다 (I too accuse) or 나도 말한다 (I too speak out) as the Korean expression to accompany MeToo, which many media outlets and academic publications have since adopted (Jang and Bak 2018; Jin 2018).

How did "I too accuse" or "I too speak out" become a more proper feminist translation of MeToo when this expression diverges from the intended meaning of the term in the versions of both Burke and Milano, to which the acknowledgment of shared sexual victimization is central, with no mention of speaking out in public or accusing the abuser? What social, cultural, and political conditions in South Korea made "I too accuse" a more feminist choice than "I too was victimized?" And what are the implications of this choice for how #MeToo has been shaped in South Korea? Examining these questions means echoing the call by South Korean feminist scholars to situate #MeToo within the context of South Korean feminist politics and activism instead of considering it as an "import" from the United States (Kwon Kim 2020; Lee 2018).

The push to translate MeToo as "I too speak out" or "I too accuse" emphasizes the act of speaking rather than being victimized. This political choice is in line with the genealogy of South Korean feminist activism on the need to break the silence around sexual violence. Such activism has included, since the 1990s, condemnation of military sexual violence in the case of the "comfort women" under Japanese colonial rule, named by the feminist scholar Na-Young Lee (2018) as "South Korea's first MeToo." Another example is the work of the Korea Sexual Violence Relief Center (KSVRC), a prominent feminist organization in the field of sexual violence. Established in 1991, the KSVRC has organized annual public "speak out" events since 2003 as well as monthly peer support groups for survivors from 2007. Speaking out, whether in public or in small circles, is highlighted by the KSVRC (2020) as a transformative act, through which one becomes "the agent of the experience," giving rise to "healing as well as movement" based on "sisterhood and solidarity."

The translation "I too accuse" also resonates with other times when feminists have collectively accused the perpetrators of sexual violence, such as the Hundred Member Committee (백인위) that named abusers within social movement organizations in the early 2000s or the Twitter hashtag campaigns that disclosed sexual violence in various fields, such as literature and theatre, in 2015–16, igniting a new wave of feminist consciousness among young women (Lee 2018). As feminist scholar Hyun-young Kwon Kim (2020, 134) argues, the essence of #MeToo is the act of breaking silence, in that those who have endured sexual violence "can now speak not only from the position of a victim, but also from the position of an accuser."

While #MeToo is a continuation of this long-standing legacy, it has mainstreamed the issue of sexual violence for the public, in contrast to prior feminist campaigns that had a narrower reach. Beginning with the prosecutor Seo Ji-hyun in 2018, who spoke about her experiences with workplace sexual harassment, countless women came forward under the banner of #MeToo in different sectors and institutions, including theater, sports, film, literature, politics, and education. As the daily news of #MeToo led prominent politicians, university professors, and theatre directors to resign, or even be convicted in court, #MeToo has become part of everyday conversations among South Korean public across generations, from high school students to older women shopping in a local market (Kwon Kim 2020). No longer a discussion limited to the women's studies university classroom or to a twitter hashtag, #MeToo brought the issue of sexual and gender-based violence to the forefront of public conversation.

#MeToo South Korea, however, did not encompass all speech against sexual violence; rather, it has emerged specifically to refer to issues of *power-laden* sexual violence (권력형 성폭력), where gendered power is compounded by authority in male-dominated organizations. With the notion that it is more feminist to translate MeToo as "I too accuse," this phrase then came to refer to a public accusation toward a sexual abuser in a position of power *and* of the institution that enabled a violent act in the first place. In the next section, I discuss how this conceptualization aptly highlights the connection between sexual violence, everyday sexism, and other forms of abuse of institutional power yet still needs to reckon with gender itself as a relation of power operating in all realms across the public and private divide.

#MeToo as an Institutional Critique: Exposing Sexual Violence Embedded in Male-Dominated Organizations

#MeToo South Korea emerged as a powerful force after January 2018, when Seo Ji-Hyun, a prosecutor with a fifteen-year career in the Korean Prosecution Service (KPS) disclosed, on national television, her experience of sexual harassment by a high-ranking prosecutor, leading to retribution against her within the KPS. While the first wave of #MeToo, which began mainly in the United States in October 2017, was reported widely in South Korea as an issue of global concern, it was the landmark case of Seo that defined the trajectory of #MeToo South Korea—how it is understood by the public and feminist counterpublic alike. What is distinctive about #MeToo South Korea is the way it has linked sexual violence to the everyday sexism and gender discrimination that women routinely face within male-dominated organizations, like workplaces, sports teams, universities, and schools, while offering an institutional critique as whistleblowers call attention to workplace abuse and other injustices within these organizations.

Seo spoke about the incident of sexual harassment she experienced— being groped by a drunk senior prosecutor while surrounded by her male colleagues—not as an isolated act, but one embedded in the hostile sexist climate at the KPS. Most media reporting of her account focused on the act of unwanted touching, but the setting in which it took place is just as significant as an indicator of the treatment of women in the KPS and, by extension, male-dominated organizations at large.

Disrespect toward women permeated the KPS to a great extent, such that male prosecutors believed the presence of women signaled the reduced status of the KPS in society and projected hostility toward the women colleagues to counter their perceived threat to masculinity. They openly expressed this opinion in front of the women they worked with, who were junior in rank and often isolated as the only women prosecutors in their assigned district offices. This sexist treatment not only came from male prosecutors, but the community as well. For example, Seo (2020) recalled multiple incidents when she called to inquire about a case and received a response questioning whether she was really a prosecutor because of her gender, with comments such as "If you are a prosecutor, I am the president of South Korea."

After Seo's disclosure of her own harassment in 2017, the Ministry of Justice conducted a climate survey of all women prosecutors and found that more than 70 percent responded that they had experienced sexual harassment or other forms of sexual violence. While such a high number might be surprising to people outside the organization, Seo added that many women prosecutors were rather surprised that the result was not 100 percent (Kim and Choi 2018). As Hyun-Mee Kim (2018, 4) noted about #MeToo South Korea, what the KPS case shows is that "sexual violence is not a matter of unwanted sexual contact between men and women, but rather one of gendered power deeply entrenched in the workplace and other parts of the public sphere as well as a matter of gender inequality that forces women into the dual role of sexual trophies in male homosocial society as well as devalued labor."

In speaking out and becoming a public figure in #MeToo, Seo not only extended her support to individual women but leveraged a powerful critique of institutionalized sexism. She posted a lengthy statement on an internal KPS online board, which was later published in national newspapers. In this statement, she positioned herself as a member of the KPS demanding institutional reform: "I write with the wish that we would no longer stay silent and reform ourselves from within. . . . I now think that simply enduring the injustice and unfair treatment that happened to me is not serving the organization. Rather, placing them out in the open will enable the organization to move forward. It is my sincere wish that we will be reborn as the KPS that deserves the nation's love and trust and works for justice" (Seo quoted in Kim and Choi 2018). Here, "we" are not women as a collective, but rather the members of the KPS, to whom she appealed from the position of an insider. Seo (2018a) ended her statement with three hashtags: #MeToo in English and #HRsystemKPS and #SexualViolenceKPS in Korean. Here, the HR (human resources) system is noted as a particular target for change, since Seo argued that it was abused as a tool for retaliation against her, showing its arbitrariness and lack of transparency. This combination of hashtags shows, through Seo's landmark case, how #MeToo South Korea firmly situated the issue of sexual violence within a concrete organizational context with a specific demand for institutional reform.

The Aftermath of #MeToo: From Madwomen to Whistleblower Subjects

After confronting her organization's failure rather than an individual perpetrator, Seo was labeled within the KPS as a 미친년 ("madwoman," or to be precise, a "crazy bitch"). She faced ostracization as a "traitor" who brought shame to the organization and who harbored ulterior motives. Dealing with countless harsh rumors about her career and character in the aftermath, Seo realized, "Ah, this is a spider web that I cannot escape; the more I struggle, the stronger it will entangle me, and eventually it will take my life. I've gotten rid of the illusion that I can escape this web now. Rather than fighting the web, I should squarely face the spider and find a way not to be eaten at the last minute" (Seo quoted in Jang 2018).

Seo's metaphor of a spider web highlights the ubiquitous nature of gendered hierarchy and violence as a pervading structure that confines and silences women. Explaining who the spider is, Seo elaborated on this structural understanding: "In a narrow sense, it is the perpetrator himself and the KPS, and in a broader sense, this society. Do you think the victims went through unspeakable suffering because of the sexual violence? Or did they wither because of the suffering caused by a community that neglected the sexual violence and actually criticized the victims while protecting their assailants? Was it the victims' weakness and fear that silenced them? Or was it because of this cruel community that doubted and condemned the victims, calling them whores and gold diggers rather than facing the truth?" (Seo quoted in Jang 2018). By bringing attention to the spider web, Seo laid bare that the issue of sexual violence is not limited to the perpetrators as individuals or the act itself, but the "cruel community" that enables it and continues to protect the assailants as an organization rather than the victims.

Following Seo, many women in South Korea spoke out under the banner of #MeToo and continued the challenge against gender-based violence, a spider web that spans organizations and broader society. Kim Ji-eun, a political aide, became another key symbol of #MeToo a few months later in March 2018, when she accused the prominent politician Ahn Hee-jung, then the governor of Chungnam Province, of sexual assault on national television, which led to his immediate resignation and later criminal conviction. Kim Ji-eun (2020) also echoed Seo's structural understanding of sexual violence, stating that "power-laden sexual crime is not simply a problem of the perpetrator as an individual. Rather, the uneven structure of power within the organization to which the victim and the perpetrator belong manifests itself in the form of criminal sexual violence." In coming forward, these women refused to play along with the rules of their male-dominated organizations, which meant keeping silent about sexual violence and everyday sexism. As prosecutors, athletes, actresses, political aides, or poets, these women risked their personal reputations and professional careers. When they spoke out, the society that could no longer hold them in the spider web called them "mad" because their conduct was not intelligible according to the dominant logic, where violence against women is entrenched within the normal order (Jông 2019, 80).

The label of "madwomen," however, began losing its power when these women came together in support of one another. Just one day after Seo spoke out, Im Eun-Jông—a more senior prosecutor who was known to be a vocal critic within the KPS on social justice issues—supported Seo in public by speaking about her own experiences of sexual harassment and assault in the KPS. Seo recalled meeting with Im afterward, where Im jokingly said, "Thank you so much. I was the number one madwoman [제1 미친년] in the KPS, but now that you have come forward, the title goes to you" (Im quoted in Horuragi Foundation 2018b). When Seo and Im laughed aloud together as they sat side by side in a public forum and told their stories, the epithet "madwoman" ceased to be a threat to isolated individuals named as such, but rather was a collective badge of honor for speaking out.

Coming together, these women were no longer simply caught in the web—they became whistleblowers who brought about an institutional challenge, often at personal cost. Jo Hyôn-wuk, the president of the Korean Women Lawyers' Association (KWLA), organized a legal defense team for the poet Choi Young-Mi, who spoke in public about the prominent poet Ko Un's sexual harassment and was subsequently sued by Ko for defamation. Jo expressed her gratitude to Choi and other victims who came forward to call for social change as part of #MeToo, which was the reason she arranged for five members of the key leadership of the KWLA to support Choi: "In ordinary legal cases, it's the plaintiff vs. the defendant, the perpetrator vs. the victim—one individual vs. another. But the #MeToo case is very different. It's Choi Young-Mi vs. the giant power within the literary field, Kim Ji-eun vs. the supporters of Ahn Hee-jung. The victim's suffering comes from this structure. . . . Our society owes a great deal to these people. For that reason, we must be mindful of the real damage inflicted on them and foster an environment where they can receive empathy, support, and solidarity" (Jo quoted in M. Kim 2020). With the support of the KWLA, Choi's legal battle was successful. While the repercussions from speaking out persist, there is increasing recognition that their actions are for the public good, and it is necessary to organize to support them.

Discussing the wave of #MeToo South Korea, Seo spoke about the pervasiveness of sexual violence and the demands of #MeToo as a call for institutional reform:

> After I spoke out, Prosecutor Im Eun-Jông said, "Why does everyone pretend to be surprised, when in fact they knew all along?" I want to say the same. Isn't this the story that everyone already knew about? The reality is that sexual violence has been rampant, not just in the field of sports, but in all sectors, including cultural industries, politics, and law. When I spoke about being a victim of sexual violence, and when other victims shouted out MeToo, society treated us as if we were freaks. But what MeToo demands is nothing special. We are not saying that the victims should receive special treatment or rights. We are simply saying, stop committing sexual violence; punish the perpetrator properly; protect the victims properly. . . . I think the success of MeToo hinges upon reform of the KPS. There is no way that MeToo can lead to a successful outcome if the KPS remains an organization where sexual violence is rampant, generously tolerated and methodically buried, and victims are systematically harassed. (*SBS News* 2019)

Seo points out that what #MeToo is asking for is simply enforcement of existing law, the Anti-Sexual Violence Act of 1994, which is the KPS's mandate, rather than a radical demand for new sexual politics. The irony of Seo's situation, where she was tasked with enforcing the law as a prosecutor but was unable to obtain justice for her own victimization, was not lost on Seo herself, nor on the broader South Korean public, as a glaring failure of the criminal justice system with respect to sexual violence. Seo, together with her allies like Prosecutor Im, used her platform as a #MeToo trailblazer in order to push for reform of the KPS, advocating for the creation of a special office that can act as a counterweight to the KPS, namely the Corruption Investigation Office for High-Ranking Officials (CIO).

In making these kinds of demands, the subjects of #MeToo South Korea have emerged not as sexualized, suffering victims, but as reformist subjects acting for the collective good. Seo called for a gender-based collectivity in South Korea and beyond by participating in multiple public forums on #MeToo and sexual violence, which she shared with other women who had come forward with their own experiences of sexual harassment and violence in diverse sectors in South Korea. Having attained a symbolic status in South Korea, Seo also met with the "comfort women" who had come forward since the 1990s to speak about sexual violence committed by the Japanese military, calling them "the pioneers of MeToo" (Bae 2018). Across national borders, Seo made connections with other #MeToo trailblazers such as Ito Shiori, a journalist who became a symbol of the #MeToo movement in Japan after bringing a prominent journalist to court for sexual assault. In a joint interview, Seo and Ito shared their experiences of sexual violence and their subsequent shaming as a "gold digger" and an "embarrassment for the nation," demonstrating that they could be "a source of courage for each other" (Jang 2018).

In addition to building a gender-based community of support, Seo also emerged as a symbol of resistance against abuse of power in the workplace, beyond the issue of gender justice or sexual violence. Seo formed a special bond with Park Chang-jin, a male flight attendant for Korean Air, who became a public figure after the "nut rage" incident in 2014. Cho Hyun-ah, then the vice president of Korean Air and the daughter of its CEO, verbally and physically attacked Park for serving her macadamia nuts improperly. She then ordered their plane to return to the gate and left him at JFK airport in New York City. When Park refused to stay silent, he was demoted and ostracized at work, making him a symbol of the victims of abuse of power by the privileged class in South Korea.

Conceptualizing #MeToo as an act of speaking out against power-laden sexual violence enabled a broader mobilization beyond gender, which pointed to abuse of power within social institutions such as the workplace. The connection between Park and Seo reveals how #MeToo South Korea is understood not only as a response to gender-based violence but as a symbol of the less powerful bringing an institutional critique to oppose the injustice of the power structure. Despite the significant differences between them with respect to occupation and gender, one journalist told Seo that they "resemble each other like twins" in the ways that their organizations tried to "kill them off systematically." Or, as Seo put it, "Korean Air systematically turned Park into a nutcase, and the prosecutor's office systematically turned me into a crazy bitch" (*SBS News* 2019). The particularly gendered insult for Seo notwithstanding, their perceived commonality as whistleblowers speaks to how #MeToo has maintained a delicate balance in appealing to the broader public while bringing attention to gendered violence as a product of the abuse of power within organizations, a testament of the polyvocality of #MeToo and its multiple audiences. It is in this context that Seo and Park were tasked with cohosting the annual ceremony to commemorate the June 10 prodemocracy movement in 2019; they spoke about how democracy has yet to be achieved from the perspective of the marginalized (Hô, Tak, and Yi 2019).

Imagining the Future of #MeToo

I have shown in this chapter that, through the Korean translation of MeToo as "I too accuse" as well as Seo Ji-hyun and Kim Ji-eun's collective stories, #MeToo South Korea came to signify the act of speaking out publicly against sexual violence as an abuse of power and authority in the context of formal institutions. The refusal to accept "I too was victimized" as a similarly relevant translation of MeToo reveals the silences within collective organizing and offers us crucial avenues to further question the nuances of feminist politics in South Korea. By equating the statement of sexual victimization with passivity, have we lost the opportunity to destigmatize sexual violence outside of institutionalized settings and the chance to see victims of violence as agents? Which forms of sexual victimization become more speakable and shareable when compared to others? In the desire to project the fantasy of a feminist speaking subject publicly and the need to assert women's voices as viable subjects that can demand justice writ large (Scott 2011), have we lost a place within #MeToo for victims who may not want to speak in these terms to make themselves known? Is there space in #MeToo and feminist politics for expressions of pain, desire, betrayal, or shame, which cause some victims to be less like proper liberal subjects, unable or unwilling to articulate rational demands for institutional reform?

The circulation and framing of #MeToo in South Korea highlight moments when women spoke out and emerged as a collective. No longer were women isolated when called madwomen. Instead, they came to together as whistleblowers. They consequently brought forth a powerful institutional critique of sexual violence as embedded in the sexist practices within male-dominated institutions. The move to frame the issue of sexual violence as a narrow version of gender politics—demanding equal treatment for women and men—and to deexceptionalize it as another form of abuse of power enabled a broader mobilization beyond gender as a language of power and injustice. Yet this articulation of #MeToo inadvertently sidelined the question of gendered power itself. It perhaps occluded how gendered power operates across the public and private divide, including sexual violence within family and intimate relationships. The potential of #MeToo to recast gender and sexual politics underscores possible avenues of social transformation still available. Understanding #MeToo's broader ethics as a departure point, then, rather than as a finite endpoint, we can begin to further elucidate the complex interplay between sexuality, agency, and victimhood. We can rethink points of affinity around gendered violence as well as its occlusions or contradictions, without surrendering the pressing need for institutional change. Framing the future of #MeToo South Korea along these openings highlights a feminist politics continually in the making.

ACKNOWLEDGMENTS

I thank the editors Chaitanya Lakkimsetti and Vanita Reddy who offered valuable comments on this chapter, and the Korean Studies community in Toronto, Canada, who has provided material and intellectual support through ongoing dialogues. I thank Choonhee Woo for superb research assistance and the feminist activists in South Korea who carry on the work of sustaining #MeToo and other gender justice projects. This work was supported by the Core University Program for Korean Studies through the Ministry of Education of the Republic of Korea and Korean Studies Promotion Service of the Academy of Korean Studies (AKS-2018-OLU-2250001), as well as a research grant by the Centre for the Study of Korea at the University of Toronto.

REFERENCES

Bae, Ji-hyôn. 2018. "Prosecutor Seo Ji-hyun Visits 'Comfort Women': 'You are the Pioneers of MeToo'" [서지현 검사, 위안부 할머니들 찾아 "미투 선구자이셨다"]. *OhMyNews*. December 31, 2018. www.ohmynews.com.

Berg, Heather. 2020. "Left of #MeToo." *Feminist Studies* 46 (2): 259–86.

Burke, Tarana, and Elizabeth Adetiba. 2018. "Tarana Burke Says #MeToo Should Center Marginalized Communities." In *Where Freedom Starts: Sex, Power, Violence, #MeToo: A Verso Report*, edited by Verso Books US, 14–17. Brooklyn: Verso.

Gill, Rosalind, and Shani Orgad. 2018. "The Shifting Terrain of Sex and Power: From the 'Sexualization of Culture' to #MeToo." *Sexualities* 21 (8): 1313–24.

Hô, Jin-mu, Ji-yông Tak, and Sang-ho Yi. 2019. "Asking Seo Ji-hyun and Chang-jin Park about the June 10th Democracy Movement" [서지현 · 박창진에게 '6·10 민주항쟁'을 묻다]. *Kyunghyang*, June 10, 2019. http://news.khan.co.kr.

Horuragi Foundation. 2018a. "Why Should Whistleblower Prosecutors Declare That They Will Not Run for a Political Office?" [공익제보 검사는 왜 '불출마 선언'을 해야 하는가?]. November 10, 2018, YouTube video, 00:51:30. www.youtube.com/watch?v=xqypqkJ6GG4.

———. 2018b. "Prosecutors Also Bully and Ostracize" [검사들도 왕따와 따돌림]. November 11, 2018, YouTube video, 00:56:59. www.youtube.com/watch?v=3BZ1or9HWCc.

Jang, Eun-gyo. 2018. "Korean and Japanese Symbols of #MeToo, Seo Ji-hyeon and Shiori Ito Speak Words of Comfort to the Victims of the World." *Kyunghyang*, December 13, 2018. http://english.khan.co.kr.

Jang, Seul-gi, and Sô-yôn Bak. 2018. "Regretting Media Reporting of MeToo in 2018" [2018년 언론의 '미투' 보도를 반성하며]. *Media Today*, December 19, 2018. www.mediatoday.co.kr.

Jin, Dal-lae. 2018. "#MeToo: It Is 'I Too Accuse,' not 'I Too Was Victimized'" [#Me too '나도 당했다' 가 아니라 '나도 고발한다' 가 맞다]. *Money Today*, March 09, 2018. http://news.mt.co.kr.

Jôn, Jông-yun. 2019. "#BrotherMeToo . . . We Can Survive Only If We Speak, Even If We Whisper" [#오빠미투 . . . 작은 목소리라도 말해야 산다]. *Hankyôre21*, August 27, 2019. http://h21.hani.co.kr.

Jông, Hee-jin. 2019. "Violence Against Women and the MeToo Movement" [여성에 대한 폭력과 미투운동], in *The Politics of MeToo* [미투의 정치학], edited by Hee-jin Jông, 76–110. Seoul: Kyoyangin.

Kim, Hyŏng-eun, and Jŏng-min Choi. 2018. "In the Aftermath of MeToo, Prosecutor Seo Ji-hyun Says 'I Will Not Stop, Despite Suffering from Secondary Victimization'" [미투 그 후 . . . 서지현 검사, '2차 가해로 고통스럽지만 그만두지 않을 것']. *BBC Korea*, October 26, 2018. www.bbc.com/korean.

Kim, Hyun-Mee. 2018. "The MeToo Movement, Why, Now and After" [미투 운동, 왜, 지금 그리고 이후]. *Gender Review* 49:4–13.

Kim, Ji-eun. 2020. "Kim Ji-eun on #MeToo: I Wanted to Shout Out 'I Too Am a Person Deserving of Respect'" [#미투 김지은 "나도 존중받아야 할 사람" 외치고 싶었다]. Interview by Hana Lee. *Women News*, May 30, 2020. www.womennews.co.kr.

Kim, Mina. 2020. "Choi Yŏng-mi, Kim Ji-eun . . . MeToo Is a Fight Between One Person vs. Many . . . Our Society Owes Them a Great Deal" [최영미 · 김지은 . . . 미투는 1 대 다수 싸움 . . . 우리 사회는 이들에게 큰 빚 지고 있어]. *Kyunghyang*, January 4, 2020. http://news.khan.co.kr.

Kim, Jinsook. 2021. "Sticky Activism: The Gangnam Station Murder Case and New Feminist Practices Against Misogyny and Femicide." *JCMS: Journal of Cinema and Media Studies* 60 (4): 37–60.

Korea Sexual Violence Relief Center (KSVRC). 2020. "A Small Speak-Out Will be Hosted in November" [11월 작은말하기가 열립니다]. November 16, 2020. www .sisters.or.kr.

Kwon Kim, Hyun-young. 2020. *We Will Find a Path as We Always Have* [늘 그랬듯이 길을 찾아낼 것이다]. Seoul: Humanist.

Lee, Na-Young. 2018. "The Social Significance of the 'MeToo Movement' from a Feminist Perspective" [페미니스트 관점에서 본 '미투 운동' 의 사회적 의미]. *Trends in Welfare Monthly* [월간 복지동향] 234:5–12.

SBS News. 2019. "Prosecutor Seo Ji-hyun of 'MeToo' Speaks after the Guilty Verdict of An Tae-geun" ['미투' 서지현 검사, 안태근 유죄 판결에 입 열다]. January 23, 2019, YouTube video, 00:00:35. https://www.youtube.com/watch?v=3c07m82QR54.

Scott, Joan. 2011. *The Fantasy of Feminist History*. Durham, NC: Duke University Press.

Seo, Ji-hyun. 2018a. "Full Text: Writings by the Prosecutor Seo Ji-hyun about Sexual Harassment by An Tae-geun" [전문: 서지현 검사가 올린 안태근 성추행 폭로 글]. *Hankyŏre*, January 30, 2018. www.hani.co.kr.

———. 2018b. "One Year after MeToo, Seo Ji-hyun Says 'It is Difficult to Tell the Victims to Be Brave'" ['미투 1년' 서지현 "피해자에게 용기 내라고 말 못하겠네요"]. *Hankyŏre21*, December 7, 2018. www.hani.co.kr.

———. 2020. "Prosecutor Seo Ji-hyun: 'I Am the Person Who Plants the Seed' . . . We Are Winning More than We Thought" [서지현 검사 "난 '씨 뿌리는 사람' . . . 생각보다 크게 이겨가고 있다"]. Interview by Kim Yŏnghee. *Hankyŏre*, January 22, 2020. www.hani.co.kr.

So, Jung-han. 2019. "Why Prosecutor Seo Ji-hyun Cried after Reading Park Chang-jin's Book" [박창진이 쓴 책, 서지현 검사가 읽고 울먹인 까닭]. *OhMyNews*, March 15, 2019. www.ohmynews.com.

Tambe, Ashwini. 2018. "Reckoning with the Silences of #MeToo." *Feminist Studies* 44 (1): 197–203.

6

Hemispheric Feminist Currents

#MeToo, Ni Una Menos, *and the Green Tide in Argentina*

BARBARA SUTTON

Feminist currents do not always follow the same path across borders. Therefore, it is important to analyze the multidirectional, relational, overlapping, and synergistic ways in which feminist activism spreads transnationally. Here I take a hemispheric viewpoint to examine the circulation of #MeToo—a US-originated hashtag and movement against sexual violence—in relation to feminist movements in Argentina. I show how the direction of influence regarding various feminist discourses and actions is not consistently North to South, as often assumed, but that other directionalities—particularly South to South and, in some instances, South to North—are also at play. Noticing these various directionalities and the significance of local developments, in this case in Argentina, helps to avoid labeling as "#MeToo" feminist interventions that, though interacting or overlapping with #MeToo, stem from previous activisms in Latin America.

The centrality often ascribed to a North-to-South directionality appears implicitly embedded in certain ways of framing questions around the dissemination of #MeToo, for example, when the question posed is about the *impact* of #MeToo—a movement emerging in the Global North—in specific countries of the Global South. However, might there be multiple flows of influence at play? Might other political developments in specific contexts, such as powerful conceptualizations and cumulative organizing by local feminisms, have greater salience than #MeToo at the local level? Would it be more appropriate to speak of *interaction* with, rather than impact on, local developments? Applying a hemispheric framework, and simultaneously looking at Argentina, is useful in this regard. This framework is imbued by a transnational perspective, helping reveal the linkages and interactions between cultures, movements, and political events across borders, while also attending to specific histories and power contestations in the Americas. Rather than assuming the primacy of the United States, this hemispheric view shows how a history of South-to-South transnational feminist solidarity, as well as the force of local feminisms in the South, has shaped responses to gender-based violence in ways that overlap with, interact with, and also exceed #MeToo.

Feminists in Argentina have long made gender-based violence a key target of critical analysis and activism (Fontenla and Bellotti 1993; Laudano 2019). Whereas their framings and actions have changed over the years, they have advanced expansive interpretations that go beyond interpersonal violence to include, for example, structural, symbolic, and state violence. By the time US #MeToo went viral in 2017 and the movement gained global traction, Argentina was already having its own visible reckoning with gender-based violence and related injustices. Thus, it would be a mistake to assume that it was due to the "landing" of #MeToo that people in Argentina had to confront these issues. As Chaitanya Lakkimsetti and Vanita Reddy (2021, 226) suggest, we need to consider how #MeToo has been "imbricated within prior histories of state responses to institutionalized violence and feminist discourses about gender-based violence." Like the "travels" of other feminist ideas and initiatives (e.g., Davis 2007), #MeToo has been adopted in nonidentical forms in different countries (Suk et al. 2023).

Moreover, while #MeToo focused on sexual violence, the case of Argentina also shows how #MeToo interacted with other causes, such as abortion politics (Garibotti and Hopp 2019), in a context in which feminists had been framing the harms of the illegality of abortion as gender violence. Still, the issue of sexual violence was not lost but rather received renewed attention amid mounting feminist activism—both local and transnational—that had been gathering steam before the dissemination of #MeToo. Accounting for the overlapping as well as longer histories of feminist struggles for gender justice in specific countries is essential to assess #MeToo from a transnational perspective.

Previous scholarship tackled aspects of #MeToo repercussions in Argentina, including works by María Cecilia Garibotti and Cecilia Marcela Hopp (2019), who draw on the framework of "political opportunities";

Marifran Carlson (2020), who considers the power of social media; and Carolina Justo von Lurzer (2020), who addresses the role of mainstream media and popular culture. I build on these and other authors' insights—as well as my own long-term research on feminisms in Argentina—to reflect on how feminist ideas, discourses, and strategies cross national borders and interact with local movements in the context of #MeToo.

Background

Mobilization around gender-based violence in Argentina needs to be understood in relation to broader feminist and women's movements. This diverse and multivocal activism has been building for a long time, particularly after the restoration of democracy, following a brutal military dictatorship (1976–83). In the name of national security, the dictatorial regime resorted to the systematic use of torture and forcible disappearance as methods of political repression against people deemed "subversive." Activist women, among others, were targeted and taken to clandestine detention centers, where they experienced various modes of sexual and gendered violence. Their stories are still emerging—in courts of justice, sites of memory, and testimonial archives—and they offer clues about the intersections of patriarchal gender ideologies and state violence in Argentina (Aucía et al. 2011; Bacci et al. 2012; Sutton 2018). The reverberations of this period are still felt, as Argentine society continues to grapple with its pernicious consequences (Bacci 2022; Escales n.d. 2022), including the traumatic effects on survivors as well as the denialism exhibited by some contemporary right-wing politicians.

State terror also left marks both on feminist perspectives on violence and the genealogy of women's movements in Argentina (Fontenla and Bellotti 1993; Bascuas, Daona, and Oberti 2020). Indeed, Mothers of Plaza de Mayo, who stood up to the dictatorship to demand the return of their "disappeared" sons and daughters, have been a reference point for generations of activists. Relatedly, Grandmothers of Plaza de Mayo organized to search for hundreds of children, now adults, appropriated by the regime (including babies born in captivity and given to other families to raise under false identities after the murder of their mothers). The social memory of this violence and the continued activism of

Mothers and Grandmothers has been enmeshed with the political life of the country. With the return of democracy, feminist organizing was able to further develop, advancing a wide variety of demands, such as legal equality, reproductive rights, economic justice, and an end to gender-based violence. Still, many forms of violence against women persisted, whether by private individuals or with the participation or complicity of state representatives.

Other countries in the region also underwent authoritarian regimes during the 1960s through the 1980s, followed by processes of democratization. Experiences of political repression and state violence have shaped aspects of feminist thought and organizing. For instance, in the first Feminist Encuentro (Meeting) of Latin America and the Caribbean in 1981, participants designated November 25 as a day of action for "Non-Violence against Women." The choice of date refers to the political assassination of the Mirabal sisters (Patria, Minerva, and María Teresa) in the Dominican Republic in 1960. In 1999, the United Nations General Assembly echoed this initiative by designating November 25 as the International Day for the Elimination of Violence against Women (Robinson 2006)—a testament of the imprint of Latin American and Caribbean feminisms. The state has been an important focus of feminist critique and adjudication of responsibility in relation to gender violence in the region (as perpetrator, accomplice, or indifferent bystander), from Mexican activists' condemnation of state-enabled impunity in response to feminicides in the Mexico-US border,[1] to Argentine activists' claims that *el Estado es responsable* (the State bears responsibility) for multiple forms of violence, to the assertion that "the oppressive state is a rapist *macho*" by the Chilean artivist group Las Tesis in their viral chant and performance *Un violador en tu camino* (A rapist in your path). An example of a transnational feminist repertoire of circulation, originating in Latin America, this performance was adapted and translated into various languages and enacted in many parts of the world. In the United States, activists performed it in the context of denunciations paradigmatic of #MeToo, such as the trial of film producer Harvey Weinstein, accused of sexual abuses (Serafini 2020).

Latin American feminist movements have been determined to challenge violence in the various spheres in which it occurs as well as the structures of inequality that sustain it. In her account of such feminist actions in Argentina, Claudia Laudano (2023) suggests that while today gender-based violence is part of the public debate, this was not always the case. She notes that the framing of violence against women "as a social problem has been the product of a long and sinuous process of meaning-making driven by the feminist movement for decades, in the country as well as in Latin America and the Caribbean" more broadly (1,214).[2] For example, among the South-to-South initiatives that Laudano highlights was a three-year campaign, "For Women's Lives: Not One More Death," launched in 2001 by the Latin American and Caribbean Feminist Network Against Domestic and Sexual Violence. The campaign aimed at recording and raising awareness of femicide in the region, and it influenced various initiatives in individual countries. Laudano describes activist efforts in Argentina to document and denounce gender-based violence during that decade and, in 2012, the creation of the National Campaign Against Violence Toward Women. The initiative brought together "a wide range of some 30 organizations, including grassroots women's and feminist groups, picketers, students, cultural organizations, and lawyers' associations" (Laudano 2023, 1226). We can think of these efforts as precursors of more massive denunciations of gender violence in Argentina in the following years, which in turn preceded the transnational spread of #MeToo.

The origin of the #MeToo movement is often credited to US actress Alyssa Milano's tweet on October 15, 2017, calling others to post "MeToo" if they had experienced sexual harassment or assault. However, Black activist Tarana Burke had started using the phrase and concept of "Me Too" about a decade earlier as part of her organizing to end sexual violence (Sayej 2017)—though without the same level of diffusion. In Argentina, by the time of Milano's tweet, an active and visible movement against femicide and other forms of gender-based violence had already been making headlines. In 2015, the movement *Ni Una Menos* (Not One [Woman] Less, *NUM*) emerged with impressive force to demand an end to the killing of women. Massive demonstrations captured the public's attention, with powerful repercussions not only in Argentina, but also in other parts of Latin America, and even beyond this region (Bidaseca et al. 2015; Gago 2019; Piatti-Crocker 2021). *NUM* also eventually coalesced with feminist demands for abortion legalization (Daby and Moseley 2021), which had been building for years, especially through the National Campaign for the Right to Legal, Safe, and Free Abortion (hereafter, the Campaign). The criminalization of abortion was framed as a form of gender-based violence, as it fostered clandestine and unsafe abortion conditions that could result in bodily injuries, mistreatment, and even death for women.

Among other things, *NUM* helped feed what came to be known as the "Green Tide" (Marea Verde) for abortion rights, the rising movement symbolized by the emblematic green kerchiefs of the abortion legalization campaign. This symbol was adopted, with variations, by abortion rights activists in other parts of the world, especially in Latin America. In the United States, green kerchiefs also appeared in various protests surrounding the US Supreme Court's 2022 decision *Dobbs v. Jackson Women's Health Organization*, which overturned abortion rights at the federal level. The adoption of the green color and symbols also suggests a different trajectory of feminist "travel," as US-based activists looked to Latin America for insights and solidarity (Avila-Guillen and Baden 2022; Schmidt 2022).

Argentina was no stranger to the global conversations spurred by #MeToo; and the debates surrounding #MeToo certainly found resonances in the local Argentine scene. However, this trend interacted with existing feminist mobilization and discourse in Argentina, which also had a momentum and power of their own and a capacity to cross national borders. For example, *Ni Una Menos*, spurred transnational solidarity and demonstrations in other localities, particularly in Latin America. There were "actions and organizations under the Ni Una Menos motto in Chile, Uruguay, Brazil, Paraguay, Bolivia, Peru, Ecuador, Colombia, Costa Rica, Guatemala, Mexico, and Dominican Republic," as well as European countries such as Spain and Italy and other parts of the world (Innocente 2020, 2–3). In other words, #MeToo entered a rich and vibrant feminist political arena that it did not create. Still, transnational awareness of #MeToo, and similar manifestations, resulted in a "positive synergy" with the movements that had already been mobilizing toward feminist social change in Argentina, including against gender violence and for abortion rights (Garibotti and Hopp 2019, 118).

Ni Una Menos, Not One Less

On June 3, 2015, hundreds of thousands of demonstrators gathered in Buenos Aires and other parts of Argentina following the rallying call #NiUnaMenos. They flooded the streets and online spaces to demand an end to the killings of women.[3] The recurrent femicides and gruesome aspects of the cases reported provoked grief and anger (Cosecha Roja 2015). Reacting to one of the latest brutal femicides—specifically, that of pregnant fourteen-year-old Chiara Páez by her boyfriend—*NUM* swelled in numbers, attracting throngs of supporters, even those of a young age (Friedman and Rodríguez Gustá 2023). In retrospect, one can see how the ground was being prepared in previous months, as activists, researchers, journalists, and writers gathered at a plaza on March 26, 2015, under the motto *Ni Una Menos*, for a "marathon of readings" concerning the murders of women (at that time, in response to the murder of nineteen-year-old Daiana García) (Cosecha Roja 2015; Ni Una Menos 2015a). Theory and action, bodies and voices, emotion and resonant experiences combined powerfully as *NUM*'s call gained traction, helping mount public pressure for the state and society to address violence against women. These mobilizations were amplified through both online and offline coordination and protest (Laudano 2019; Friedman and Rodríguez Gustá 2023).

NUM demonstrations in Argentina additionally found resonance and solidarity across Latin America, where countless women have been killed, disappeared, and sexually assaulted with impunity, prompting cross-border feminist dialogues and calls for action (Fregoso and Bejarano 2010, ECLAC 2022). Transnational currents in the region influenced *NUM*'s discourse. For example, Laudano (2023, 1,228) recounts that "the phrase 'Not one woman less, not one more dead' was used by the Mexican poet and activist Susana Chávez Castillo in 1995, to protest the systematic crimes against women, framed in relation to feminicide in Ciudad Júarez [Mexico]. From that moment, and limited to 'not one less,' it began to circulate and spread as a slogan throughout different feminist spaces in Latin America, until it became an emblem of the fight after the femicide of the poet herself in 2011 in Mexico." In 2015, *Ni Una Menos* spread as a hashtag and began to designate a movement to end violence against women, and specifically femicides. It also names the collective of organizers spearheading *NUM* actions over the years. As mentioned, connected calls and protests emerged in other countries of the region, sometimes with variations.

In 2016, women in Argentina continued mobilizing under the banner of *NUM*, including the motto *Vivas nos queremos* (We want us alive), borrowed from Mexican activists (Palmeiro 2019). Participants from all walks of life joined in protests, and on October 19 of that year, they held a National Women's Strike consisting of both a work stoppage and demonstrations—particularly in response to the killing and sexual violence against sixteen-year-old Lucia Perez, among other femicides within just a few days (Gago 2019; *Página 12* 2016). Earlier that month women in Poland held a strike to counter political efforts to further restrict abortion, and activists in Argentina took note of the event (Laguna and Palmerio 2023). They decided to use a similar tactic to emphasize the connection between gender violence and the structural position of women in society, involving the devaluation of women's work, lives, and bodies. Repurposing the strike—a time-honored protest practice from the labor movement—and mobilizing in the streets, participants in Argentina denounced the violent treatment of diverse women, across social realms marked by intersecting injustices (Mason-Deese 2018; Gago 2019). They refused to be silenced and resorted to the power of collective action to confront intertwined forms of violence that, in extreme cases, result in the death of women.

The rising feminist mobilization against gender violence and the strategic deployment of the strike helped make the point about the need to think about violence expansively. It also centrally underscored the importance of women's labor, which is too often devalued and invisible, as evidenced by the gender wage gap; the prevalence of unpaid care work by women; the precarity that characterizes informal economies in which women are overrepresented; and the specific risks experienced by many women at work, including sexual harassment. Confronting the socially induced disposability of women's lives and bodies—symbolized by the garbage bags sometimes used to dispose of murdered women—activists responded with their massive, embodied presence in the streets, visibly reclaiming the public space.

By October 2017, as debates about sexual violence picked up in the United States, feminist organizing against gender violence and other feminist causes in Argentina had been gaining momentum, both at the local level and as part of transnational actions. Members of *NUM* and women across a broad swath of organizations participated in an International Women's Strike that took place earlier that year, on March 8 (International Women's Day), with participation of women in more than fifty countries (Palmeiro 2019). Feminist coalitional activism and participatory spaces during those years yielded expansive understandings of violence, facilitated by the process of organizing, especially public discussion gatherings known as *asambleas* (assemblies):

> It has been through a series of assemblies, in different places, bringing together different groups of women, that these activists have been able to directly map out the connections between different forms of violence, and, most importantly, to build direct links of solidarity between the women who experience it. In assemblies women share stories of facing sexual harassment on the job, of being afraid to advocate for better working conditions because of fear of violence, of staying in abusive relationships because they lack the economic means to leave. . . . These assemblies multiply in diverse spaces: in workplaces, in unions, in political organizations, in schools, in urban neighborhoods, towns, and rural areas. (Mason-Deese 2018)

This type of process enabled conceptualizations of violence that move beyond the individual to assess interconnected systems of oppression. *NUM* widened the critique of violence from femicide to the violence of financial debt, economic systems that create poverty and inequalities, reproductive injustice, repressive state institutions, racism, colonialism, and extractivism, as well as to cis-heterosexist violence against people of diverse gender and sexual identities. The manifesto for the June 3, 2023, *NUM* demonstration, endorsed by hundreds of organizations, stated: "We say enough to patriarchal, economic, sexual, institutional, political and racist violence. We say enough to everyday violence, which is part of historical forms of oppression and which serve to exploit our bodies and territories" (Télam 2023).

The Green Tide

The struggle against gender violence and for legal abortion converged as *NUM* started to include abortion rights under the umbrella of its demands. Abortion had not been explicitly mentioned in the first manifesto of *NUM*, dated June 3, 2015—the day of the first massive *NUM* demonstration. Still, in the lead up to that rally, the National Campaign for the Right to Legal, Safe, and Free Abortion sent a note of *adhesión* (support), making the following connection: "Femicides are also the dead women due to the clandestinity of abortion," and *NUM* published the note on its Facebook page (as was the case with other groups expressing their *adhesión*) (Ni Una Menos 2015c).

The Campaign for abortion rights had been launched in 2005, a decade earlier than *NUM*, and throughout the years it grew in size and recognition, gaining the support of hundreds of organizations. The Campaign employed multiple strategies to advance abortion rights, including presenting to Congress its own abortion legalization bill and many other kinds of activist interventions at the grassroots level (Zurbriggen and Anzorena 2013; Gutiérrez 2021). The Campaign brought the abortion discussion to diverse sectors of society through persistent organizing and the capillary mode of reaching different strata and institutions, with representation across the country. The green kerchief, currently widely recognized, was used by activists in the Campaign from its inception (though the symbol's first appearance was in the National Women's Encuentro in 2003 in Rosario, Argentina, before the Campaign's formal launch).

Among core organizers of *NUM* were vocal supporters of the struggle for abortion rights—such as journalists who had been reporting on feminist causes, including the legalization of abortion, for years—but as mentioned, the need to legalize abortion was not initially addressed by *NUM*. Some perceived the abortion issue as too divisive (Garibotti and Hopp 2019; Bedrosian 2022). However, by the time of its second manifesto, dated May 9, 2016, *NUM* included abortion, explicitly saying, "Without legal abortion there is no Ni Una Menos" (Ni Una Menos 2016). Discussions among activists from various sectors and movement experiences apparently contributed to the shift—conversations that also included abortion rights activists. For example, Sandra, an activist from the abortion Campaign whom I interviewed, recalled that "the first Ni Una Menos, the document that was jointly crafted, did not address abortion. Through our activism and participation in assemblies, we managed to include the right to abortion as part of Ni Una Menos. Ni Una Menos was specifically about violence and feminicides. So, why only talk about violence when a woman is killed by a man, when we know that clandestine abortion is also violence against women? Thus, we gradually achieved consensus."[4] As *NUM* expanded in reach and broadened its focus beyond the murder of women, it also helped raise support for the abortion rights struggle.

Around September 28, 2017, multiple activist initiatives focused on abortion. September 28 has been on the Argentinian feminist calendar for decades as a result of regional, South-to-South solidarities and organizing. In 1990, participants in the Fifth Feminist Encuentro of Latin America and the Caribbean chose September 28 as a date to mobilize for abortion rights ("Declaración de San Bernardo" 1991 [1990]). In 2017, the *Grito Global por el Aborto Legal* (Global Cry for Legal Abortion) took place, organized in Argentina by the National Campaign for the Right to Legal, Safe, and Free Abortion and joined by actions in various countries. The initiative, promoted as part of the broader September 28 Campaign for Latin America and the Caribbean, demanded *#NiMuertasNiPresas, ¡vivas y libres nos queremos!* (#NotDeadNotImprisoned, we want us alive and free!), alluding to the criminalization of abortion and women dying due to dangerous clandestine abortions (Campaña Nacional 2017). Indeed, in Argentina, the Penal Code criminalized abortion with few exceptions, and activists pointed to the State as responsible for the preventable deaths of women due to unsafe abortions.

Pressure mounted for Congress to debate abortion legalization in 2018. The Campaign had been working on this for years, and with the emergence of *NUM,* it was able to further draw on the strength amassed through that movement. Guillermina, a Campaign activist I interviewed in 2018, referred to the convergence of several factors in relation to the rise of the Green Tide. Among them was the importance of the activism propelled by *NUM.* According to Guillermina, *NUM* was able to contribute to a "massification" of feminist struggles, attracting a "public of *pibas*" (girls, young women) and helping to "light a spark on something that had already been cooking."[5] Mora, another abortion rights activist, also observed, "I think that Ni Una Menos began to have a poignant kind of visibility, like *minas* [slang for women] saying, 'I also want to be part of this.' Then, well, there were a lot of phenomena that converged— [in] the countries of the global North, it was all the #MeToo thing."[6]

By the time #MeToo spread globally, feminist activism in Argentina was effervescent, manifesting through multiple actions against gender violence, for legal abortion, and on behalf of various gender justice causes. As we shall see, awareness of #MeToo interacted with local developments, adding to public discussions on sexual violence, and it indirectly appeared in certain chains of events with repercussions on the struggle for abortion rights.

Locating #MeToo in the Local Argentine Scene

A series of events unfolding in Argentina in 2018 helped amplify the public discussion about feminism, gender violence, and abortion through popular mainstream media. #MeToo entered the mix, though it was not the whole or most salient part of the story of the mobilization and debates that ensued. Celebrities were involved in events and discussions regarding feminist issues that attracted media attention, and a group of actresses who initially organized for abortion rights played an active role in both the struggle for abortion legalization and later collective denunciations of sexual harassment.

As Libertad Borda and Carolina Spataro (2018) suggest, it was perhaps in the "least expected" space—a daytime TV show that usually airs celebrity gossip, *Intrusos del Espectáculo*[7]—that an impactful discussion on abortion, and feminism more generally, would be spearheaded. They recount that it was partly due to a controversy involving celebrities that the debate was catalyzed on TV and social media. Actress Araceli González, who had condemned remarks that naturalized and trivialized sexual violence (uttered at the time by singer "Cacho" Castaña[8]), still distanced herself from feminism during an interview on *Intrusos* in January 2018: "I am not a feminist. I have great respect for them, but in fact I have a beautiful son, I have a precious husband, and I have great respect for men too," González said. She added that "perhaps, during many years, women tolerated things that they did not dare to talk about, that perhaps they were afraid to talk about, out of fear of not being believed. Or perhaps many women have been harassed due to working." As part of this reflection the actress also referred to the United States, pointing out that women there had "raised their voices" against such situations (Infobae 2018). One can infer from the statement that she was taking notice of #MeToo, given the attention that denunciations of sexual violence, particularly by US celebrities, were receiving at the time. A set of contingent developments followed this interview that helped move forward feminist debates and, specifically, the struggle for abortion rights.

Araceli González's statement about feminism met significant pushback in the social media sphere, and the controversy in turn received coverage by other mainstream media channels (Borda and Spataro 2018; Justo Von Lurzer 2020). *Intrusos* then invited feminist activists, journalists, celebrities, and others to continue the conversation on feminism on the show. It was in that context that a new phase in the public debate on abortion ensued. While serendipity seemed to have played a role, the movement was ready to intervene when the opportunity arose. For example, Borda and Spataro (2018) mention that as the debate on abortion was taken up by the mainstream media, members of the abortion rights Campaign brought their materials to the TV production. Subsequently, the host of *Intrusos* even showed up with the kerchief of the Campaign tied to his wrist.

As abortion gained increased media attention, the Campaign organized a large *pañuelazo* (public demonstration raising the green kerchiefs) in February 2018, and subsequently, the president of the country (then Mauricio Macri) assented to a discussion of abortion in Congress. As the year unfolded, a spirited societal debate took place with massive demonstrations, activist performances, educational events, and public hearings about abortion. Congress debated the legalization of abortion for the first time, and the lower house approved the bill, though the Senate later rejected it. Despite the setback, feminist activism did not stop, and during the COVID-19 pandemic, it included strategies adapted to the constraints of the public health emergency. In 2020, a new president (Alberto Fernández) spearheaded a bill supporting abortion rights, which gathered many of the movement's demands, and the legalization of abortion was finally approved by Congress in December 2020 (the law, No. 27.610, went into effect in January 2021). This legislation constitutes a milestone for the abortion rights movement and is part of a broader history of feminist activism in Argentina—one that also included cumulative, increasingly resonant, and massive demonstrations against gender violence.

#MeToo denunciations of gender-based violence in the United States—broadcasted in US and international media—coincided with a time in which local grievances by women, LGBTQ+, and feminist activists in Argentina had been mounting. Before the viral spread of #MeToo, and even *NUM,* public debates and campaigns about gendered forms of harassment captured the public's attention. For instance, in 2014, a public controversy followed comments by Mauricio Macri, then chief of government of the City of Buenos Aires, who said that all women like to receive *piropos* (unsolicited remarks, often about their physical appearance or of a sexual nature, or both) and that he did not believe those who say otherwise (Canal 10 Córdoba 2014). Topics such as *acoso callejero* (street harassment) also gained attention and prompted legislative proposals (CEPAL 2015). In 2015, *NUM* further opened a space for women to speak out about their experiences of gendered violence. In 2016, public denunciations of sexual abuse within the rock music scene appeared on the website Ya No Nos Callamos Más (We No Longer Stay Silent), later adding accounts of abuses by men beyond rock musicians (Erbetta 2018). Around the time of #MeToo, some Argentine celebrities also engaged the conversation on sexual harassment, including specific denunciations by actresses, which were "met with backlash" (Garibotti and Hopp 2019, 188). Still, in December 2018, a group of actresses participated in a visible and impactful collective action against sexual abuse in the industry. As we shall see, this intervention cannot be interpreted as simply caused by or replicating the actions of their US counterparts. Among other things, a process of organizing for other feminist causes—namely abortion rights—seems important to the way these actresses came together to make such denunciations later.

Among the hundreds of groups and organizations that were mobilizing for the legalization of abortion in 2018—amid the acceleration of the public debate—was the collective Actrices Argentinas (Argentine Actresses).[9] What was distinctive about this group was the potential of its members to reach a wide audience and be heard by certain political leaders by virtue of their popular recognition. For María Cecilia Garibotti and Cecilia Marcela Hopp (2019, 191), #MeToo created a political opportunity in relation to abortion "by attracting the mainstream media's attention and through the emergence of the Actresses Association, which actively promoted the legalization of abortion, using strategies inspired by the Hollywood actresses' uprising." At the same time, the Argentine actresses drew on local repertoires, and the robust activist infrastructure that was already in place was a critical factor. This infrastructure could be traced to years of organizing, forming networks, developing expertise, lobbying, and demonstrating for abortion rights by the Campaign as well as the groundswell of popular support and movement building garnered through *NUM* in more recent years.

Actresses-turned-abortion-rights activists—like other celebrities and journalists—have access to the media and the public's attention in ways that other activists usually do not. So, in that sense, the contributions of Argentine Actresses were particularly noteworthy. Carola, an activist I interviewed from the Campaign, observed, "What happens in 2018 is that we started February with a *pañuelazo* in a context where some public figures who later became great, and are great, allies—Argentine Actresses—began to take up the issue and came out to say that they had had an abortion, they went out to fight with some actors who were saying nonsense, and then—it seems silly, gossipy—but suddenly one day at 2:00 in the afternoon on the Argentine gossip show, they take out a green kerchief and start talking about misoprostol [abortion medication], you see?"[10] Carola contrasted this situation with her own experience as a grassroots activist, many times having taken out the kerchief "during activities and then stor[ing] it back." In 2018, it was quite a different scene: the kerchief was ubiquitous in the public sphere, as abortion rights supporters, including celebrities on TV, proudly donned the symbol in the streets, workplaces, education establishments, and movement events.

The actresses contributed to the struggle for abortion rights by using the skills and tools of their trade for feminist messaging on abortion, including video appearances and media production in favor of legalization, and additionally drawing on the knowledge and support from non-celebrity activists. Members of the Campaign for abortion rights were in contact with some of the actresses, providing training of sorts through workshops, phone conversations, and information exchanges. Mia, a Campaign activist I interviewed, recalled that Campaign members met with the actresses "to share certain tools to develop their organization and such."[11]

Guillermina, also from the Campaign, referred to conversations with the actresses in which Campaign activists shared some of the arguments and ideas they had honed over the years. These encounters served as a space of transmission of feminist knowledge and helped to amplify the message in support of legal abortion via the visibility and clout afforded to celebrities. Guillermina clarified, "I mention the actresses' collective because it was like the most . . . what precipitated [things] the most and suddenly . . . and in a very specific way, given that they are very *mediáticas* [in the media spotlight] and because they can have an impact on discourse very quickly. It worked very well. The actresses wrote a letter, and with it, a series of letters of support to the [abortion] bill followed."[12] The encounters between noncelebrity members of the Campaign and Argentine Actresses are important to highlight because it shows productive interactions that helped advance the abortion legalization cause as part of a much wider mobilization. This kind of organizing was also taking place in a context in which discourse about abortion rights was connected, in the public debate, with that on gender violence (including TV shows mentioning actresses' experiences, both from Argentina and the United States).[13] Activists had developed skills, arguments, analyses, coalitions, and outreach in different sectors of society over many years—all of which became useful at this particular juncture. In thinking about the rising Green Tide, Guillermina reflected on the difficulty of attributing a single cause, but noted how momentum was building. She included #MeToo in her analysis, mentioning its contribution among other factors:

> It also starts with the gender violence issue, when women start to speak out, the #MeToo, all those things—which although it was not due to that, it was not due to Ni Una Menos, it was not due to #MeToo, it was not due to . . . All those things started unfolding, and getting entwined in a kind of, well, "This happened to her, the same happened to me, and so I am going to denounce it, and I will gather courage and I will speak out," and women started raising their consciousness about the power that

they could have and the support that they will have from other networks of women.[14]

In this vein, another spinoff of these developments was how Argentine Actresses, which originally organized for abortion rights, came together in December 2018 to issue a #MeToo type of denunciation (Camezzana 2020; Justo von Lurzer 2020). This time, it was in support of actress Thelma Fardin who accused former costar Juan Darthés of having raped her years earlier when she was sixteen and he was forty-five, during a tour of the show *Patito Feo* (Ugly Duckling) in Nicaragua. Among other things, Fardin mentioned that Darthés said "*Mirá como me ponés*" ("Look what you do to me") in the context of the abuse. In response, Argentine Actresses issued the rallying call *Mirá Como Nos Ponemos* ("Look How We Get"), a play on words that turns the tables around, underscoring women's voices, agency, and collective organizing against sexual violence. Other actresses had also accused Darthés of sexually abusive behavior, including references to the same phrase (Perfil 2018). In the case of Fardin, Argentine Actresses issued a collective and public response, with a press conference to accompany her decision to file criminal charges.

As Daniella Camezzana (2020) argues, though there might be some overlaps with #MeToo US, the actions of Argentine Actresses cannot be equated to the latter. This is partly due to certain aspects of Argentine public conversations and responses to violence, for instance, the precedent of public denunciation strategies known as *escraches*. These naming and shaming practices were originally deployed by human rights organizations for children of the disappeared in Argentina to expose the repressors of the dictatorship in the context of impunity. Women have also resorted to *escraches*—in person and online—to denounce sexual and gender violence in Argentina and other places, such as Mexico (González-López and Cordero Cabrera 2021) and Colombia (Castellanos Forero 2022), underscoring the regional traveling and adaptation of movement discourse and actions. While the actresses' action is inscribed in a moment of heightened national and international awareness of feminist issues, the recourse to naming and shaming in the face of faulty justice systems was already available as part of social movement repertoires in Argentina. Around the time of the actresses' denunciation, Claudia

Korol—an Argentine feminist and popular education activist—referred to the actresses' action in relation to a wider array of gendered identities marked by capitalist, racist, colonial, patriarchal, and cis-heterosexist oppression: "Look how we get. We get angry, we echo all the complaints that suddenly overflow, because we have them tattooed like wounds on our bodies, in our memories. We get into 'enough is enough' mode. We get into 'we believe ourselves' mode. We get into the mode, 'if there is no justice there is *escrache*'" (Korol 2018, emphasis mine).

Additionally, the plural call of Argentine Actresses (the "we" in "Look how we get") contrasts with the individual "me" in mainstream understandings of #MeToo. That call was not just about the aggregation of individual complaints, but about standing together in solidarity. At the same time, it is important to note that, according to Shireen Roshanravan's (2021) scholarly analysis, the "me" in the hegemonic version of #MeToo that followed Hollywood actresses' denunciations can be interpreted as different from the original "me too" in Black activist Tarana Burke's organizing to end sexual violence against Black women and girls. Drawing on Black epistemologies and history of resistance, Roshanravan (2021, 246) points out that the "me too" in Burke's activism implies a collective self and that "the white Western incorporation of Burke's Black feminist 'me too' politics erases the Black feminist communal self-understanding of the 'me' committed to connection and solidarity against antiblack and heteropatriarchal publics."

The collective nature of the "Look how we get" intervention by Argentine Actresses also has its own cultural and political specificities, as is evident in the enunciation and presence of a "we" and in the action's links to the broader feminist movement in Argentina. Commenting on the actresses' press conference that accompanied Thelma Fardin's denunciation of sexual violence, Camezzana (2020, 8–9) observed that the event "combined significant elements of the mobilizations of street feminisms (the kerchief tied on the wrist, the choral reading of the document, the sound that emulates the *zaghareet* and the songs of the 8A vigil) with television resources such as the *insert* or video in which the young woman recounts the events, a segment of questions for the accredited journalists and the statements of certain members in the foyer of the theater [where the event took place]."[15] One of the actresses emphasized, "Today we are together and organized, and we will fight for our rights," and another asserted, "We no longer stay silent" (Televisión Pública Noticias 2018). The power of this action stems to a large extent from its collective character, striving to avoid the "breaking of bonds of community and solidarity among gendered workers" (Camezzana 2020, 8). In her study of the digital activism of Argentine Actresses, Raquel Tarullo (2023, 63) also observes that on Instagram, "the actresses do not operate individually. They manage to attract the attention of traditional media, but as members of a collective, not in a personalistic way." The "Look how we get" intervention exemplifies the collective approach and was part of broader debates about gender-based violence, which were unfolding at various levels of society. In social and mainstream media, workplaces, political gatherings, and education institutions, the issue of violence—and ways of dealing with it—came into sharp relief, also involving concomitant issues such as the role of the justice system, feminist protocols for workplaces and education institutions, the role of *escraches* and punitivism, and other sorts of responses to patriarchal violence.

So, what can we say about #MeToo in relation to feminist debates and actions in Argentina? The spread of #MeToo was among a range of social developments happening at a time that coincided with growing awareness and public conversations about feminist causes in Argentina. #MeToo added fuel to such discussions, in turn generating new spirals. Yet the powerful feminist uprising already visible in the public sphere had arguably broader and deeper significance in the Argentine context. In other words, #MeToo appeared in an existing feminist scene of great magnitude, and even actions that bear resemblance in content (sexual violence denunciations) or players involved (celebrities) should not be automatically labeled as a manifestation of the #MeToo movement or assumed to have been merely caused by #MeToo's spread.

Conclusion

As the global dissemination and uptake of #MeToo attests, sexual violence is a serious and widespread social problem in diverse societies, and women around the world resonated with the need to confront it. Similarly, the previous diffusion of *Ni Una Menos* across borders, particularly in Latin America, also speaks of the continued need to end other forms of gender-based violence embedded in intersecting systems of oppression. Through its participatory process and intersectional analysis, *NUM* advanced an expansive understanding of gender-based violence in connection to state violence, exploitative economic systems, racist relations, extractivism, and oppressive financial institutions, among others. *NUM*'s wide-ranging approach contrasts with the narrower focus of #MeToo in its mainstream version.

In Argentina, the connection between diverse types of violence helped raise awareness about the injustice of punitive abortion laws enabling clandestine and dangerous practices—an argument that the National Campaign for the Right to Legal, Safe, and Free Abortion had been making for years. The Green Tide for abortion rights spread in various places of Latin America, too, in turn drawing on previous local activisms as well as transnational feminist solidarities. In the last few years, important reforms toward abortion liberalization happened not only in Argentina but also in Colombia and Mexico (Sutton and Vacarezza 2023). Still, activists across the hemisphere face many challenges when it comes to abortion access. The reversal of abortion rights in the United States, particularly following the Supreme Court's *Dobbs* decision in 2022, is a reminder of the continued need to defend basic rights and to engage in feminist dialogues across the hemisphere. The appearance of green kerchiefs for abortion rights in the United States points in that direction. Furthermore, in the context of such events and mounting conservative attacks against LGBTQ+ rights, critical race theory, inequality reduction efforts, and the basic functioning of democracy, we can see that interconnected fronts of struggle are necessary.

The history of feminist solidarity and collaboration in Latin America and the Caribbean—including Feminist Encuentros, regional campaigns for reproductive rights or gender-based violence, networks to exchange information and strategies on abortion accompaniment, and the circulation and adaptation of symbols and tactics of protest across borders—speaks of the need to pause before making assumptions about the influence of movements spreading from the Global North, including #MeToo. A hemispheric framework that pays attention to the powerful feminist activism and expansive analyses of violence that emerged in Argentina and other Latin American countries helps counter common notions ascribing the greatest significance and impact to hegemonic

Global North feminisms. In that sense, we can think of #MeToo both as internally contested and as part of multidirectional, overlapping, and mutually reinforcing feminist efforts toward more just societies, free from violence.

ACKNOWLEDGMENTS

I thank activists in Argentina who have shared their experiences and knowledge with me, and Chaitanya Lakkimsetti, Vanita Reddy, Oscar A. Pérez, and Silvia Mejía for valuable feedback. This work also benefited from the research assistance of Alex Perry and Jamie Ackerman and funding from the Faculty Research Award Program (FRAP B) at the University at Albany.

NOTES

1 In this chapter, I use the terms "feminicide" or "femicide," following different contexts' usage. For a conceptual distinction, see Fregoso and Bejarano 2010.

2 This and other quoted extracts originally in Spanish are my translation.

3 For a list of demands, including the full implementation of law 26.485/2009 (Comprehensive Protection Law to Prevent, Punish and Eradicate Violence against Women in the Areas in which they Develop their Interpersonal Relationships), see Ni Una Menos 2015b.

4 Sandra, interview by the author, July 5, 2018, Argentina. The name of this and other interviewees are pseudonyms.

5 Guillermina, interview by the author, June 27, 2018, Argentina.

6 Mora, interview by the author, July 30, 2018, Argentina.

7 In English, "Showbiz Intruders."

8 In an interview, Castaña said, "If rape is inevitable, then relax and enjoy" (A24 .com, "Cacho Castaña: 'Si la violación es inevitable, relajate y goza'").

9 For an account of the emergence and activities of Argentine Actresses, see Justo von Lurzer 2019. For an explanation of what the group is about, see also Actrices Argentinas 2019.

10 Carola, interview by the author, December 23, 2019.

11 Mia, interview by the author, December 19, 2019, Argentina.

12 Guillermina, interview by the author, June 27, 2018, Argentina.

13 See, e.g., El Show del Día 2018.

14 Guillermina, interview by the author, June 27, 2018, Argentina.

15 Presumably, "8A" is August 8, the day when the Senate debated the legalization of abortion in 2018.

REFERENCES

A24.com. "Cacho Castaña: 'Si la violación es inevitable, relájate y goza.'" Facebook, January 8, 2018. https://www.facebook.com/A24com/videos/1810026745738533/.

Actrices Argentinas. 2019. "¿Qué es Actrices Argentinas?" YouTube video, 00:02:03. January 21, 2019. www.youtube.com/watch?v=YUmYPfVaQOI.

Aucía, Analía, Florencia Barrera, Celina Berterame, Susana Chiarotti, Alejandra Paolini, Cristina Zurutuza, and Marta Vassallo, eds. 2011. *Grietas en el silencio: Una investigación sobre la violencia sexual en el marco del terrorismo de Estado*. Rosario: CLADEM.

Avila-Guillen, Paula, and Kelly Baden. "The Case for an Inter-American Green Wave for Abortion Rights." *Ms. Magazine*, April 3, 2023. http://msmagazine.com.

Bacci, Claudia Andrea. 2022. "Políticas feministas y memorias del terrorismo de Estado en la Argentina." *RevIISE—Revista de Ciencias Sociales y Humanas* 20 (20): 157–72.

Bacci, Claudia, María Capurro Robles, Alejandra Oberti, and Susana Skura. 2012. *Y nadie quería saber: Relatos sobre violencia contra las mujeres en el terrorismo de Estado en Argentina*. Buenos Aires: Memoria Abierta.

Bascuas, Maisa, Victoria Daona, and Alejandra Oberti. 2020. "Insumisas, encuentros del feminismo y el movimiento de derechos humanos." *Revista Haroldo*, July 8, 2020. www.revistaharoldo.com.ar.

Bedrosian, Alyssa. 2022. "How #NiUnaMenos Used Discourse and Digital Media to Reach the Masses in Argentina." *Latin American Research Review* 57 (1): 100–116. http://dx.doi.org/10.1017/lar.2022.6.

Bidaseca, Karina, Celina Vacca, Mirtha Mestre, Lucía Nuñez Lodwick, Agustina Veronelli, Leticia Virosta, Estefanía Verónica Santoro et al. 2015. *#NiUnaMenos: Vivxs Nos Queremos*. Buenos Aires: Milena Caserola.

Borda, Libertad, and Carolina Spataro. 2018. "El chisme menos pensado: El debate sobre aborto en Intrusos en el espectáculo." *Sociales en Debate*, December 2018. http://ri.conicet.gov.ar.

Camezzana, Daniela. 2020. "Mirá como luchamos: Reflexiones sobre la acción de repudio a Darthés en Brasil." *Avatares de la Comunicación y la Cultura* 11 (19): 1–21.

Campaña Nacional por el Derecho al Aborto Legal, Seguro y Gratuito. "#UnGritoGlobal por el #AbortoLegal." *Campaña Nacional por el Derecho al Aborto Legal, Seguro y Gratuito*, September 23, 2017. www.abortolegal.com.ar.

Canal 10 Córdoba. "Macri Sobre Los Piropos: 'A Todas Las Mujeres Les Gustan.'" YouTube, 00:02:17, April 23, 2014. www.youtube.com/watch?v=Br2LPiGaLHU.

Castellanos Forero, María Camila. 2022. "Motivaciones y consecuencias de usar el escrache feminista como mecanismo de denuncia pública por parte de víctimas de violencia sexual en Colombia, un análisis crítico del sistema penal patriarcal." *Nuevo Foro Penal*, 98 (January–June): 115–67. https://doi.org/10.17230/nfp18.98.4.

Carlson, Marifran. 2020. "#MeToo Argentina: A Protest Movement in Progress." In *The Routledge Handbook of the Politics of the #MeToo Movement*, edited by Giti Chandra and Irma Erlingsdóttir, 410–22. New York: Routledge.

Comisión Económica para América Latina (CEPAL). 2015. "Acoso sexual en el espacio público: La ciudad en deuda con los derechos de las mujeres." Observatorio de Igualdad de Género de América Latina y el Caribe, November 18, 2015. http://oig .cepal.org.

Cosecha Roja. 2015. "Todo Sobre #NiUnaMenos." *Cosecha Roja*, May 19, 2015. www .cosecharoja.org.

Daby, Mariela, and Mason W. Moseley. 2022. "Feminist Mobilization and the Abortion Debate in Latin America: Lessons from Argentina." *Politics & Gender* 18 (2): 359–93. http://dx.doi.org/10.1017/S1743923X20000197.

Davis, Kathy. 2007. *The Making of Our Bodies, Ourselves: How Feminism Travels across Borders*. Durham, NC: Duke University Press.

"Declaración de San Bernardo." 1991 [1990]. *Nuevos aportes sobre aborto: Publicación de la Comisión por el Derecho al Aborto* 3 (5): 2.

Economic Commission for Latin America and the Caribbean (ECLAC). 2022. "Femicidal Violence in Figures: Latin America and the Caribbean." *Bulletin No. 1.* https:// oig.cepal.org.

El Show del Día. 2018. "La Señorita Bimbo se sentó en intrusos y dio cátedra: No esquivó ningún tema." YouTube, 00:28:10 February 6, 2018. www.youtube.com/watch ?v=l6xnaEhNvQY&t=1323s.

Erbetta, Emilia. 2018. "Ya No Nos Callamos Más: La historia detrás de la red que destapó los abusos en el rock." *La Nación* and *Rolling Stone*, June 5, 2018. www .lanacion.com.ar.

Escales, Vanina, ed. n.d. 2022. *Ser Mujeres en la ESMA II: Tiempo de Encuentros*. N.p.: Museo Sitio de Memoria ESMA and Centro de Estudios Legales y Sociales.

Fontenla, Marta, and Magui Bellotti. 1993. "La resistencia tiene múltiples voces." *Travesías: Temas del debate feminista contemporáneo* 1 (1): 31–42.

Fregoso, Rosa-Linda, and Cynthia Bejarano. 2010. *Terrorizing Women: Feminicide in the Américas*. Durham, NC: Duke University Press.

Friedman, Elisabeth Jay, and Ana Laura Rodríguez Gustá. 2023. "'Welcome to the Revolution': Promoting Generational Renewal in Argentina's Ni Una Menos." *Qualitative Sociology* 46 (2): 245–77. https://doi.org/10.1007/s11133-023-09530-0.

Gago, Verónica. 2019. *La potencia feminista: O el deseo de cambiarlo todo*. Buenos Aires: Tinta Limón.

Garibotti, María Cecilia, and Cecilia Marcela Hopp. 2019. "Substitution Activism: The Impact of #MeToo in Argentina." In *#MeToo and the Politics of Social Change*, edited by Bianca Fileborn and Rachel Loney-Howes, 185–99. Switzerland: Palgrave Macmillan.

González-López, Gloria, and Lydia Cordero Cabrera. 2021. "The Borders of #MeToo: A Conversation about Sexual Violence Against Women in Ciudad Juárez." *Feminist Formations*, 33 (3): 333–50. https://doi.org/10.1353/ff.2021.0036.

Gutiérrez, María Alicia. 2021. "Rights and Social Struggle: The Experience of the National Campaign for the Right to Legal, Safe, and Free Abortion in Argentina."

In *Abortion and Democracy: Contentious Body Politics in Argentina, Chile, and Uruguay*, edited by Barbara Sutton and Nayla Luz Vacarezza, 157–74. New York: Routledge.

Innocente, María Valeria. 2020. "Ni una menos ¿Politización transnacional del femicidio?" Master's Thesis, Facultad Latinoamericana de Ciencias Sociales, FLACSO Ecuador. https://repositorio.flacsoandes.edu.ec.

Infobae. 2018. "La frase de Araceli González sobre el feminismo que causó indignación en las redes sociales." *Infobae*, January 23, 2018. www.infobae.com/.

Justo von Lurzer, Carolina. 2020. "Del #MeToo al #MiráComoNosPonemos: Un año de feminismo celebrity en la cultura masiva Argentina." *Temas y Problemas de Comunicación* 18:68–82.

Korol, Claudia. 2018. "No hables de punitivismo para garantizar la impunidad. Mirá cómo nos ponemos." *Marcha*, December 20, 2018. https://marcha.org.ar/.

Lakkimsetti, Chaitanya, and Vanita Reddy. 2021. "#MeToo and Transnational Gender Justice: An Introduction." *Feminist Formations* 33 (3): 224–38. https://doi.org/10.1353/ff.2021.0046.

Laguna, Fernanda, and Cecilia Palmeiro. 2023. *Mareadas en la marea: Diario íntimo y alocado de una revolución feminista*. Buenos Aires: Siglo Veintiuno.

Laudano, Claudia. 2019. "#Ni una menos en Argentina: Activismo digital y estrategias feministas contra la violencia hacia las mujeres." In *Internet e feminismos: Olhares sobre violências sexistas desde América Latina*, edited by Graciela Nathansohn and Florencia Rovetto, 149–173. Salvador: EDUFBA.

———. 2023. "Acciones colectivas contra la violencia hacia las mujeres en Argentina." In *Cuestiones de teoría social contemporánea*, edited by Antonio Adolfo Marcial Camou, 1214–36. La Plata: EDULP.

Mason-Deese, Liz. 2018. "From #MeToo to #WeStrike: A Politics in Feminine." *Viewpoint Magazine*. March 7, 2018. http://viewpointmag.com.

Ni Una Menos. 2015a. "Maratón de lectura." Ni Una Menos, March 26, 2015. http://niunamenos.org.ar.

———. 2015b. "Manifiestos." Ni Una Menos, June 3, 2015. http://niunamenos.org.ar.

———. 2015c. "Recibimos la adhesión de la Campaña Nacional por el Derecho al Aborto Legal, Seguro y Gratuito." Facebook, May 15, 2015. www.facebook.com/NUMArgentina.

———. "El grito en común." Ni Una Menos, May 9, 2016. http://niunamenos.org.ar.

Página 12. "La cifra de los femicidios." October 18, 2016. www.pagina12.com.ar.

Palmeiro, Cecilia. 2019. "Ni Una Menos: Las lenguas locas del grito colectivo a la marea global." *Cuadernos de Literatura* 23 (46): 177–95.

Perfil. 2018. "'Mirá como me ponés': La frase que las actrices denunciantes le adjudican a Darthés." *Perfil*, December 11, 2018. www.perfil.com.

Piatti-Crocker, Adriana. 2021. "Diffusion of #NiUnaMenos in Latin America: Social Protests Amid a Pandemic." *Journal of International Women's Studies* 22 (12): 7–24.

Roshanravan, Shireen. 2021. "On the Limits of Globalizing Black Feminist Commitments: 'Me Too' and Its White Detours." *Feminist Formations* 33 (3): 239–55. https://doi.org/10.1353/ff.2021.0047.

Robinson, Nancy P. 2006. "Origins of the International Day for the Elimination of Violence Against Women: The Caribbean Contribution." *Caribbean Studies* 34 (2): 141–61.

Sayej, Nadja. 2017. "Alyssa Milano on the #MeToo Movement: 'We're not Going to Stand for It Any More.'" *The Guardian*, December 1, 2017. www.theguardian.com.

Schmidt, Samantha. "How Green Became the Color of Abortion Rights." *Washington Post*, July 3, 2022. www.washingtonpost.com.

Serafini, Paula. 2020. "'A Rapist in Your Path': Transnational Feminist Protest and Why (and How) Performance Matters." *European Journal of Cultural Studies* 23 (2): 290–95. https://doi.org/10.1177/1367549420912748.

Suk, Jiyoun, Yibing Sun, Luhang Sun, Mengyu Li, Catalina Farías, Hyerin Kwon, Shreenita Ghosh et al. 2023. "'Think Global, Act Local': How #MeToo Hybridized across Borders and Platforms for Contextual Relevance." *Information, Communication & Society*. https://doi.org/10.1080/1369118X.2023.2219716.

Sutton, Barbara. 2018. *Surviving State Terror: Women's Testimonies of Repression and Resistance in Argentina*. New York: NYU Press.

Sutton, Barbara, and Nayla Luz Vacarezza, eds. 2023. "Abortion Rights Activism in Latin America." *South Atlantic Quarterly* 122 (2). http://dx.doi.org/10.1215/00382876-10405133.

Tarullo, Raquel. 2023. "El activismo de celebridades desde el Sur Global: El caso de @actricesargentinas en Instagram." *Zona Franca* 31: 48–69. doi: https://doi.org/10.35305/zf.vi31.361.

Télam. 2023. "El documento que será leído en el cierre de la movilización." *Télam*. June 3, 2023. www.telam.com.ar.

Televisión Pública Noticias. 2018. "Denuncia de Thelma Fardin contra Juan Darthés." *YouTube*, 00:24:27, December 11, 2018. www.youtube.com/watch?v=SMS63IQXLm4.

Zurbriggen, Ruth, and Claudia Anzorena, eds. 2013. *El aborto como derecho de las mujeres: Otra historia es posible*. Buenos Aires: Herramienta.

PART III

Recognizing

7

#AidToo

Reckoning with Power and Privilege in the International Development Industry

DINAH HANNAFORD

In 2018, British crime reporter Sean O'Neill published a front-page article in the *Times of London*, detailing abuses perpetrated in 2011 by employees of one of the leading international charities, Oxfam. Oxfam was in Haiti ostensibly helping with relief efforts in the wake of the devastating 2010 earthquake. As the article revealed, in the aftermath of this crisis, where survivors were grappling with lost homes, lost jobs, and lost loved ones, aid workers from Oxfam were taking advantage of that poverty and desperation by paying people (some underage) for sex, including trading relief supplies for sex. The director of operations in Haiti, Roland van Hauwermeiren, was chief among those involved in the sexual exploitation (O'Neill 2018).

The article noted that Oxfam had performed an internal investigation of these events in 2011 and van Hauwermeiren had admitted to the misconduct. Instead of firing him, the charity allowed him to resign, offering him a "phased and dignified exit" (O'Neill 2018). This process left his professional reputation intact, so that after this resignation, van Hauwermeiren took a job as country director for a French charity in Bangladesh (Heffer 2018). Furthermore, the article revealed that van Hauwermeiren had only landed in his leadership role in Haiti after a long track record of previous abuses; he had been dismissed from a previous organization for accusations of sexual misconduct in Liberia in 2004 and faced further allegations of sexual misconduct while working for Oxfam in Chad in 2006 (O'Neill 2018). His history of abuse failed to keep him from being placed in positions of power among vulnerable people in poor countries; indeed, it seems to have expanded his geographic access to new communities of potential victims.

The publication of this article in the *Times* coincided with the rise of the #MeToo movement, and that timing was crucial in the sustained attention that the story was given in the global press and the subsequent fallout in the aid industry. In 2018, the hashtag #AidToo began trending among current and former development professionals working for the United Nations (UN), global charities, and international and local nongovernmental organizations (NGOs) and nonprofit organizations, collecting and eliciting stories of sexual misconduct in the development industry. The movement quickly became a repudiation of not just Oxfam; in the direct aftermath of the Oxfam revelations came allegations of abuse and harassment by senior executives at Save the Children UK, World Vision UK, the United Nations, and Médecins Sans Frontières (Cooper 2021). The momentum of #MeToo gave power to those seeking to uncover the poorly kept secret of aid agencies' mishandling of sexual exploitation and represented a potentially pivotal moment of reckoning in the aid industry.

This chapter argues that a real reckoning within the aid industry will not come from the #AidToo momentum. Echoing other critiques of the #MeToo movement (Lakkimsetti and Reddy 2021; Roshanravan 2021; Choo 2021; Tambe 2018), I contend that the lack of an explicit analysis of the intersections of race, patriarchy, and colonialism in development leaves the movement ineffectual in addressing the root causes of sexual exploitation in aid work. Though initiatives such as new codes of conduct, new channels of reporting, and new monitoring systems are laudable and long overdue, the crux of the aid industry's tendency toward abuse lies in the aid industry's foundations on gendered, class-based, and racial inequities of power and its perpetuation of these inequities. I show that calls to decolonize the development industry dovetail with calls for a decolonial approach to #MeToo and for a decolonial feminist resistance to gendered violence more broadly (see Lukose 2018).

Exposing a Long History of Abuse

In some ways, the Oxfam revelations were a rather mundane event, as the kind of exploitation unveiled was by no means new in the aid world.

A 2002 report by the UN High Commissioner for Refugees (UNHCR) and Save the Children found widespread sexual exploitation of refugee children in West Africa by aid workers, peacekeepers, and community leaders (UNHCR and Save the Children 2002). Subsequent investigations have documented the banality of sexual abuse at the hands of UN peacekeepers in particular, such as an investigation by the Associated Press that reported more than two thousand cases of sexual abuse and exploitation by UN peacekeepers between 2004 and 2014 (Petesch 2019). The United States Institute for Peace, in a 2013 special report titled *Criminalizing Sexual Exploitation and Abuse by (UN) Peacekeepers* chronicled sexual abuse by UN peacekeepers in the Democratic Republic of Congo, Mozambique, Eritrea, and Somalia; the solicitation of prostitution and trafficking in Bosnia and Liberia; and abuse of minors in Sierra Leone (Ferstman 2013). Since then, the incidents of sexual abuse have continued to accrue. In February 2017, before the #AidToo hashtag took off, the secretary general of the UN reported 145 incidents of sexual abuse involving 311 victims, all but two of whom were girls (UN Secretary General 2017). It is unlikely that these numbers capture the full breadth of the abuse given the tremendous vulnerability of victims and lack of channels for reporting abuse, especially in the wake of conflict. Because UN peacekeepers enjoy near immunity, very few of the perpetrators ever face accountability for their actions (see Westendorf 2020).

While the stories that sparked the #AidToo movement in this period were about the aid industry's abuses against the supposed "beneficiaries" of aid—vulnerable local people in the communities that aid workers had purportedly come to support—the #AidToo hashtag began to highlight and reveal long-standing abuses within development agencies, where aid workers themselves were harassed, discriminated against, and assaulted by those in their organizations. Women in development work face some of the same kinds of discrimination, lack of promotion, and harassment as women and nonbinary workers in other fields do (Humanitarian Women's Network 2016), and sexual assault against female aid workers has been demonstrated to be both widespread and underreported in the aid sector (Mazurana and Donnelly 2017). The sector is known to be particularly hierarchical and patriarchal (see Lokot 2021; Rolstad 2020, 66; Gillespie, Mirabella, and Eikenberry 2019, 2), and stories of aid workers' personal experiences of mistreatment and their organizations' mishandling of these incidents piled up as thousands of contributors used the hashtag in its first few months (Cornaz 2019, 58). Megan Norbert, a Canadian humanitarian worker who was drugged and raped by a fellow humanitarian worker while posted in South Sudan, became a leading face and voice of #AidToo (77). Whistleblowers came forward in numerous organizations, bolstered by the wave of reckonings happening as a direct result of #MeToo in other industries. In social media circles both public and private, women aid workers shared their histories of harassment and assault with one another (Cooper 2021).

Aid agencies tried to minimize bad press and stop the flow of information that poured out in the wake of #AidToo, lawyering up against newspapers and hiring pricey crisis management consultants (Cooper 2021, 757), but this only led to more women coming forward. In the scramble to show their ability to hold people accountable, agencies themselves revealed publicly how many cases of abuse by their own staff they were investigating. This only served to underline how widespread and entrenched the problems are. In the UK in particular, the fallout included the resignation and firing of many leaders in top NGOs and charities.

Barriers to Transparency in Aid

The stories of abuse and cover-up were of little surprise to most who work in development, but many felt ambivalent about the industry's dirty laundry being aired in public (Cooper 2021, 752). Though of course there was an acknowledgment of the need for change, many in aid worker circles saw the "scandals" as fodder for right-wing politicians who wanted to cut federal spending to development. A whistleblower who had worked at Save the Children, for example, explained her own reluctance to undermine the mission of the organization: "Save the Children do amazing work . . . and you don't want to go against that good work" (Riley 2020, 51). Aid workers from the Global North generally see their work as underfunded, underrespected by their home countries, and perpetually in danger of being cut by those who would rather fund military operations abroad than charitable works and infrastructure projects. In online fora where aid workers discuss their industry, like 50ShadesofAid, aid professionals voiced these ambivalences and weighed the costs and benefits of publicly condemning agencies that allowed for abuse.

This ambivalence is common for aid workers who among themselves indulge in self-aware cheek about the aid industry, while at the same time feeling self-righteously defensive about the moral good of their vocation (see Hannaford 2023, 127). Many a meme is posted and shared among aid workers that pokes fun at the absurdities of their work or the self-seriousness of their profession. Among aid workers, however, knowing winks and jabs at the profession build community and a sense of inclusion. This is an insider game—the same aid worker Facebook groups that lampoon their own through silly memes and biting satire also passionately decry journalistic stories that they view as cherry-picking the worst cases of development incompetence or corruption and excoriate politicians who target development for criticism and drive down public support.

As Charlotte Lydia Riley (2020, 50) notes, international NGOs "gain power from the projection of moral authority" and thus have much to lose from cracking that veneer of goodness. The moral associations with aid work are part of what those who would silence bad behavior use to continue the cover-up. In this way, sexual abuse in the aid industry functions like sexual abuse in the Catholic church: offenders are quietly moved around instead of exposed, all for the good of protecting the mission. The transitory nature of aid work, with a high rate of turnover and "chronic mobility" (Nowicka 2006), only offers further cover for the phenomenon of "powerful men failing upward" (Riley 2020).

For the general public, the Oxfam scandal held some interest because of the perceived "moral untouchability of humanitarianism" and commonly held conceptions of aid workers as altruists that were so at odds with this story of predatory behavior (Fassin 2011; Shutt 2012, 1532; Fechter 2012). Even the aid industry's loudest critics usually come from the perspective not that aid does harm to the nations it is supposed to serve, but that it takes precious national resources away from donor countries that could be used for their own populations. That aid work is beneficial or well-meaning is generally taken for granted, and this sense of aid as a benign force for good allows for nefarious actors to get away with a wide range of bad behavior, including sexual predation.

Moreover, accountability is generally lacking in development projects and oversight is minimal, allowing for both ineffective (mis)uses of funds at one end of the spectrum and egregious human rights abuses at the other. Take, for example, the same Haitian earthquake response that begins this chapter. Oxfam was only one of many development organizations that descended upon Haiti in the aftermath of the earthquake. USAID, the United States' development agency, awarded some $450 million in contracts to development organizations—with 70 percent of them going to DC-area contractors like the project management company Chemonics, which received a large percentage of that total. A 2011 investigation by USAID's inspector general found that Chemonics had grossly misused millions of dollars of funding for earthquake relief, performing very little oversight of their partners and producing few beneficial results to the people of Haiti (Ramachandran and Walz 2015, 44). Despite this finding, USAID then awarded over $50 million more to Chemonics the next year for projects in Haiti. This lack of consequences is not unique to Chemonics, nor to Haiti. When development projects fail, mismanage funds, and eat money earmarked for disaster relief without any tangible benefits to victims of disaster, they are not put out of business; they are not brought to trial. They continue to apply for and receive funds with little accountability or consequences.

Two recent scandals involving young, white American women represent further examples of the malevolence of the "white savior" narrative that presumes that any Western action in poor countries is morally righteous and thus permissible. These examples, which feature women aid workers, also underline the idea that simply putting leadership in (white) women's hands will not automatically resolve issues of abuse of power and the coloniality of aid (see Lugones 2010). American Katie Meyler opened schools for vulnerable girls in Liberia despite lacking any background or training in education or management. The charity raised $8 million and Meyler herself earned praise and an invitation to the White House, before a ProPublica investigation revealed that students had been sexually assaulted and infected with HIV by a staff member while Meyler ignored evidence of the crimes and then sought to cover them up for the sake of her organization's reputation (Young 2018). Renee Bach moved to Uganda at eighteen years old to work as a missionary and decided to play doctor through an NGO she created called "Serving His Children." With no medical training, no accreditation, and no permission from Uganda's Ministry of Health, Bach began experimenting with medical procedures she had learned from YouTube, including giving blood transfusions to babies. More than a hundred children died in her center's care between 2010 and 2015 (Levy 2020). Before these abuses were exposed and lawsuits ensued, both women were the subjects of glowing, congratulatory media attention about their "good works" in Africa and operated for years before facing any scrutiny or pushback.

Even the most well-meaning do-gooder would not think of opening their own medical clinic in Canada or Germany to practice blood transfusions on babies without any formal medical training or licensing. The arrogance of doing so in Uganda comes from the assumption that Western people can play fast and loose with the law in poorer countries. Aid workers can behave with relative impunity in poor countries, undertaking all manner of irresponsible actions that would be unthinkable in their countries of origin simply because they are granted access to vulnerable populations. Van Hauwermeiren and his Oxfam colleagues' actions in Haiti point to this presumption of untouchability and immunity.

Not only do individuals behave in this manner, but Western NGOs act with presumed immunity as well. In the aftermath of the Oxfam scandal's exposure, then-president of Haiti Jovenel Moise called for more investigations of the abuses of other agencies that were engaged in relief efforts following the 2010 earthquake. Moise claimed that Médecins Sans Frontières repatriated seventeen of their staff for misconduct and that the Haitian authorities were not privy to explanations of said misconduct to pursue their own investigations and criminal charges (Delva 2018). The organization simply repatriated their own staff and kept their investigations internal, as though the Haitian government had no authority over aid workers working on their soil. This attitude of entitlement is grounded in an imperial history and only bolstered by the vague assumption that aid work is morally good.

Good Intentions?

It is important to move away from this understanding of development work as morally good for a number of reasons, including but not limited to the need for more scrutiny about what people are doing under its banner in poor countries. That work begins with an examination of the origins of the development industry. The development industry grew out of and, indeed, within the colonial project. In Africa, as just one example, development ideology emerged in direct overlap with and service of colonization. In the postwar period of European colonialism particularly, there was a distinct turn to focus rhetorically on the good works of colonialism. This period—referred to as "welfare colonialism" by M. Crawford Young (1994) or even "developmental colonialism" by Fredrick Cooper (2002)—put a charitable face on imperialism in large part in response to the growing criticism of colonialism at home and in the colonies (Beeckmans 2017, 360). A strategic rebranding focused on benevolent projects of lifting people up, rather than on the realities of labor extraction (including military labor in the form of soldiers) and resource extraction. In Africa and beyond, these "humanitarian 'good works' of empire were part of its very durable architecture—with exacting exclusions and inequities structured through them" (Stoler 2010, xii).

These exclusions and inequities flowed neatly into the postindependence pivot to "development" interventions in the same places by the same architects. As Cooper (2002, 16) reminds us, even for postindependence African governments, development, in its most top-down constructions, was a continuation of most of the principles of colonial-era projects (see also Renders 2002, 61). The continuities between the colonial era and the present push us to think of these two periods not as wholly separate; as Uma Kothari (2009, 161) puts it, "the trajectory from colonialism to development is more usefully characterized as a shift in emphasis." "Coloniality" continues to shape global dynamics of power and their consequences, and this has clear expression in the contemporary development industry.

The development industry employs the same "hierarchy of humanity" that upheld, legitimated, and excused imperial conquest in foreign lands (Fassin 2010, 239). This hierarchy of humanity still permeates the development project both in its logics and its everyday practice. The foundational concepts of "developed" and "underdeveloped" that underlie the aid industry's mission are not objective categorizations; they are socially constructed designations that have a history rooted in a colonial understanding of the world as organized by a split between civility and primitivity. The conceit of development presumes a ladder to modernity on which certain countries are at the top and others are at the bottom. The "development" metaphor itself is a biological one: poor people should "develop" from childhood (poverty) into adulthood (prosperity). The vernacular of development is, as Jemima Pierre (2020, 87) convincingly argues, a "racial vernacular" whose very terminology works to "reinforce patterns of racial (dis)advantage, global inequality, and relations structured in dominance."

The technocratic terminology of development acts explicitly to depoliticize poverty and obscure its racial ideology and its colonial origins. Development still suffers from what Robtel Neajai Pailey (2020) calls the "white gaze" problem. The depoliticization and deracialization of discourses of poverty and development insidiously frame continued power imbalances as being outside racial dynamics while perpetuating them. This allows practitioners and scholars of development to be silent on questions of race and therefore to avoid confronting the uncomfortable reality of the "the powers, privileges and inequalities that continue to flow from whiteness" (Pailey 2021, 732).

That Western development experts have tools to "build capacity" in poorer countries who are assumed to lack the tools for their own advancement has meant that "poverty became the basis of a lucrative industry for planners, experts, and civil servants" (Escobar 1999), largely from the Global North. Arturo Escobar (1999) credits the creation of this lucrative industry as the only real success of development work; the "problems" of global poverty still exist, while the development industry thrives, with master's programs in development practice proliferating—86 percent of these programs are based in the West—and a steady offering of jobs for the technicians of poverty management. This reminds us that the development industry itself is just one engine of global capitalism in which the global inequalities of race, nationality, and gender are not neutralized but are in many ways reproduced and heightened. The entitlement that shaped imperial intervention continues to shape Western understandings of poor nations as open to their interventions and authority.

It is perhaps not surprising that this industry "structured around hierarchies of race and place" should also contain profound inequities between local workers and expat or "international" staff (Pailey 2021, 32). Within the development industry's hierarchy of personnel, "deciding what to do becomes the component presumed to require real skill and expertise, presumably foreign, while carrying out what has been decided is presumed to be the work of mere practice, performable by undifferentiated masses of national staff" (Peters 2020, 20). In other words, expatriate aid workers are privileged as the all-important deciders, and the local staff are mere doers. They are compensated as such, with international staff receiving not only exponentially higher salaries but also considerable perks and amenities that can include housing, private security, relocation costs, and copious paid leave (see Hannaford 2023). As a result of this coding of only certain qualifications and provenances as valuable expertise, local aid workers are given relatively limited authority, pay, and professional mobility, not to mention few channels to challenge abuses by their senior, expat colleagues that they have observed or suffered.

The mismatched authority and rewards that the development industry brings to its Western practitioners versus its target beneficiaries has direct relevance for questions of sexual violence in development contexts. When Western practitioners can draw from wells of colonial power and authority, behave with impunity, and treat the populations they ostensibly serve as exploitable and expendable, sexual violence will be one form of domination and exploitation that flourishes. In the section that follows, I draw together critiques of the #MeToo movement's Western feminist hegemony and calls for the decolonization of development to argue that without a real reckoning with development's situation at the nexus of colonialism, white supremacy, and patriarchal capitalism, #AidToo is unlikely to change the fate of those most vulnerable to sexual abuse.

Decolonizing #MeToo and Decolonizing Development

Intersectional lines of feminist critique of the #MeToo movement assert that the movement is limited by its framing, which is based on a Western feminist idea of justice and neoliberal cultural logics (Gill and Orgad 2018; Ghadery 2019); by its focus on white and privileged victims thus leaving out many of the most marginalized victims of sexual violence (de la Garza 2019; Phipps 2020; Fraser, Bhattacharya, and Arruzza 2019; Onwuachi-Willig 2018; Tambe 2018); and by the way it distracts from an interrogation of the structural frameworks of sexual violence (Adetiba and Burke 2018, 32). Recently, scholars have called for a decolonial approach to studies of sexual violence, one that underlines gender violence as a tool of colonial violence both historically and in the present moment (Dougherty and Calafell 2019; Mack and Na'puti 2019; Rowe 2019). Approaching sexual violence from this orientation will "require resisting the reproduction of colonial logics" (Mack and Na'puti 2019, 348).

Similarly, many scholars have in recent years called for a decolonization of development. Decolonization of development starts from an understanding that the contemporary aid industry is rooted in the framework of European imperial conquest. Decoloniality seeks to interrogate how knowledge is produced about non-Western countries and who has a hand in producing that knowledge. It demands an evaluation of what we consider expertise and how decisions are made regarding the future and self-determination of various nations (Rutazibwa 2019, 66). In a decolonial approach, Western ideology must be displaced from the center of development metrics and decision-making to give room for alternative modes of evaluation of value (Mignolo and Walsh 2018, 17).

In a more radical vein, some scholars believe that decolonization of development does not go far enough. The colonial foundations of development are so insidious as to make the entire project not worth saving (for example, see Ziai 2013). In her elegant essay "On Babies and Bathwater," Olivia Rutazibwa (2018) takes this position seriously, ultimately advocating for the need to demythologize the development industry. She points to the "colonial amnesia" that allows for "a continuation of the Western self-image as the 'good guys' of history (with the exceptional hiccups)" and leads naturally to Western interventions being conflated with unimpeachable moral goodness (167). This is the same shield that allows for sexual abuses by Western aid workers to go so often unchecked and unpunished. A widespread perception of aid as "morally untouchable," the culture of benign celebration of aid work and a lack of scrutiny, as well as the fear of aid work being defunded as a sector, and protectionism all create a cover for all kinds of abuses of power including sexual violence.

#AidToo helped lift the curtain and demanded a closer, critical look at how the foundations of aid allow for abuses of power. However, the hashtag quickly moved from addressing victims, such as those coerced into transactional sex by Oxfam workers in Haiti, to addressing the aid workers themselves in the workplace, replicating the hierarchies of race, class, citizenship, and privilege that continue to shape the development industry. Aid beneficiaries' voices were largely silent in the online discussions on, tweets about, and media coverage of the hashtag (Cornaz 2019, 43). One of the leading demands from the movement was for development organizations to do a better job protecting their own staff members from sexual abuse. Though new rules and reporting channels within aid organizations are commendable, how can such measures address the extreme and entrenched imbalances of power and access that subject women in conflict zones to sexual violence at the hands of itinerant, powerful aid workers? These concerns were decentered from the #AidToo discussions, as aid workers themselves—especially Western women aid workers—became the loudest voices in online discourse (Cornaz 2019, 43).

The #MeToo movement has been criticized not only for erasing the foundational role that women of color played in its creation but for continuing to ignore and decenter the particular experiences women of color face (Onwuachi-Willig 2018). The movement and the media coverage of the movement has repeatedly centered the experiences of wealthy white women at the expense of a focus on the nuances that make nonwhite and poor women particularly vulnerable (Tambe 2018; Phipps 2020). This mirrors a larger tendency in what is labeled as "white feminism," which situates "white women's experiences as the basis for feminist engagements" (Oyěwùmí 2003, 4). As the #AidToo hashtag gained momentum, a similar shift in emphasis toward the sexual and gender harassment experiences of professional aid workers usurped attention from what had been a discussion about the aid industry's abuse of power against local communities. Though the racist and misogynistic cultures of aid industry workplaces certainly deserve attention and scrutiny and are doubtlessly entangled with the industry's racist and patriarchal foundations, the kinds of accountability called for by centering the experiences of aid industry employees won't address the larger fundamental problem of colonial amnesia that structures the industry.

Without a decolonial approach to development, it is unlikely that #AidToo can lead to a substantial reordering of power that would lead to meaningful change for those most vulnerable to sexual abuse at the hands of the development industry. Real change will only come with the shattering of the image of the development industry as an unquestioned beacon of moral goodness and an engaged public desire for oversight of the industry's actions. Viewing the aid industry's motivations as based in colonial aspirations for domination and subjugation can engender a new kind of scrutiny for the actions of aid workers abroad. This perspective shift, grounded in decoloniality, is an inherently feminist project akin to the calls for a decolonization of #MeToo, "dismantling what has already been assembled" in the hopes of building back on equitable foundations (Ahmed 2017, 91).

REFERENCES

Adetiba, Elizabeth, and Tarana Burke. 2018. "Tarana Burke Says #MeToo Should Center Marginalized Communities." In *Where Freedom Starts: Sex, Power, Violence in #MeToo*, edited by Verso Books US, 8–37. London: Verso.

Ahmed, Sara. 2017. *Living a Feminist Life*. Durham, NC: Duke University Press.

Beeckmans, Luce. 2017. "The 'Development Syndrome': Building and Contesting the SICAP Housing Schemes in French Dakar (1951–1960)." *Canadian Journal of African Studies / Revue Canadienne des Études Africaines* 51 (3): 359–88. https://doi.org/10.1080/00083968.2017.1411820.

Choo, Hae Yeon. 2021. "From Madwomen to Whistleblowers: MeToo in South Korea as an Institutional Critique." *Feminist Formations* 33 (3): 256–70. https://doi.org/10.1353/ff.2021.0048.

Cooper, Fredrick. 2002. *Africa since 1940: The Past of the Present*. Cambridge: Cambridge University Press.

Cooper, Glenda. 2021. "#AidToo: Social Media Spaces and the Transformation of the Reporting of Aid Scandals in 2018." *Journalism Practice* 15 (6): 747–66. https://doi.org/10.1080/17512786.2020.1851611.

Cornaz, Natacha. 2019. "An Analysis of the #AidToo Movement on Twitter: What Impacts Can a Hashtag Achieve on Sexual Exploitation and Abuse in the Aid Sector?" Master's thesis, Malmö University.

de la Garza, Sarah Amira. 2019. "No More Magic Mirrors: Confronting Reflections of Privileged Feminisms in #MeToo." *Women and Language* 42 (1): 175–81. https://doi.org/10.1080/17475759.2020.1806099.

Delva, Joseph Guyler. 2018. "Haiti's President Says Oxfam Claims are 'Tip of the Iceberg' as He Accuses Medecins Sans Frontieres." *The Independent*, February 17, 2018. www.independent.co.uk.

Dougherty, Cristy, and Bernadette Marie Calafell. 2019. "Before and Beyond #MeToo and #TimesUp: Rape as a Colonial and Racist Project." *Women and Language* 42 (1): 213–18.

Escobar, Arturo. 1999. "The Invention of Development." *Current History* 98 (631): 382–86.

Fassin, Didier. 2010. "Inequality of Lives, Hierarchies of Humanity: Moral Commitments and Ethical Dilemmas of Humanitarianism." In *In the Name of Humanity: The Government of Threat and Care*, edited by Ilana Feldman and Miriam Ticktin, 238–55. Durham, NC: Duke University Press.

———. 2011. "Noli Me Tangere: The Moral Untouchability of Humanitarianism." In *Forces of Compassion: Humanitarianism Between Ethics and Politics*, edited by Erica Bornstein and Peter Redfield, 35–52. Santa Fe: School for Advanced Research Press.

Fechter, Anne-Meike. 2012. "'Living Well' while 'Doing Good'? (Missing) Debates on Altruism and Professionalism in Aid Work." *Third World Quarterly* 33 (8): 1475–91. https://doi.org/10.1080/09700161.2012.698133.

Ferstman, Carla. 2013. "Criminalizing Sexual Exploitation and Abuse by Peacekeepers." *United States Institute of Peace Special Report 335*. Washington, DC: United States Institute of Peace.

Fraser, Nancy, Tithi Bhattacharya, and Cinzia Arruzza. 2019. *Feminism for the 99%: A Manifesto*. London: Verso.

Ghadery, Farnush. 2019. "#Metoo—Has the 'Sisterhood' Finally Become Global or Just Another Product of Neoliberal Feminism?" *Transnational Legal Theory* 10 (2): 252–74. https://doi.org/10.1080/20414005.2019.1630169.

Gill, Rosalind, and Shani Orgad. 2018. "The Shifting Terrain of Sex and Power: From the 'Sexualization of Culture' to #MeToo." *Sexualities* 21 (8): 1,313–24. https://doi.org/10.1177/1363460718794647.

Gillespie, Elizabeth M., Roseanne M. Mirabella, and Angela M. Eikenberry. 2019. "#Metoo/#Aidtoo and Creating an Intersectional Feminist NPO/NGO Sector." *Nonprofit Policy Forum* 10 (4): 1–9.

Hannaford, Dinah. 2023. *Aid and the Help: International Development and the Transnational Extraction of Care*. Stanford: Stanford University Press.

Heffer, Greg. 2018. "Oxfam's Shamed Ex-Haiti Chief Roland van Hauwermeiren Hits Back at 'Lies.'" *Sky News*, February 15, 2018.

Humanitarian Women's Network. 2016. *Humanitarian Women's Network Full Survey Results*. N.p.: Humanitarian Women's Network. http://interagencystandingcommittee.org.

Kothari, Uma. 2009. "Spatial Practices and Imaginaries: Experiences of Colonial Officers and Development Professionals." In *Empire, Development and Colonialism: The Past in the Present*, edited by Mark Duffield and Vernon Hewitt, 161–75. Rochester, NY: Boydell & Brewer.

Lakkimsetti, Chaitanya, and Vanita Reddy. 2021. "#MeToo and Transnational Gender Justice: An Introduction." *Feminist Formations* 33 (3): 224–38. https://doi.org/10.1353/ff.2021.0046.

Levy, Ariel. 2020. "A Missionary on Trial." *New Yorker*, April 13, 2020. https://www.newyorker.com/.

Lokot, Michelle. 2021. "From the Inside Out: Gender Mainstreaming and Organizational Culture Within the Aid Sector." *Frontiers in Sociology*. 6:664406. https://doi.org/10.3389/fsoc.2021.664406.

Lukose, Ritty. 2018. "Decolonizing Feminism in the# MeToo Era." *Cambridge Journal of Anthropology* 36 (2): 34–52. https://doi.org/10.3167/cja.2018.360205.

Lugones, María. 2010. "Toward a Decolonial Feminism." *Hypatia* 25 (4): 742–59. https://doi.org/10.1111/j.1527-2001.2010.01137.x.

Mack, Ashley Noel, and Tiara R. Na'puti. 2019. "'Our Bodies Are Not *Terra Nullius*': Building a Decolonial Feminist Resistance to Gendered Violence." *Women's Studies in Communication* 42 (3): 347–70. https://doi.org/10.1080/07491409.2019.1637803.

Mignolo, Walter, and Catherine E. Walsh. 2018. *On Decoloniality: Concepts, Analytics, Praxis*. Durham, NC: Duke University Press.

Mazurana, Dyan, and Phoebe Donnelly. 2017. *STOP the Sexual Assault Against Humanitarian and Development Aid Workers*. Somerville, MA: Tufts University.

Nowicka, Magdalena. 2006. *Transnational Professionals and their Cosmopolitan Universes*. Frankfurt am Main, Germany: Campus.

O'Neill, Sean. 2018. "Top Oxfam Staff Paid Haiti Survivors for Sex." *The Times*, February 9, 2018. www.thetimes.co.uk.

Onwuachi-Willig, Angela. 2018. "What about #UsToo? The invisibility of race in the #MeToo movement." *Yale Law Journal Forum* 128: 105–20.

Oyěwùmí, Oyèrónke. 2003. *African Women and Feminism: Reflecting on the Politics of Sisterhood*. Trenton, NJ: Africa World Press.

Pailey, Robtel Neajai. 2020. "De-centering the 'White Gaze' of Development." *Development and Change* 51 (3): 729–45. https://doi.org/10.1111/dech.12550.

———. 2021. "Race in/and Development." In *The Essential Guide to Critical Development Studies*, edited by Henry Veltmeyer and Paul Bowles, 31–39. 2nd ed. Abingdon: Routledge.

Peters, Rebecca Warne. 2020. *Implementing Inequality: The Invisible Labor of International Development*. New Brunswick, NJ: Rutgers University Press.

Petesch, Carley. 2019. "Leaked UN Report Shows Failed Investigation on Sexual Abuse." *APNews*, October 31, 2019. https://apnews.com.

Phipps, Alison. 2020. *Me, Not You: The Trouble with Mainstream Feminism*. Manchester, UK: Manchester University Press.

Pierre, Jemima. 2020. "The Racial Vernaculars of Development: A View from West Africa." *American Anthropologist* 122 (1): 86–98. https://doi.org/10.1111/aman.13352.

Ramachandran, Vijaya, and Julie Walz. 2015. "Haiti: Where Has All the Money Gone?" *Journal of Haitian Studies* 21 (1): 26–65. https://doi.org/10.1353/jhs.2015.0003.

Renders, Marleen. 2002. "An Ambiguous Adventure: Muslim Organizations and the Discourse of 'Development' in Senegal." *Journal of Religion in Africa* 32 (1): 61–82. https://doi.org/10.1163/15700660260048474.

Riley, Charlotte Lydia. 2020. "Powerful Men, Failing Upwards: The Aid Industry and the 'Me Too' Movement." *Journal of Humanitarian Affairs* 2 (3): 49–55. https://doi.org/10.7227/JHA.052.

Rolstad, Vilde. 2020. "Humanitarian Organisations' Experience with and Response to Sexual Harassment in the Aftermath of #AidToo: The Case of NORCAP." Master's thesis, Norwegian University of Life Sciences.

Roshanravan, Shireen. 2021. "On the Limits of Globalizing Black Feminist Commitments: 'Me Too' and its White Detours." *Feminist Formations* 33 (3): 239–55. https://doi.org/10.1353/ff.2021.0047.

Rowe, Aimee Carrillo. 2019. "A Long Walk Home: Decolonizing #MeToo." *Women and Language* 42 (1): 169–74.

Rutazibwa, Olivia U. 2018. "On Babies and Bathwater: Decolonizing International Development Studies." In *Decolonization and Feminisms in Global Teaching and Learning*, edited by Sara de Jong, Rosalba Icaza, and Olivia U. Rutazibwa, 192–214. London: Routledge.

———. 2019. "What's There to Mourn? Decolonial Reflections on (the End of) Liberal Humanitarianism." *Journal of Humanitarian Affairs* 1 (1): 65–67. https://doi.org/10.7227/JHA.010.

Shutt, Cathy. 2012. "A Moral Economy? Social Interpretations of Money in Aidland." *Third World Quarterly* 33 (8): 1527–43. https://doi.org/10.1080/01436597.2012.698139.

Stoler, Ann. 2010. *Carnal Knowledge and Imperial Power*. 2nd ed. Berkeley: University of California Press.

Tambe, Ashwini. 2018. "Reckoning with the Silences of #MeToo." *Feminist Studies* 44 (1): 197–203. https://doi.org/10.1353/fem.2018.0019.

UN Secretary General. 2017. *Special Measures for Protection from Sexual Exploitation and Abuse: A New Approach*. Report of the Secretary General, No. A/71/818. http://undocs.org.

UNHCR (UN High Commissioner for Refugees) and Save the Children UK. 2002. *Sexual Violence and Exploitation: The Experience of Refugee Children in Liberia, Guinea, and Sierra Leone*. New York: WomenWarPeace.org (UNIFEM—a Portal on Women, Peace, and Security). http://www.womenwarpeace.org.

Westendorf, Jasmine-Kim. 2020. *Violating Peace: Sex, Aid, and Peacekeeping*. New York: Cornell University Press.

Young, M. Crawford. 1994. *African Colonial State in Comparative Perspective*. New Haven, CT: Yale University Press.

Young, Finlay. 2018. "Unprotected." *ProPublica*, October 11, 2018. https://www.propublica.org.

Ziai, Aram. 2013. "The Discourse of 'Development' and Why the Concept Should be Abandoned." *Development in Practice* 23 (1): 123–36. https://www.doi.org/10.1080/09614524.2013.752792.

8

#MeToo from the Margins

Rethinking Consent-Coercion Binaries with Commercial Sex Work in India

SUDESHNA CHATTERJEE

During the 2017 resurgence of the MeToo movement, you may not have heard much from sex workers. Were we there? Did you somehow miss us?
—Selena the Stripper

A critical intervention in the #MeToo movement has been brought forth by sex workers, who point out that #MeToo doesn't adequately complicate binary coding of consent and coercion and of sex and work that underlie this movement, the feminist movement broadly, and the legal infrastructure which regulates sexual commerce (Cooney 2018; West and Horn 2021). An article published by *Time* magazine in early 2018 highlighted how several sex workers who came out on Twitter to recount their #MeToo stories, faced severe stigma-driven backlash and subsequently felt that they had "been excluded from the public conversation around #MeToo" and the "nationwide reckoning on workplace harassment" (Cooney 2018). Selena the Stripper's questions in the epigraph, about whether sex workers were "there" in #MeToo discourses, pave the way for a critical feminist inquiry into a seemingly paradoxical situation, whereby sex workers find themselves most vulnerable to sexual assault and gender-based violence as well as quite overlooked and excluded from media, policy, and academic narratives on #MeToo. In this paper, I discuss sex workers' critiques of #MeToo by highlighting how the movement does little to disrupt the binary coding of consent and coercion. This is further reflected in and complicated through similar dualistic notions about sex and work underlying legal systems and moral norms that govern sexual commerce and continue to hinder sex workers' demands for rights and justice. I ground these critiques in a study of sex work activism in India to identify thematic continuities between sex workers' critiques of #MeToo and similar concerns raised by Indian sex work activists.

To formulate sex workers' critiques of the #MeToo movement, my paper draws on works by sex work activists and works that highlight sex workers' voices, such as works by Jessie Patella-Rey (2018), Samantha Cooney (2018), and Natalia West and Tina Horn (2021). I theorize consent and coercion in sex work based on works in critical and feminist literature that assert that consent and coercion must be understood as a continuum rather than a binary (Anitha and Gill 2017) and as products of conducive contexts rather than an event (Kelly 2016). Here, Michelle Dempsey's (2021) framework for theorizing consent and coercion by distinguishing three norms (wrongfulness, excusability, and accountability) that govern shifts in discourses and responses to sexual misconduct in the era of #MeToo is particularly valuable. While Dempsey's framework is far from foolproof (I disagree with Dempsey's oversweeping generalization that #MeToo has brought forth a "cultural reckoning" in terms of how people view all instances of sexual violation), her theoretical model nonetheless provides some concrete parameters against which we might measure normative transformations (or lack thereof) brought about by the #MeToo movement. The normative shifts in how we perceive wrongfulness (coercion) and excusability (consent) of and public accountability for acts of sexual transgressions did not happen for all women. If #MeToo's significance lies in legal and social norm transformations, the limitations of the movement become obvious in the way sex workers as a subject group are still struggling to justify wrongfulness, inexcusability, and public accountability for acts of sexual assault and aggression against sex workers. All three norms converge to discount violence and sexual assault against sex workers.

In this paper, I discuss three major conceptual critiques raised by sex workers against #MeToo and by sex work activists in India. First, I provide a brief overview of why the wrongfulness of acts of sexual violence against sex workers is underplayed because sex workers don't fit the imagery of "perfect victims." I specifically discuss how the gendered assumptions underlying the legal infrastructure and even various strands of the feminist movement frame sex trafficking (and coercion) and sex work (and consent) in oppositional terms and reserve outrage for pain and sexual violence experienced only by perfect victims. Second, I explore how defining wrongfulness is closely linked to reading consent and, hence, (in)excusability of an act of aggression. I discuss how sex workers push back against excusability norms governing sexual violence discourses against sex workers by challenging (mis)interpretations of transactional sex as unconditional, irreversible consent and conflations of sex with selfhood. Last, I discuss how wrongfulness and excusability norms converge with public accountability norms (or the lack thereof) and how sex work activists resist systemic silencing and discrimination by upholding individual agency, community solidarity, and legal and social accountability.

Gauging Wrongfulness: Sex Workers Are Not Perfect Victims

Accounts of sexual violence and transgressions against sex workers do not elicit the same response of wrongfulness—when defined as undermining the voluntariness of consent—as those encountered by women who are not sex workers. At the heart of their systemic exclusion lies the idea that sex workers are not the "perfect victims" when it comes to sexual assault, which furthermore feeds the deleterious, gendered notion that sex workers cannot be sexually assaulted (see Jordan 2008, 2004). The general unease to consider sex workers as perfect victims stems from a complicated web of gendered and racialized norms regarding what is considered coercion, what are considered legitimate forms of work, how we read consent and how we read the role of sex in the market and polity. Sex work is defined as the exchange of sexual services, performances, or products for material compensation (Weitzer 2000), and it has long been a subject of conflicting theorizations across disciplinary boundaries. The feminist movement itself is greatly divided over its characterization of sex work. Western feminist deliberations in the 1980s viewed any form of sexual commerce as either oppressive and inherently violent (dominance/abolitionist and radical feminists) or agentic (sex positivists). Abolitionist narratives and policies primarily focus on the trafficking aspect of sexual commerce, conflate sex work with sex trafficking, and view sex workers as sex slaves (Kotiswaran 2011). Here, consent is deemed to be irrelevant, given the inherently discriminatory and violent nature of sexual transactions. Since sexual transactions are deemed inherently violent, folks who "are usually totally aghast at the idea that a woman has somehow asked for it" don't show equal support towards sex workers who chose the profession by their own volition and refused to be rescued (Cooney 2018). Hence, sex workers' critiques of #MeToo must be viewed as historically embedded in critiques of (neo) abolitionist perspectives on sex work, highlighting how activism around trafficking and sexual violence has the tendency to fall prey to rescue politics centered around a "perfect," believable victim, which doesn't really uproot gender norms. Thus, while sex trafficking victims are perfect victims, sex workers who refuse to be rescued and mainstreamed are not.

The consent-coercion binary operationalized through "perfect victim" narratives are also observed in legal and policy discourses that render consensual sex work invisible. In India, for instance, the invisibility of sex workers as a legal subject group is intimately tied to the sole visibility accorded to sex trafficking victims in legal and policy discourses on sexual commerce. The women's movement largely ignored conversations on nonmarital, nonheterosexual, and nonmonogamous sex until the 1908s, and sexual minorities (including sex workers) were not recognized as political communities with the moral standing to make legitimate demands from the state (Lakkimsetti 2020). Even then, discourses on prostitution and sex work came to be framed through narratives of harm, coercion, and victimhood. This led sex work activist organizations such as Veshya Anyay Mukti Parishad (VAMP), Sampada Grameen Mahila Sanstha (Sangraam), and Durbar Mahila Samanwaya Committee (DMSC) to subsequently push back against the victim mentality implicit in mainstream feminist narratives in the 1990s (Gangoli 2007). During my field research, I observed that state officials readily recognized trafficked victims as a subject category but not sex workers. In an interview with the spokesperson of the National Minister of Women and Child Welfare in 2017, I was explicitly told that the Government of India was "aware" of sex work activism but it was outside the area of concern for the ministry, which was focused on trafficking in women and children. The spokesperson refused to address any questions related to sex work activism and the conversation was nudged toward national policies which exist for the prevention of human trafficking and rehabilitation of trafficked victims. Similarly, a high-level bureaucrat at the West Bengal Department of Women and Child Development and Social Welfare stated that "there is no direct interface" between the Department's scope of work and sex workers. While he agreed that "it is difficult to say" if sex work should be recognized as legitimate work, he refused any knowledge of sex workers movements in West Bengal or any other part of the country.

Sex workers are not simply ignored by the law, they also face active persecution as a result of their invisibility. A study in 2014 found that the risk of physical and sexual violence against sex workers was amplified seven times among sex workers who operate in spaces where sex work is criminalized or semicriminalized. "Whore stigma" plays a significant role in supporting a culture of impunity for violence and aggression against a range of vulnerable women and children who engage in illicit sex, particularly street-based workers, migrant workers, drug-addicted workers, and transgender workers (Deering et al. 2014; Vanwesenbeeck 2017). In #MeToo conversations, sex workers especially harp on how the movement ignores the issue of the legally precarious foundation of sex work which further prevents reporting of sexual harassment for fear of facing legal and criminal charges. J. Brantley, alternative sexualities advisor at Sharmus Outlaw Advocacy and Rights (SOAR) institute, states that "there's no HR department in the strip club. . . . You think we're going to go to the cops? Hell no. . . . You have to out yourself, and you lose your credibility—now we're not the perfect victim anymore" (Cooney 2018). Sex work activists associated with DMSC in Kolkata also highlighted similar struggles against discrimination, which they attribute to their invisibility to the law: "Before 1992 [formation of DMSC], sex workers had no rights. They faced violence from the police, local goons and brothel madams. There was rampant sexual abuse of these girls, and they felt hopeless, that they weren't a part of society, that they weren't worth living" (Focus Group with anonymous participants, DMSC 2017).

Thus, binary positioning of sex trafficking vis-à-vis sex work plays a central role in underplaying the wrongfulness of sexual assault and harassment faced by sex workers. This necessitates that #MeToo become mindful of experiences of legally precarious subjects such as sex workers, especially in non-Western contexts where they are typically viewed as victims of modern slavery and in dire need of rescue or as law-breaking individuals who consented to violence by virtue of their individual choice to engage in sex work.

(Un)reasonable Belief: Can Sex Workers Be Sexually Assaulted?

Allegations of sexual assault against sex workers are almost always challenged by virtue of the believability of such claims, especially because sex workers are far from fitting the role of perfect victims. Melony Hill, a sex worker whose #MeToo tweets received backlash on Twitter, articulates how the believability of sex workers facing sexual assault is unapologetically questioned by the movement. She states that "they don't want to include women like me. . . . They'll say we're just whores anyway . . . 'how can you sexually assault a whore?' I've had that said to me multiple times" (Cooney 2018). This disbelief, I argue, is deeply rooted in two things: first, misreading transactional sexual encounters as blanket consent and, second, conflating sex with selfhood, which requires a complication of the ways in which we understand consent in sexual encounters more broadly (Tambe 2018).

According to Dempsey, excusability norms that "concern the reasonableness of mistaken beliefs regarding what is, in actuality, wrongful conduct" might help lend clarity about mistaken beliefs regarding consent to sex (Dempsey 2021, 354). Unlike wrongfulness norms, the issue under consideration here is not the wrongfulness of the act but rather the believability of the claim that a certain encounter was mistaken to be consensual, when in fact it was not. However, a striking flaw in Dempsey's framework is the absence of a gendered approach to understanding how nonverbal gestures are "honestly mistaken" and misinterpreted to mean consent. Mistaking transactional sex as unconditional sexual consent is a deeply gendered and racialized process and perpetuates the conflation of sex with selfhood, more so for some subjects than for others.

Despite their unique qualification to speak about sexual consent, sex workers have been kept out of feminist discussions on sex and consent. A consent violation for sex workers occurs when clients go outside the bounds of the agreement of "what is about to transpire—if a client touches a part of the body or attempts to engage in a sexual act that's off-limits. Sometimes, clients become violent. Or they may fail to pay for services" (Cooney 2018). Assumptions underlying these instances of consent violations are manifold and range from the systemic conflation of sex with selfhood to presuming voluntary consent on the part of an individual who is habituated to have sex (Tambe 2018; Nigam 2017). This, in turn, leads to the perpetuation of harmful notions such as "men wouldn't rape if they seek a sex worker to get it all out" (Cooney 2018). Hence, the automatic assumption that sex workers are exclusively sexual subjects, rendering unconditional and irreversible consent, makes sex workers extremely vulnerable to assault and violence from several actors, and not just from those who have been approved as clients (such as the police, pimps, etc.). Here, sex workers call out both abolitionist feminists as well as sex positivists. Let us consider, for instance, how anti-trafficking activists in India perceive the relationship between #MeToo, sex work, and consent. Ruchira Gupta stated in an interview that "it's (#MeToo) is a fantastic campaign, and it's really given women a voice. . . . Where are the voices of prostituted women? They are the most abused and exploited, but when they are called sex workers, implying they are doing this out of choice, then how can they say, 'me too'?" (Chandran 2017). Gupta's statement highlights the problematic notion that sex workers consent is ubiquitous, constant, and irreversible. For sex workers in India, (un)believability of assault and violence claims is closely tied to systemic and legal recognition, visibility, and social stigma. Yet, systemic conflation of sex and selfhood is not simply restricted to deliberations on sex work. In fact, legal and juridical discourses on rape highlight how patriarchy and misogyny are still deeply institutionalized in India's legal system, such that courts often challenge the believability of sexual assault claims by questioning a woman's sexual (and therefore personal) character and placing the onus of communicating consent on the woman (Nigam 2017). Sex workers in India are thus compelled to negotiate consent on a number of fronts with a wide variety of actors and collectively operationalize consent by consistently pushing back against being reduced to helpless victims of sex trafficking or aberrant sexual subjects in need of disciplining. Rather, they uphold that sex work must be recognized as consensual, legitimate labor with regulatory standards and sex workers as active political and social agents who are capable of choosing the terms of sexual transactions and performing multiple roles such as parents, activists, and citizens.

Over the course of my field research I found that sex workers at VAMP/Sangram and DMSC explicitly laid out the terms of their consent starting from a broader consent to engage in sex work as adults and more specific issues of consent such as the use of condoms, as well as major systemic obstacles which render sex workers' consent invisible.

> Trafficking and sex work are different. They must not be conflated. The SRV board at Durbar works to prevent trafficking of minors and second-generation prostitution. If it is an adult, who is consenting, to the proper documentation, they must be allowed to go into the profession. (Focus Group with Anonymous Participants, Durbar, 2017)

> We can identify several challenges . . . goon and police violence, as women in this profession are used as disposable bodies so they are continuously subject to goon and police violence. Another challenge our sex workers face is sex without condoms or money. (Focus Group with Anonymous Participants, VAMP/Sangram, 2017.)

Sex workers also caution against the imagery of the "happy hooker," which forms the cornerstone of sex positivism and third wave feminism. West and Horn state how consensual sex workers are often projected to be united with their clients in terms of interests and constructed in opposition to the hapless trafficked victim. This only deepens the consent-coercion binary by portraying sex workers as either self-directed individuals choosing sex work as a "joyful project of selfhood" or as victim-criminals in need for carceral reform (West and Horn 2021, iv). Hence, discourses on #MeToo must be read as a unique blend of carceral and neoabolitionist feminist narratives about sexual commerce, which distinguishes between sex work as a form of consensual labor that is a product of irreversible, individual choice and as the coercive experience of sexual slavery or sex trafficking that rescue politics hinges on.

Accountability and Sex Work Activism: Sex Workers Are in the Frontline of Consent Wars

One of the most dramatic normative shifts in the post-#MeToo era has occurred in the realm of public accountability. Dempsey's model defines accountability norms as those which guide "our practices of holding others to account for past wrongdoing" (Dempsey 2021, 358). Sex workers are not the perfect victims and the believability of their claims are systematically challenged, challenges that further converge into the substantial lack of legal, public, and third-party accountability when it comes to sexual assault and violence faced by sex workers. Much like victim-blaming discourses like "She asked for it," sex workers are held accountable for their own vulnerability to violence, especially by virtue of the consensual choices they made not to be rescued and mainstreamed. If a spurt in public accountability is one of #MeToo's most prized achievements, sex workers' blatant exclusion from public accountability discourses most obviously limits #MeToo's potential to become truly inclusive.

As a pathway to demand public accountability, sex workers are now reclaiming their pivotal role in the #MeToo movement by articulating individual strategies, emphasizing community-building and solidarity, and demanding systemic legal and social changes. At the individual level, several sex work activists are coming out to recount their personal stories and sharing advisory opinions based on personal experiences, which is further closely tied to community-building initiatives. As Jessie Patella-Rey, a sex work activist and community organizer writing for the *Washington Post* lays out, consent in the sex work industry is viewed as a collective responsibility, which further shapes individuals' interactions with clients and other sex workers. "Sex workers organize to build their power and the ability to prevent abuse. . . . In some cases, [this] might involve exchanging information about bad customers, workplaces or managers. In others, it might be about collaborating to improve workplace conditions" (Patella-Rey 2018). Patella-Rey calls out the rescue industry by explicitly stating that sex workers spend a great deal of time exercising and practicing consent. It is particularly noteworthy how Cooney and Patella-Rey's op-ed pieces emphasize voices of sex workers by drawing upon interviews with and literary works by sex workers (such as Lola Davina's *Thriving in Sex Work: Heartfelt Advice for Staying Sane in the Sex Industry*) that advise sex workers how to protect themselves against law and stigma and conduct negotiations with clients. West and Horn here write about the value of community solidarity in the face of legal coercion and invisibility. West and Horn (2021, 22) state, "We try our best to protect each other—through community support networks, client lists, and sharing the best practices to keep us safe from law enforcement—but the state seems hell bent on passing legislation that keeps us from doing so."

Despite individual and community resilience, sex work activists emphasize the ultimate importance of challenging legal and moral criminalization and systemic discrimination, both of which exacerbate sex workers' precarity and must be addressed if #MeToo aims to become truly inclusive. West and Horn write that the contention over recognizing sexual labor as work makes movements against workplace harassment a particularly vexing terrain for sex workers. They state that "without seeing sex work as work, sex workers cannot be seen as laboring subjects in need of rights, not rescue" (West and Horn 2021, 20). This line of argument has long formed the core of the sex workers movement. Furthermore, sex workers point out how the feminist movement at large has often marginalized and erased sex workers' narratives and how public voices during #MeToo (such as Oprah's acclaimed Golden Globes speech) have failed to highlight issues faced by sex workers, which is unlike the case for domestic workers or farmworkers (Cooney 2018). In India, for instance, sex workers emphasize how this legal discrimination distinguishes sex work from other forms of informal labor: "The social perception of sex work makes this profession unique compared to other jobs in the informal sector. . . . In sex work major obstacles are structural and social. The law is detrimental and criminalizing. . . . This helps people in power to exploit them" (anonymous interviewee 19, 2016). On October 7, 2020, at the height of the COVID-19 pandemic, the National Human Rights Commission of India issued an advisory titled "Human Rights of Women in the context of Covid 19," in which it extended recognition of sex workers as informal workers. However, this invited pushback and backlash from certain sections of the feminist movement, especially from anti-trafficking, abolitionist activists. Thus, deliberations over recognizing sex work as labor (formal or informal) remains the axis of contention among various feminists and activists in India. This has led sex workers to uphold an intersectional, multipronged approach toward understanding accountability for sex work precarity. Their accounts show that it is crucial not just to hold individuals (such as clients and pimps) accountable but also to demand public accountability for systemic exclusion, violence, and discrimination by the state as well as social emancipatory movements such as #MeToo.

Concluding Thoughts

Circling back to Selena's question then, about where sex workers in the #MeToo movement were, the answer is clear but complicated. Despite its emancipatory intentions, the #MeToo movement did not adequately give voice to vulnerabilities that confront sex workers. The movement did not displace the binary coding of coercion and consent and of sex and work that underlies anti-trafficking and sexual harassment laws and forms the basis of that precarity. As evidenced in several legal, social, and political discourses, sex workers are rarely viewed as perfect victims and rather always as sexual bodies rendering unconditional and irreversible consent. Thus, the accountability for being subject to sexual violence almost always lies with sex workers rather than the aggressor. And yet, sex workers' activism, mobilization, and critiques also provide a robust space to (re)imagine transnational feminist praxis. As the sex work movement in India indicates, sex workers' critiques of mainstream feminist theorization and practice have also pushed the boundaries of how we define consent and coercion, agency, and transactional sex and practice feminist politics. Only by challenging assumptions about sex and labor that underlie discussions on sex work and #MeToo can a movement against sexual harassment truly become inclusive and universal.

REFERENCES

Anitha, Sundari, and Aisha Gill. 2017. "Coercion, Consent and the Forced Marriage Debate in the UK." In *Marital Rights*, edited by Sundari Anitha and Aisha Gill, 133–52. New York: Routledge.

Anonymous. 2017. "Focus Group on Sex Work and Sex Work Activism." Focus Group discussion at Durbar, conducted by Sudeshna Chatterjee, January 2017.

Anonymous. 2017. "Focus Group on Sex Work and Sex Work Activism in VAMP/Sangraam." Focus Group discussion at VAMP/Sangram, conducted by Sudeshna Chatterjee, January 2017.

Anonymous Interviewee 19. 2016. "Discussing sex work at Sanlaap Kolkata." Interviewed by Sudeshna Chatterjee in November 2016.

Chandran, Rina. 2017. "MeToo Campaign Excludes India's Most Vulnerable Women, Activists Say." *Reuters*, December 18, 2017. https://www.reuters.com.

Cooney, Samantha. 2018. "'They Don't Want to Include Women Like Me.' Sex Workers Say They're Being Left Out of the #MeToo Movement." *TIME*, February 13, 2018. https://time.com/5104951/sex-workers-me-too-movement.

Deering, Kathleen N., Avni Amin, Jean Shoveller, Ariel Nesbitt, Claudia Garcia-Moreno, Putu Duff, Elena Argento, and Kate Shannon. 2014. "A Systematic Review of the Correlates of Violence against Sex Workers." *American Journal of Public Health* 104 (5): 42–54. https://doi.org/10.2105/AJPH.2014.301909.

Dempsey, Michelle Madden. 2021. "Coercion, Consent, and Time." *Ethics* 131 (2): 345–68. https://doi.org/10.1086/711212.

Gangoli, Geetanjali. 2007. "Immorality, Hurt or Choice: How Indian Feminists Engage with Prostitution." *International Feminist Journal of Politics* 9 (1): 1–19. https://doi .org/10.1111/j.1467-9299.2008.00749.x.

Jordan, Jan. 2004. *The Word of a Woman? Police, Rape and Belief*. Basingstoke: Palgrave Macmillan.

———. 2008. "Perfect Victims, Perfect Policing? Improving Rape Complainant's Experiences of Police Investigations." *Public Administration* 86 (3): 699–719.

Kelly, Liz. 2016. "The Conducive Context of Violence against Women and Girls." *Discover Society*, March 1, 2016. http://archive.discoversociety.org.

Kotiswaran, Prabha. 2011. *Dangerous Sex, Invisible Labour: Sex Work and the Law in India*. Princeton, NJ: Princeton University Press.

Lakkimsetti, Chaitanya. 2020. *Legalizing Sex: Sexual Minorities, AIDS and Citizenship in India*. New York: New York University Press.

Nigam, Shalu. 2017. "From Mathura to Farooqui Rape Case: The Regressive Patriarchy Found Its Way Back." *Social Science Research Network*, October 9, 2017. https://dx .doi.org/10.2139/ssrn.3049756.

Patella-Rey, Jessie. 2018. "Want to Figure Out the Rules of Sexual Consent? Ask Sex Workers." *Washington Post*, May 21, 2018. www.washingtonpost.com.

Tambe, Ashwini. 2018. "Reckoning with the Silences of #MeToo." *Feminist Studies* 44(1): 197–202. Doi: 10.1353/fem.2018.0019.

Vanwesenbeeck, Ine. 2017. "Sex Work Criminalization is Barking Up the Wrong Tree." *Archives of Sexual Behavior* 46 (6): 1631–40. https://doi.org/10.1007%2Fs10508-017 -1008-3.

Weitzer, Ronald. 2000. *Sex For Sale: Prostitution, Pornography, and the Sex Industry*. New York: Routledge.

West, Natalie, and Tina Horn. 2021. *We Too: Essays on Sex Work and Survival*. New York: Feminist Press at CUNY.

9

Troubling Gendered Scripts of Rape in #MeToo Television

I May Destroy You *and Consent as Constellation*

LANDON SADLER

Written, created, and codirected by Michaela Coel, *I May Destroy You* (2020) follows Arabella Essiedu, a British social media influencer who strives to rebuild her life after being raped at a nightclub in London. Fans and critics of *I May Destroy You* have referred to the twelve-episode miniseries as a "consent drama." The term "consent drama" is hard to define owing largely to its newness. Of course, film and television have long featured plotlines about sexual violence, from *The Birth of a Nation* (1915), which depicts two racialized rape attempts, to the long-lasting *Law & Order: Special Victims Unit* (1999–). However, the term "consent drama" was popularized in 2020 to describe a spate of recent films and television series that, implicitly or explicitly, engage the #MeToo movement and comment on such issues as sexual harassment and rape culture. Willa Paskin (2020) broadly defines the consent drama as one "that takes a prismatic view of sexual assault and its ramifications"; here, a "prismatic view" is constituted by depth, illumination, and nuance. Nevertheless, those who deploy the term have no universal standard for "prismatic" or comprehensive, so texts that have been labeled consent dramas vary in length, tone, and ideological message. Sometimes, consent dramas are relegated to standalone episodes in a series that do not center on sexual violence, such as *Brooklyn Nine-Nine*'s "He Said, She Said" (2019) and *Grey's Anatomy*'s "Silent All These Years" (2019), which both feature victims of sexual assault in guest roles helped by the main cast. Comparatively, the seven-episode miniseries *The Loudest Voice* (2019) and the film *Bombshell* (2019) dramatically retell the sexual harassment at FOX News by CEO Roger Ailes. The television series *The Morning Show* (2019–) focuses on the fallout of a sexual misconduct scandal caused by a character like Harvey Weinstein, while *She Said* (2022) is a biopic that directly confronts Weinstein's abuses.

Also referred to as "MeToo television," these consent dramas tend to reaffirm the biases and blind spots of the movement that inspired them. Notwithstanding the important work that consent dramas do in spreading awareness about and destigmatizing sexual assault, they often perpetuate the "oppression reproduced within #MeToo by the combination of nominally inclusive frameworks, the centering of white women, and the context of a neoliberal society in which the accused are discursively constructed as individual 'bad men' rather than part of a broader systemic problem" (Trott 2021, 1,139). In the coverage of #MeToo and its filmic and televisual representations, a common narrative emerges: the victim is a white, straight, cis woman who retains some class privilege but is outranked by her male victimizer who is also white, straight, and cis and occupies an important position in a public-facing field such as entertainment, news, or politics. In this binary, gender is depicted as the only social marker that matters, which ignores how a person can be more vulnerable to sexual violence depending on their race, class, sexuality, disability, and country of origin. Additionally, this binary equates womanhood with victimization and so conceals how men and nonbinary people can be victims and women can be victimizers. Last, as Caetlin Benson-Allott (2020, 100) observes, *I'll Be Gone in the Dark* (2020), *Unbelievable* (2019), *Jessica Jones* (2015–19), and other consent dramas "privilege white victims, perpetrators, and investigators." Investigators play a crucial role in consent dramas as far as many consent dramas resolve violations of consent through the law, putting a specific man— instead of a larger system or ideology—on trial. By framing consent mainly through police investigations and courtroom cases, consent dramas take a carceral approach to justice that risks reducing a survivor's journey to a piece of testimony, pressuring them to report their assault, and depicting the criminal justice system as the proper, if not infallible, arbiter of truth, justice, and consent.

In contrast to carceral approaches to violence and consent, *I May Destroy You* upends such myopic conventions and offers a blueprint for sexual assault activism and recovery from sexual trauma. Unlike other consent dramas that perpetuate the racial, sexual, and class biases of #MeToo, Coel's series critiques and rejects #MeToo's tendencies to center white women's experiences; flatten the differences of sexuality, class, and nation when it comes to sexual assault; and premise justice and closure on legal and carceral systems. Focusing on the sexual traumas of three Black Brits of Ghanaian descent with working-class backgrounds—Arabella's being the most prominent—*I May Destroy You* demonstrates that sexual assault is not a problem limited to the individual victim of assault; rather, it emerges from specific intersecting systems and oppressive structures that do not erase a survivor's subjective experiences. This notion is illustrated by Arabella's recovery process: to heal and move on, Arabella must relate her sexual assault by a white male stranger in a suit to the sexual violence experienced by others in her community, including a case in which a young Black man is wrongfully accused of rape by his white female classmate. Doing so allows Arabella to envision consent in a way that is distinct from other consent dramas. Whereas other consent dramas typically confine consent to the deracialized, concentrated domain of white female victim, singular white bad man, and unbiased, authoritative judicator, Arabella understands that consent is always already racialized and that who is believed, who can give consent, and who is expected to receive consent are all filtered by categories of race, gender, sexuality, and class. Rather than being romanticized as punishers of injustice, the Metropolitan Police are incapable of helping Arabella, for they are unable to identify her perpetrator and are further shown to be perpetrators of systemic violence themselves when they act homophobic and racist to Kwame, Arabella's gay male friend whose sexual assault is one of the three highlighted in the miniseries.

"I Thought You Were Writing About Consent?"

I May Destroy You has received overwhelmingly positive reviews and major awards for acting, directing, and writing (Framke 2020; Jung 2020; and St. Félix 2020), and yet little scholarship exists on the miniseries. This dearth may stem from the show's recency, its graphic nature—the show asks its audience to witness and work through sexual violence—and the marginalization of Black sexual assault survivors in life and art. The unfortunate reality of #MeToo is that the people who are most likely to be victimized—lower-class women of color (Jones and Wade 2020, 209)—are also the ones most likely to be ignored and drowned out. The little attention, both popular and scholarly, that the show has garnered does engage with gender and to a lesser extent queerness and race as units of analysis. However, there remains a lack of engagement with how the show treats consent as a concept despite its genre as a consent drama and despite how the show explicitly calls attention to misunderstandings and misapplications of rape, sexual assault, and consent. That most popular writing about the show takes consent for granted evinces a larger problem that is illuminated by a growing number of feminist scholars including Janet Halley (2016), Cyndi Darnell (2019), and Erinn Gilson (2016) who show a pressing need to rethink key concepts in feminist discourses on sexual violence, including consent, vulnerability, and victimization.

In general, #MeToo, consent dramas, and mainstream feminist activism have contributed to the perception that consent is merely a yes-no binary, which consigns both men and women to socially conservative roles: men as aggressors and women as victims. Darnell (2019) historicizes this yes-no binary, noting that mainstream feminists have traditionally taken an approach to consent that is predicated on violence prevention as opposed to erotic motivations; this approach views power within eroticism as dangerous and violent because this power, as the dominant thinking goes, occurs under patriarchy and belongs chiefly to men. Darnell (2019, 253) outlines that our "current obsession with yes/no versions of consent leaves women with few avenues to experience pleasure, eroticism, and power (over self and others) on their terms, men with little incentive nor methods to explore sex outside of the aggressor/initiator role, while those outside the gender binary are rendered invisible." Darnell's sketch of the consent binary has much in common with #MeToo's model of sexual assault in which the victim is a (white, straight, cis) woman and the perpetrator a (white, straight, cis) man; again, gender is the privileged analytic. Halley (2016) is correct in her claim that these framings of consent are socially conservative as far as they paint women as passive, reactive, and susceptible to male domination and, in effect, give credence to laws and policies that are repressive and sex negative. Halley (2016, 262) traces the punitive history of American sexual harassment laws to conclude that consent is largely regarded as an action instead of a desire, affect, or state of mind. These codes are cis-heteronormative, basing rape on sexual penetration, and they empower the state to police and judge consent. While violating consent is wrong and categorically should not be tolerated, Halley is rightfully concerned with the recent push by some feminists for affirmative consent requirements: laws or campus policies that require a person, through clear words or actions, to give permission before engaging in any sexual activity with a partner. Although well-intentioned, these requirements expand the carceral project by "grounding women's emancipation, sexual and otherwise, on . . . a sweeping use of criminal punishment and civil incapacitation" (Halley 2016, 264).

In privileging gender as the primary mode of analysis, this discourse forwards a "color-blind" view of consent that especially harms women of color. Of course, white femininity is not immune to structural inequalities of consent; intersections of class and sexuality, among others, prevent all white femininities from being equally placed. At the same time, the color-blindness of this discourse positions white women as the default, ideal victims of sexual assault, which affords them some protections in the eyes of the law and media in comparison to women of color whose accounts of sexual assault are less likely to be seen as legitimate and trustworthy. Maria Ontiveros (1993) stresses the importance of seeing race and culture in sexual harassment and abuse. Ontiveros writes, "From the viewpoint of the harasser, women of color appear to be less powerful, less likely to complain, and the embodiment of particular notions of sexuality" (818). These "particular notions of sexuality" largely construe women of color, with their deviant bodies and sexualities, as eternally consenting. Ontiveros, for example, calls attention to how histories of racism, slavery, and colonialism have marked Black women as sexually available and naturally lascivious, Latinas as hot-blooded and exploitable, and "Asian American women as exotic, submissive, and naturally erotic" (819). These histories also paint men of color—particularly Black men—as lecherous and predatory, especially threatening to idealized white women. In sum, the yes-no binary creates scripts that narrowly allow white women to express their victimhood at the expense of men of color and male, queer, and women of color survivors.

Challenging consent orthodoxy, even among feminists, *I May Destroy You* expands audiences' understanding of consent. If the dominant understanding of consent is a yes-no action between a (white) man and (white) woman that must be sanctioned by the state to protect the woman, then *I May Destroy You* reveals consent to be a constellation made up of multiple interconnecting factors and dimensions including gender, race, sexuality, class, nation, place, desire, intention, language, history, technology, and state of mind. This constellation is not static but constantly in flux, and if there is a polestar, it is indubitably not a paternalistic and racist criminal justice system. By "constellation," I am not suggesting that consent is nebulous or a configuration of blurred lines, but that it is a cluster of factors in which the presence of one node does not necessitate the absence or diametrical opposition of another. I use the constellation model to capture the complexity of consent and reveal the different intersecting powers, desires, and vulnerabilities each person has, especially in relation to another person. Thus, this model moves us away from the straight line between yes and no that produces the quintessential (white, cis, straight) victim so embedded in socially conservative laws. Like a web, constellations are formed by interconnections, and *I May Destroy You*'s portrayal of consent breaks free from simple binary rigidity and disjunction.

The semi-autobiographical miniseries begins with Arabella, played by Coel, who has translated her viral tweets about social justice and Black British culture into a bestselling book, *Chronicles of a Fed-Up Millennial*. Seeking to become more established financially and socially, Arabella starts drafting her second book. However, paralleling Coel's own experiences writing the script of a prior show—the cringe comedy sitcom *Chewing Gum* (2015–17), which is infamous for the racism that Coel and other Black actors routinely endured on set (Dawson 2020)—Arabella suffers from writer's block and tries to alleviate it by taking a break at a nightclub where her drink is spiked and where she, like Coel, is sexually assaulted by a stranger: in Arabella's case, an unknown white man in a business suit (Miller 2020). At first, the issue of consent appears straightforward and familiar. The main difference from typical #MeToo coverage is that the victim is a Black woman, not white, and she could not consent because she was under the influence of a substance, a classic drug-facilitated sexual assault.

Based on other consent dramas, one might expect Arabella to next report her case to the police, which she does. Nonetheless, while another consent drama might have rewarded Arabella with a happy ending in the form of a successful police investigation and fair trial, *I May Destroy*

You demonstrates that, for Arabella and other members of her Black, working-class community, the Metropolitan Police will not bring them closure or justice and should not be considered the authority on consent. While the two officers assigned to Arabella's case—Officer Funmi who is Black and Officer Beth who is white, both pregnant women—are sympathetic to and appreciated by Arabella, their hard work to apprehend Arabella's rapist is ultimately fruitless. Although Arabella behaves like an ideal victim by reporting her assault and subjecting herself to a rape kit, the system fails her as there is insufficient DNA evidence to identify the perpetrator (Miller and Coel 2020d). Although the specter of policing hangs over every episode, the police officers are merely supporting characters, and much of Arabella's learning about consent and her recovery process happen outside the police station or other formal expressions of state force. Instead, Arabella spends much of her time with her friends on walks, in shops, or at her flat; she tweets, goes to birthday parties, and attends therapy in addition to a survivor's support group. Although Arabella's recovery process is marked by progress and regress, these more intimate and private interactions in her community are forms of healing that she cannot access from the carceral state.

Arabella's interactions with members of her community form the basis of her second novel, *January 22nd*, which is named after the night of her assault and is an autobiographical retelling of it and the ramifications. *January 22nd* is a consent drama in novel form that treats Arabella's everyday life with her friends and family—several of whom are dealing with their own sexual traumas impacted by their different identity markers—as central to her understanding of consent that complicates the yes-no binary. Accordingly, Arabella incorporates the microaggressions and overt instances of oppression that she and her community members face, understanding that her assault is not an isolated incident limited to her and her perpetrator. Rather, her assault is connected to the assaults of other Black Brits in her community and beyond and is produced by larger social forces such as sexism, racism, classism, and colonialism. This can be seen when a pastor from Ghana talks to Arabella at a birthday party. Pastor Samson teaches her about how Western environmental nonprofits in Africa often economically exploit the native people they claim to aid; he says that their present actions reflect "the same manipulative and sociopathic mind that helped them invade, exploit, and rape all but twenty-two countries in the world" (Miller and Coel 2020c). Hearing "rape," Arabella grows quiet as she confronts whether her rape by the posh white man in a business suit is part of this colonial mindset. Similarly, when Arabella hears from a podcast host about stealthing—the secret removal of a condom during sex—Arabella notes the conspiratorial nature of how men help other men stealth women, how "there are actual Reddit forums where men share tips and tricks and even phrases like . . . 'I thought you knew. You mean, you didn't feel it?'" (Miller and Coel 2020a). These instances push Arabella to view sexual assault through a structural, intersectional lens.

When Zain, another writer at Arabella's publishing house, reads the outline of her novel, he is confused about her inclusion of interactions with friends and family and why she discusses racism and colonialism, remarking, "I thought you were writing about consent?" (Miller and Coel 2020e). Zain's question represents the common color-blind understanding of consent as a binary and reveals that he is largely unaware of systemic biases, instead considering sexual assault to be the product of two people's regrettable actions. But Arabella is of course writing about consent: her novel signals an evolution in thinking about sexual assault from amorphous individual problem to concrete structural issue. To tell her story, Arabella must tell the stories of others and acknowledge their sociopolitical interconnections. Arabella does so in part by remembering a case from her high school in which a white female classmate falsely accuses a Black male classmate of rape. The quickness of the school's teachers to believe the white student's rape script causes Arabella to examine the role race plays in accusations of sexual assault, and it makes Arabella reckon with how her own Black femininity makes her particularly vulnerable to white male domination. The writing of her novel serves to engage with systemic forces while offering Arabella an outlet for healing that reaches beyond carceral models of justice.

This departure differentiates *I May Destroy You* from other consent dramas, but Arabella does not arrive at this "intersectional consciousness" overnight. By "intersectional consciousness," I recall Gloria Anzaldúa's (2012) "mestiza consciousness" to refer to how the woman of color becomes "vulnerable to foreign ways of seeing and thinking" (104); Anzaldúa's "mestiza consciousness"—like the constellation model of consent—tolerates ambiguity and breaks down duality "to create a new

value system with images and symbols that connect us to each other"
(103). As Anzaldúa sees herself as a mestiza, an Indian, a Mexican, and a
lesbian, Arabella comes into her consciousness when she makes a statement about realizing she is a woman and not just Black, which is the
predominant way she understood herself as a teen. Arabella verbalizes
this paradigm shift after hearing different sexual assault narratives in her
support group and participating in the police investigation. Showcas-
ing this intersectional consciousness, Arabella reads part of a draft of
January 22nd:

> Before my rape, I never took much notice of being a woman; I was busy
> being Black and poor. . . . The Bible says, 'You cannot serve two masters.'
> Am I too late to serve this tribe called women? . . . A little rape in the
> mouth is a walk in the park when other girls are currently being stoned
> to death for having mobile phones, are bleeding to death after genital
> mutilation, are looking at a womb irreparably destroyed by militias sys-
> tematically raping them during times of civil conflict and war. Are these
> facts a humbling reminder not to be so loud about my experiences, or are
> they a reminder to shout? Can my shout help their silent screams? . . . I
> hope one day to know. (Miller and Coel 2020c)

In this monologue, Arabella displays a consciousness around the intersectional nature of social violence toward her, and *I May Destroy You*
functions as a meditation on this consciousness. Her comments about
being too Black and poor to notice that she was a woman illustrate that
Arabella arrived at this consciousness, not that she was naturally pre-
disposed to it as a Black woman. Kimberlé Crenshaw (1991, 1,244), who
coined the term "intersectionality," first uses the concept to "denote
the various ways in which race and gender interact to shape the multiple dimensions of Black women's . . . experiences." Arabella follows
Crenshaw's call to map the intersections of race and gender, resisting dominant assumptions—such as those encouraged by the yes-no
binary—that race, gender, and other identity markers are separate
categories or do not matter. Connecting her experiences to other girls
who suffer from genital mutilation and wartime sexual violence—
victims often excluded from #MeToo discussions—Arabella identifies
her rape as both caught within and hypervisible in comparison to

state-sponsored and patriarchal violence, thus expanding our under-standing of rape as not just patriarchal violence but also a form of racial terror. Arabella's specific subject formations—her Blackness, poorness, and Englishness—are not erased or made irrelevant when she implicitly invokes how nation, culture, religion, and age affect the aforementioned victims. Altogether, this monologue shows the developing intersectional consciousness that expands Arabella's radical understanding of consent.

"The Alliance"

One of the primary factors that leads Arabella to an intersectional con-sciousness around consent more broadly is her recollection of an alleged sexual assault from her teenage years. The flashback episode "The Alli-ance," in which Arabella recalls her high school years, contrasts sharply with the #MeToo movement's downplaying of race and the essentialist, oversimplified decree to believe the (white) woman. One of the central figures in this allegation is Theodora, who, in the present timeline, is the leader and founder of Arabella's support group for sexual assault survi-vors. In the flashback to high school, Theodora is one of the few white students who attend Arabella's school, which affords her some privilege in the eyes of her mostly white teachers and classmates of color. As a student, Theodora often had consensual sex with her classmate Ryan, who is Black and male; however, when Ryan takes pictures of Theodora having sex with him without her permission, her trust in him is broken. At first, Theodora is confused, disgusted, and horrified, but when Ryan offers to pay for the pictures, Theodora hesitantly accepts. After they awkwardly finish having sex and exchange money, Theodora steals and breaks Ryan's phone and then tells a teacher that Ryan violently raped her, a lie that she apparently tells out of shame for selling the sexually explicit pictures and anger over Ryan's initial betrayal.

Through the character of Theodora, a victim and victimizer, *I May Destroy You* complicates and problematizes #MeToo's tendency to privi-lege gender as a unit of analysis at the expense of other identity markers. After all, Theodora is initially and quickly believed by the white fac-ulty because her accusation draws on the myth of the Black male rapist and the presumption that sexual assault victims are white, cis, straight women. To be clear, false allegations of rape are vanishingly rare; about

2 percent of rape allegations are estimated to be false (Norton and Grant 2008, 275), which is much smaller than many other crime allegations. The takeaway from Theodora's lie is not that women who make accusations of rape should be viewed suspiciously, but rather that the social categories of all involved shape whether the accuser is believed and what happens afterward. Tracey Patton and Julie Snyder-Yuly (2007) examine the impact of the 2003 false rape accusations by a white female former Iowa State University student in a mostly white community against four Black males. They trace the stereotype of the Black male criminal who preys on white female victims from the Ku Klux Klan's *The Birth of a Nation* (1915) to the murder of Emmet Till (1955) to the case of the Central Park Five (1989). Patton and Synder-Yuly clarify how "taken-for-granted White supremacist, patriarchal, mythological frames . . . made African American men a hyper visible threat" (2007, 889). This frame is what makes it so easy for Theodora to be believed as a victim and not Ryan, given that white supremacist patriarchy paints Black men as bestial, lustful, aggressive, and violent and white women as delicate, dependent, and naïve. If Theodora is the ideal victim, then Ryan is the ultimate ideal threat, not only because of her race but also because she scripts her rape in a particular way. Furthermore, for the racist white vigilantes in *The Birth of a Nation* and the extrajudicial killers of Emmet Till, it is inconceivable that a white woman would desire a Black man, and therefore, if the two had sex, it must not have been consensual. The idea that a white woman would and could never consent to sex with a Black man makes the white faculty more easily believe Theodora's rape script. Because of #MeToo's focus on upper-class individuals and celebrities in particular, many of the accused men are white, not Black, and the default to white victims and perpetrators leaves the myth of the Black male rapist unexamined and unchallenged.

"The Alliance" derives its name from the verbatim "alliance" that Arabella and her best friend Terry—another Black classmate—form with other Black students to protect themselves and show solidarity after Arabella and Terry obtain video evidence that Theodora is lying about being raped by Ryan. Although Theodora broke Ryan's phone, Ryan unbeknownst to Theodora and against her wishes had already sent their sex video to one of his friends, an example of nonconsensual pornography. Before Theodora learns that Ryan sent the video to his friend, she steals a knife from the cafeteria and cuts herself on the back of her thigh; she then takes her seat in class as blood slowly drips down her leg. When Terry alerts their white female teacher that Theodora is bleeding, the teacher rushes over and asks Theodora what had happened. Pained and exhausted, Theodora sobs, "Ryan. I didn't want to. He made me. He had a knife" (Miller and Coel 2020b). The teacher, panicky and indignant, shouts at other students to run and get help from the nurse and other teachers. When discussing why the white, middle-class teachers as a whole were so quick to believe Theodora's rape script, Terry remarks, "White girl tears have high currency," alluding to Patton and Synder-Yuly's findings, before contrasting to how when "I [Terry] sneeze, Miss Mott is talking about [how] I'm showing signs of intimidation. . . . I swear down, if I cry, all Miss Mott would see is weapons of mass destruction leaking out of my eyeballs" (Miller and Coel 2020b). Forwarding an intersectional framework, Terry observes how "white girl tears"—not just "white tears" or "girl tears"—have high currency. Although a white boy's tears may be read as effeminate and pathetic and Terry's as abhorrent due to her Blackness, Theodora's tears are moving and worthy of protection because she is white and female, symbolizing the particular vulnerability of white femininity to Black masculinity.

Although Terry and Arabella form a group called "the alliance," the title of the episode also alludes to the unnamed strategic alliance that Arabella forms, somewhat unexpectedly and surprisingly, years later with Theodora and her support group. One might expect Arabella to want nothing to do with Theodora after she falsely accused Ryan of rape; Terry, who is still Arabella's best friend in the present, resents Theodora. But Arabella and Theodora become comrades, friends even, as it seems that Theodora recognizes that what she did to Ryan was inexcusable and that Arabella's experience of sexual assault helps her connect to Theodora whose own consent was violated by the video. While Theodora's choice to exchange money for sexual favors places her outside ideal victimhood, the simplistic narrative of the Black male rapist does allow her to claim some aspects of ideal victimhood. Another reason for this strategic partnership between Arabella and Theodora is that, after recalling how Ryan's Black masculinity was seen as dangerous to Theodora's white femininity, Arabella begins to see the intersections of gender and race in her own assault. Black femininity makes her uniquely vulnerable to white masculinity. Catherine Clinton (1994, 206) writes, "Within the Old South, a slave woman was denied the power of consent by legal definition: she could not be raped." Clinton maintains that the rape of Black women by their white male masters was an integral means of social control, not an aberration or dysfunction in the context of slavery. Hence, because Black women were seen as property, not fully human, they supposedly could not consent or be raped. Arabella's alliance with Theodora is conditioned by and conditions her own awareness of racialized gendered violence.

In *I May Destroy You*, Arabella must deal with the legacy of this racist, sexist denial of consent. She does not meet her unnamed rapist after he violates her, although in the last episode, "Ego Death," she fantasizes meeting him and imagines multiple scenarios in which she can exact revenge, sometimes with Theodora or Terry, or both, assisting her. The viewer never directly meets "David," the name Arabella gives her rapist, or learns why he raped Arabella; however, in one of Arabella's revenge fantasies, David treats Arabella much like his slave or property. He handles her roughly and closes her mouth: "Stupid bitch!" David says, "Fucking self-entitled whore. That's what you are. You're a dumb little whore" (Miller and Coel 2020f). In this instance, David's mistreatment of Arabella is gendered and racialized: his pejoratives are misogynistic— "bitch" and "whore"—but he also invokes the "Jezebel" stereotype, the image of Black women as lascivious, vacuous, and seductive. He implies that Arabella is "asking for it," that she is so sex-crazed that she wants him to rape her. To what extent "David" targeted Arabella and why are unknown, but throughout her imaginings, Arabella is mindful of a longer history of racialized and gendered violence in which her Black womanhood renders her particularly vulnerable to white male domination, even though and precisely because she is not a white female like Theodora, the default #MeToo victim.

"Hornyman808"

Another key character that Coel uses to develop consent as a gendered and racialized concept is Kwame. Like Theodora and Arabella, Kwame is a victim of sexual violence, but unlike either of them, he is mistreated by officials, in his case the police. When he reports his sexual assault, his homosexuality compounds the police's understandings of the Black male as assailant. Like Theodora, Kwame may also be considered victim and victimizer, an uncommon role in consent dramas. Mainstream representations of #MeToo tend to portray victims and victimizers as separate, so audiences sympathize or identify with victims. *I May Destroy You* complicates this dichotomy and urges viewers to examine their own subject positions without making normative moral judgments. Theodora and Kwame's simultaneous positions as victim and victimizer result from their intersectional identities and subject formations; thus, the miniseries moves from the moral to the intersectional. After Kwame is sexually assaulted by Malik, a queer Black man, he becomes anxious about having sex with other men and wants to experiment with women. His first female partner is Nilufer, a white woman who, Kwame finds out, fetishizes Black men and is homophobic. When Nilufer finds out Kwame is gay and was experimenting with her, she is repulsed and indignant, believing that Kwame deceived her and violated her "consent" by keeping his sexuality and motives a secret (Miller and Coel 2020d). Identifying with the perceived violated woman, Arabella takes Nilufer's side and accuses Kwame of rape, although she soon forgives Kwame, and they return to being friends after he apologizes. Kwame's storyline with Nilufer raises the question of what is legible as sexual violence in the first place. Must an experimenting person declare their sexual orientation before having sex with their partner(s)? When, if at all, should a trans person disclose their gender identity to their partner(s), a question that arises when Terry unsuspectingly goes on a date with Kai, a trans man? What must be verbalized before consent can be achieved?

In fleshing out an intersectional constellation model of consent, *I May Destroy You* ponders these questions and raises the core question of who gets to decide what is and is not consent. In many consent dramas that take a carceral approach to justice and truth, legal officials are the adjudicators of consent, but, as Theodora's false accusation of Ryan shows, racism, sexism, and classism are systemic issues, and elites in education, law, and media are not excluded from this carceral system. In ". . . It Just Came Up," the fifth episode, Kwame's interactions with the police further demonstrate that those representing the law often define "consent" in ways that disempower and exclude men and queers.

In this episode, Kwame is surprised to learn through Google that non-consensual humping—what he previously experienced in a traumatic Grindr encounter with Malik—is in fact sexual assault and a crime. Kwame's surprise and the police's subsequent mistreatment of him reflect a dominant and exclusionary understanding of rape and victimhood in which the rapist is always a man with a penis and the victim a woman with a vagina.

Kwame's experience as a gay male victim helps Arabella understand her experience of rape by broadening her understanding of rape and dispelling rape myths. Her learning exemplifies relationality since this connection exists across lines of gender and sexual orientation. Moments before Kwame discovers that he has been victimized, Arabella remarks, "[I] didn't even know you could get raped in the mouth" (Miller and Coel 2020a), referring to her own assault in the nightclub in which, drugged, she was forced to perform oral sex. Arabella's prior belief exemplifies a rape myth: "False beliefs that are widely accepted, [which] contribute to the justification and normalization of sexual violence by offenders and [which] focus on the actions and behavior of victims while minimizing the harm" (Walfield 2018, 6,391). One of the most pervasive and pernicious rape myths is the belief that men cannot be raped, that it does not happen to them. The centering of white, straight, cis women by #MeToo and consent dramas paired with their emphasis on courts and the police place Black gay male victims in precarious relation to the concept of consent, as the legal and media systems were not designed with their type of victimhood in mind.

Kwame's interaction with Officer Tom, the one assigned to record Kwame's account, makes these biases and shortcomings clear. Both Arabella and Kwame have traumatic experiences reporting their assaults, but whereas the police are professional and considerate to Arabella—Arabella's trauma coming from having to recount her rape—Kwame is met with suspicion and condescension; his masculinity is questioned and his justifiable concerns are downplayed. Although both Arabella and Kwame are Black, the intersections of Kwame's queerness and manhood, in contrast with the heteronormative conditions of Arabella's assault, make Arabella—not Kwame—a believable, legitimate victim in the eyes of the police. The first microaggression Kwame suffers comes after Officer Tom asks Kwame the name of his victimizer; Kwame cannot provide his name, explaining they met on Grindr and used aliases to have anonymous (gay) sex, to which the officer emphatically scoffs (Miller and Coel 2020a). Reflecting a moral expectation of monogamy and a police culture rooted in homophobia, particularly when it comes to male victims of rape (Rumney 2008, 80), Officer Tom is shocked and disgusted upon learning that Kwame knows his victimizer as only "hornyman808."

The officer then begins victim blaming Kwame, pressing him about why he didn't bother learning the name of the accused upon meeting him and talking over a rattled and offended Kwame who tries to helpfully give the officer hornyman808's address. The questioning devolves from bad to worse, and the mortifying interaction culminates when the officer dismisses Kwame's case, saying that, because Kwame had consensual sex with his victimizer before expressing a lack of consent as the hook up sex continued, "there's no point in . . . doing a DNA sample" (Miller and Coel 2020a). While a DNA sample may have not proved Kwame was assaulted, the officer's emphasis on Kwame's prior consent coupled with his own homophobia underscores the police's particular difficulty in conceptualizing male rape victims, even, or especially, gay ones. After all, in dominant ideas that sanitize sex, victims of sexual assault are innocent straight women, not promiscuous men who have anonymous, risky sex with other men. Further complicating consent is Kwame's Blackness, which constructs him as the "straight" assailant, not the "queer" victim.

I May Destroy You ends not with a guilty verdict nor the rapist being handcuffed and led into a police car. Instead, after imagining the different ways that she could find and exact revenge on her rapist—including turning him into the police or simply killing him herself—Arabella decides to give up on her search and spend a cozy night watching TV with her flat mate, Ben. Months later, Arabella and her circle of friends—Kwame, Terry, Theodora, Ben, and Kai—watch a commercial together, in which Terry, an emerging actor, stars; afterward, Arabella reads the finished version of *January 22nd*, self-published, in front of a packed audience. The finale is a celebration of friendship, care, interconnection, solidarity, and community: Arabella could not have told her story or moved on without the help of her friends. These themes are encapsulated by the dedication page on *January 22nd*: "Your birth is my birth, / your death is my death. / This book is dedicated to Terry, / my best friend." (Miller and Coel 2020f). Terry and Arabella often say to each other, "Your birth is my birth, your death is my death, G!" to show their love for and dependence on each other, the "G" part of their Black vernacular. The two support each other so much that it is difficult to tell where one ends and the other begins, a motif that might not have existed in a consent drama in which the carceral project, and not Terry, was the pillar that uplifts, validates, and empowers Arabella. In other words, this healing embrace of friendship, community, and solidarity in the denouement is what *I May Destroy You* offers as a path forward in place of a clichéd consent drama ending that privileges whiteness, heteronormativity, and the carceral system.

Ultimately, the good that the #MeToo movement has created in highlighting the pervasiveness of sexual assault and making it more acceptable for survivors to come forward should not be undervalued. Nevertheless, reaffirmed by many recent texts in popular culture, the #MeToo movement, like every movement, has blind spots and biases, namely the marginalizing of working-class women and queers of color and the framing of sexual assault in depoliticized individual terms to be resolved by authoritative police and courts. By theorizing race, class, and sexuality and reenvisioning consent through a constellation rather than a binary, *I May Destroy You* occupies a disruptive place in #MeToo popular culture, upholding the too often absent values of intersectionality and solidarity.

REFERENCES

Anzaldúa, Gloria. 2012. *Borderlands/La Frontera: The New Mestiza*. 4th ed. San Francisco: Aunt Lute Books.

Benson-Allott, Caetlin. 2020. "How *I May Destroy* You Reinvents Rape Television." *Film Quarterly* 74 (2): 100–105. https://doi.org/10.1525/fq.2020.74.2.100.

Clinton, Catherine. 1994. "'With a Whip in His Hand': Rape, Memory, and African-American Women." In *History and Memory in African-American Culture*, edited by Genevieve Fabre and Robert O'Meally, 205–18. Oxford: Oxford University Press.

Crenshaw, Kimberlé. 1991. "Mapping the Margins: Intersectionality, Identity Politics, and Violence against Women of Color." *Stanford Law Review* 43 (6): 1,241–99. https://doi.org/10.2307/1229039.

Darnell, Cyndi. 2019. "Consent Lies Destroy Lives: Pleasure as the Sweetest Taboo." In *#MeToo and the Politics of Social Change*, edited by Bianca Fileborn and Rachel Loney-Howes, 253–66. London: Palgrave Macmillan.

Dawson, Brit. 2020. "Michaela Coel Shares Stories of Racist Incidents on Set of *Chewing Gum*." *Dazed*, July 7, 2020. www.dazeddigital.com.

Framke, Caroline. 2020. "How Michaela Coel Processed Trauma and Fought to Own Her Story with 'I May Destroy You.'" *Variety*, August 19, 2020. www.variety.com.

Gilson, Erinn Cuniff. 2016. "Vulnerability and Victimization: Rethinking Key Concepts in Feminist Discourses on Sexual Violence." *Signs* 42 (1): 71–98. https://doi.org/10.1086/686753.

Halley, Janet. 2016. "The Move to Affirmative Consent." *Signs* 42 (1): 257–79. https://doi.org/10.1086/686904.

Jones, Trina, and Emma Wade. 2020. "Me Too?: Race, Gender, and Ending Workplace Sexual Harassment." *Duke Journal of Gender Law and Policy* 27 (203): 203–25.

Jung, E. Alex. 2020. "Michaela the Destroyer: How a Young Talent from East London Went from Open-Mic Nights to Making the Most Sublimely Unsettling Show of the Year." *Vulture*, July 6, 2020. www.vulture.com.

Miller, Sam, dir. 2020. *I May Destroy You*. Season 1, episode 2, "Someone Is Lying." Aired June 9, 2020, on BBC One.

Miller, Sam, and Michael Coel, dir. 2020a. *I May Destroy You*. Season 1, episode 5, ". . . It Just Came Up." Aired June 22, 2020, on BBC One.

———. 2020b *I May Destroy You*. Season 1, episode 6, "The Alliance." Aired June 23, 2020, on BBC One.

———. 2020c. *I May Destroy You*. Season 1, episode 7, "Happy Animals." Aired June 29, 2020, on BBC One.

———. 2020d. *I May Destroy You*. Season 1, episode 8, "Line Spectrum Border." Aired June 30, 2020, on BBC One.

———. 2020e. *I May Destroy You*. Season 1, episode 11, "Would You Like to Know the Sex?" Aired June 23, 2020, on BBC One.

———. 2020f. *I May Destroy You*. Season 1, episode 12, "Ego Death." Aired July 14, 2020, on BBC One.

Norton, Russell, and Time Grant. 2008. "Rape Myth in True and False Rape Allegations." *Psychology, Crime & Law* 14 (4): 275–85. https://doi.org/10.1080/10683160701770286.

Ontiveros, Maria. 1993. "Three Perspectives on Workplace Harassment of Women of Color." *Golden Gate University Law Review* 23 (3): 817–28.

Paskin, Willa. 2020. "*I May Destroy You* Is about More than Consent." *Slate*, June 22, 2020. www.slate.com.

Patton, Tracey, and Julie Snyder-Yuly. 2007. "Any Four Black Men Will Do: Rape, Race, and the Ultimate Scapegoat." *Journal of Black Studies* 37 (6): 859–95.

Rumney, Philip. 2008. "Policing Male Rape and Sexual Assault." *Journal of Criminal Law* 72 (1): 67–86. https://doi.org/10.1350/jcla.2008.72.1.478.

St. Félix, Doreen. 2020. "Michaela Coel's Chaos and Charisma in 'I May Destroy You.'" *New Yorker*, June 29, 2020. www.newyorker.com.

Trott, Verity. 2021. "Networked Feminism: Counterpublics and the Intersectional Issues of #MeToo." *Feminist Media Studies* 21 (7): 1,125–42. https://doi.org/10.1080/14680777.2020.1718176.

Walfield, Scott. 2018. "'Men Cannot Be Raped': Correlates of Male Rape Myth Acceptance." *Journal of Interpersonal Violence* 36 (13–14): 6,391–417. https://doi.org/10.1177/0886260518817777.

10

"Na Tuttiya Ve"

Spiritual Activism and the #MeToo Movement in Pakistan

AYESHA KHURSHID

Coke Studio 2020, one of the most popular music shows in Pakistan, opened its special pandemic year season with a powerful homage to the suffering, anguish, and strength of everyday women in Pakistan. The song "Na Tuttiya Ve" (Unbroken) narrates the story of the wounded hearts and unbroken spirits of the resilient women for whom both home and street are devoid of love, recognition, and respect. "Na Tuttiya Ve" became an instant hit upon its release, garnering more than six million views on YouTube within one month. All the women singers of the show sang it. The most visible among this group of six singers was Meesha Shafi, a thirty-nine-year-old singer whose name has become synonymous with the #MeToo movement in Pakistan. Shafi, known for her powerful vocals, is considered one of the leading musicians in Pakistan. Hailing from a family of well-known artists and writers, Shafi is known for bringing her own distinct flair to folk, pop, and eastern classic music genres. This song was originally meant to be a solo performance by Shafi. However, she and Rohail Hyatt, the founder and producer of *Coke Studio*, decided to make it a "collective" voice of all women singers. Shafi's participation in the song included a rap segment, a relatively less common genre in the Pakistani music scene, especially for women singers. But Shafi lived up to her reputation of fusing disparate elements in her music.

In addition to her reputation as a musician, Shafi is also the face of the #MeToo movement in Pakistan. In 2018, Shafi came forward with allegations of sexual harassment against another popular singer and actor, Ali Zafar. She posted a statement on Twitter stating how she had been subjected to "sexual harassment of a physical nature on more than one occasion." She emphasized how it happened to her despite being an "empowered, accomplished woman" known for speaking her mind and "as a mother of two children." She called it a betrayal and "an extremely traumatic experience" inflicted by the person she had known and worked with for many years. By breaking this "culture of silence" that surrounds sexual harassment, Shafi wanted to set an example for youth, especially girls, in Pakistan to carve their own path in life. Zafar categorically and vehemently denied all these allegations in his social media posts as well as through the traditional media.

This chapter explores how and why one of the most prominent figures of the #MeToo movement in Pakistan has been demarcated in this manner. It explores the way that Shafi's rise to prominence as a feminist public figure raises questions about how and why have certain *modalities of self* have been embraced by the #MeToo movement whereas others have been rendered irrelevant. Why have the secular dimensions of Meesha Shafi's work been highlighted, while her spiritual expressions have been made invisible in relation to her status as a prominent #MeToo activist in Pakistan? In other words, how have certain presentations of feminist selfhood become intelligible (or not) under the umbrella of this new feminist movement that has gone truly global?

Shafi has engaged with #MeToo through pursuing her case in the Pakistani judicial system as well as through her music. On social media, Shafi identifies as a feminist and a cultural icon. Whereas her music does not explicitly mention feminism or the #MeToo movement, the themes of suffering, empowerment, and healing in her song lyrics have been dominant in her post-#MeToo activism. Her music seamlessly transcends the boundaries of two apparently different worlds, the political and the musical, as she has spoken about the exploitation and strength of women in both spheres. However, it is primarily her engagement with Pakistani legal institutions and her explicitly feminist public persona that have been understood by the public as being relevant to the #MeToo movement. Meanwhile, her musical expressions, like "Na Tuttiya Ve," remain invisible in relation to their potential contributions to the movement.

I argue that the exclusion of Shafi's nonsecular expressions from the Pakistani feminist movement are neither coincidental nor ahistorical. Shafi's musical expression, including "Na Tuttiya Ve" and some of her other post-#MeToo work, speaks of a vulnerable self that defies the cultural norms in her quest for love. In this modality of self, power comes from surrendering to a nonsecular power, referred to as *taqdeer* in "Na Tuttiya Ve," rather than to an institution. "Na Tuttiya Ve" presents women as formidable subjects, not merely for pursuing love against the patriarchal norms but also for surrendering to *taqdeer*, the higher power, as the true source of love. This spiritual love is a fluid dance of resistance and surrender, notions that stand in tension rather than in opposition to each other. This call for embracing vulnerability as strength echoes the Sufi thought (a spiritual tradition that Shafi draws on) that speaks of surrender to the Divine as the highest form of empowerment. The popular folk stories about Heer, Sassi, and Sohni mobilize the same themes of surrender and power. The vulnerable self that emerges in these narratives is neither a victim of nor separate from an empowered subjectivity. This nonseparation is also manifested by the women of "Na Tuttiya Ve," as they embrace even those who embody patriarchal norms while following their path of love.

Spiritual Activism: Healing the Split

The separation of religion from science and of spirituality from rationality has been central to the secular enlightenment projects that have shaped feminist movements all over the world (Mahmood 2005). Liberal feminist movements in North America mobilize these colonial imaginations in their expectations, for example, for Indigenous women to prioritize their gender identity over their Indigenous identity (Arvin, Tuck, and Morrill 2013). This split enables them to tie gender identity to feminist projects while positioning the "spiritual" Indigenous identity in the cultural realm. It is thus no surprise that even culturally transformative feminist movements like #MeToo are unable to recognize forms of activism that embrace thinking that goes beyond secular modes of self-making as a source of empowerment and healing. Gloria Anzaldúa (2012) as well as Anzaldúa's (2015) work with AnaLouise Keating calls the healing of such splits, through integration of activism and spirituality, a form of decolonization. Such integration constitutes "spiritual activism," a combination of traditional practices of spirituality (contemplation, meditation, and private rituals) with the technologies of political activism. Anzaldúa and Keating (2015, 19) argue that this split is a colonial wound that can be healed through "*conocimiento* (knowing action) [that] pushes us into engaging the spirit in confronting our social sickness with new tools and practices whose goal is to affect a shift. Spirit-in-the-world becomes conscious, and we become conscious of spirit in the world. The healing of our wounds results in transformation, and transformation results in the healing of our wounds." Anzaldúa's and Keating's notion of spirit transcends the categories and identities that govern our material reality. This notion of spiritual activism offers a path to radical transformation through acknowledging different modalities of power, such as the life force of earth and cosmos as science, which can shape different forms of self-making (Schaffer 2018). Using the metaphysics of interconnectedness, Anzaldúa's spiritual activism actively engages with modern institutions as potential spaces for transformation while acknowledging and recognizing their oppressive politics and practices. For instance, this spiritual activism is embodied in the peaceful collective action taken by Native people in North Dakota and many other places to resist the oil pipeline that is threatening to their beliefs, practices, and land (Schaffer 2018). This is a departure from secular feminist politics and thought that extensively focus on institutional reform as the key to gaining better gender representation in these institutions and to supporting socioeconomic transformation (Mahmood 2005). Such institutional reforms are meant to protect "vulnerable" victims through enabling them to claim rights and empowerment (Gilson 2016). The notion of vulnerability in Shafi's spiritual activism, however, is not equated with weakness, but rather presented as an ability to surrender to realities that might go beyond rational thinking. Whereas the contemporary #MeToo movement has been equated with speaking up and holding the perpetrators of sexual violence accountable, the desire for individual and collective healing has been foundational for the movement (Daily Show 2018; Roshanravan 2021).

I contend that Shafi has, intentionally or unintentionally, responded to Anzaldúa's call of spiritual activism by imploring modern institutions to "speak up" while surrendering to an invisible and nonsecular higher power. She transcends the boundaries of secular feminist thought and politics by simultaneously holding empowerment and vulnerability in tension as part of her identity. Shafi's integration of an empowered and accomplished self, which stands firm in the face of online trolling and legal setbacks, with a vulnerable self, which seeks healing through surrendering to a higher power, problematizes narrow understandings of vulnerability, victimhood, and empowerment.

#MeToo in Pakistan = Meesha Shafi

In Pakistan, a large number of women and some men responded to the global #MeToo movement by using social media to share their own experiences of facing sexual harassment. Shafi's became a landmark case for being the first, and one of the very few ones to date, in which a public figure accused another public figure of sexual harassment in a public forum. She received support for her courage but also faced intense backlash. The public reaction to these allegations was swift and strong. Social media forums exploded with people sharing their shock, disbelief, support, and critique of both Shafi and Zafar. Some social media users questioned how an "empowered" woman like Shafi could have allowed for such a thing to happen to her, whereas others called her choice of "revealing" clothing an invitation for such attention. "They [feminists in Pakistan] want their *azadi* [freedom] to be vulgar," was one of the responses to Shafi's post (Ali 2018). Another stated, "She is too bold of a person to let it happen firstly; and then do nothing to counter it" (Mansoor 2018). Others cast doubt on how a successful, young, and good-looking celebrity like Ali Zafar could do something like this. One comment, "[Ali Zafar] has never been scandalize[ed] throughout his career, so you must be damn sure about what you are saying about (a) superstar of pak(istan) [*sic*]," captures this sentiment (Abbas 2018).

The electronic media jumped on the issue and started covering all the details of the allegations in a sensational manner. Many TV channels used a picture of a smiling Shafi in a sleeveless fitted top with Zafar standing next to her with his arm around her waist. The image was meant to invoke the same questions about Shafi's morality, as reflected in her choice of what would be considered revealing clothing in Pakistan, and to invoke her consent, as she looked friendly and comfortable with Zafar. Shockingly, in 2020, the Pakistani state decided to confer the prestigious Pride of Performance award to Ali Zafar for his services in the field of art.

In addition to the media and public debates around this issue, Shafi and Zafar have filed their own legal cases against each other. Both of them have received some relief but have also faced setbacks as their cases are being tried in multiple courts and under complex laws. In 2010, the Pakistani state celebrated the passing of a law called the Protection Against Harassment of Women at the Workplace Act. This law makes sexual harassment at the workplace a punishable offense and includes provisions for protection against harassment. Such provisions include the institution of sexual harassment inquiry committees and the appointment of an ombudsperson at the federal and state levels who can oversee these inquiry committees as well as serve as an adjudicating agency. In 2018, Shafi filed a sexual harassment case against Zafar under this law. The case was rejected by the provincial ombudsman as well as by the provincial governor on technical grounds. Given that Shafi and Zafar did not have an employee-employer relationship, the ruling declared that the alleged harassment did not occur in what could be qualified as "the workplace." Shafi challenged this decision in the provincial high court to argue that her case could in fact be heard under this law. The Higher Court, however, also agreed with the previous ruling. Her partial victory came in January 2021 as the Supreme Court of Pakistan, the highest judicial authority in Pakistan, agreed to deliberate whether her case could indeed be heard under this law. Despite facing multiple losses, Shafi's litigation brought national attention to the vague definition of "workplace" in this law meant to protect women in the workplace.

Shafi versus Zafar also highlighted the clash of free speech and digital rights under another law called the Prevention of Electronic Crimes Bill (2015). In 2018, soon after Shafi made allegations against Zafar, Zafar's legal team used this new cybersecurity law to sue Shafi and a number of other women who had also used social media to raise similar allegations against Zafar for defamation. This is an ongoing case, but the majority of women withdrew their claims and issued unconditional apologies in order to avoid further litigation and possible heavy fines. This incident also brought public attention to the claims made by human rights activists about the sweeping powers that this controversial law had extended to the regulatory authorities to block any private information they deemed "illegal." The ongoing litigation between Shafi and Zafar thus became a site to apply and test the limits of these new laws meant to combat sexual harassment and protect digital rights.

Shafi's case became a rallying cry for the Aurat March (Women's March) first held in 2018 and then followed by marches in all the major cities of Pakistan in 2019, 2020, and 2021. The Aurat Marches have focused on a wide array of issues, such as gendered domestic labor, sexist employment practices, sexual harassment, and honor killings, among others. Despite fierce opposition from some extremist groups, as well as conservative sections of Pakistani society, the March events have attracted a large number of women from all backgrounds throughout the country. The backlash that Shafi faced for breaking the "culture of silence" seemed to have touched a nerve as *Mera jism meri marzi* (My body, my choice) became a popular and controversial slogan at the 2019, 2020, and 2021 Aurat Marches. Shafi's case has become a lightning rod as the organizers and participants have frequently cited her case as an example of what women have to endure for speaking up against sexual harassment. Shafi's case has thus shaped not only the #MeToo movement, but also the public, legal, and feminist discourses about women's bodies and rights in Pakistan.

It is not an overstatement to call Meesha Shafi one of the pioneers of the #MeToo movement and an emerging feminist icon in Pakistan. Shafi has emerged as an articulate, assertive, and unapologetic activist fighting her case on social media and other public forums, as well as through the bureaucratic legal system. She has made her individual fight public and collective. This pioneer status, however, is often not put in dialogue with another, and no less important, dimension of her identity. In November 2020, Shafi announced the upcoming release of her *Coke Studio* music by quoting the Quranic verse in Urdu, "beshak izzat denay wali zaat sirf Allah kee hai" (No doubt it is only Allah who can bestow honor on whomever He wills). In the face of constant scrutiny and abuse for her #MeToo activism, Shafi's participation in the prestigious music show was indeed a matter of celebration. She announced this "victory" by surrendering to what she called the will of Allah (Shafi 2020). This reference to religion and spirituality makes Shafi an unlikely icon for the conventional feminist movement in Pakistan.

Fiercely secular, the feminist movement emerged in response to the Islamization project initiated by the brutal military regime (1977–88) in Pakistan. This Islamization relied on targeting women through discriminatory laws as well as through strict moral and dress codes. Farida Shaheed (2019) calls the feminist movement state-focused, reactive, and adversarial, led primarily by a cohesive group of urban, educated, and middle-class women. Over time, the leaders and activists of this movement have become the face of feminism in Pakistan and continue to represent women and gender issues in national and international policymaking and media. Despite going through multiple transitions since the 1980s, this secular feminist movement continues to be guided by the liberal frameworks of institutional reforms to empower women and transform patriarchal structures. It is thus no surprise that Shafi's articulation of vulnerability as strength and her engagement with nonsecular higher power remains unintelligible within this feminist discourse.

It is, however, important to mention that though not widely recognized by the state or society, in recent times there has been a steady increase in the number of feminist groups that are more interested in self-expression and less occupied with institutional reforms, engagement with the state, or formation of a movement with cohesive leadership. Some of these groups engage in artistic endeavors like standup comedy or theater whereas others aim to create safe social spaces for women (Shaheed 2019). This newness has also been evident in the diverse participation in the Aurat Marches as well as the wide range of issues that the Aurat Marches have raised. However, despite this shifting landscape, the organizational, institutional, and social influence of the conventional feminist movement remains intact in terms of shaping public, policy, and media discourses about women's issues. The #MeToo movement in Pakistan, thus, remains a reflection of these complex dynamics that include on-the-ground diversity that is not fully captured or articulated by the leaders and activists of the conventional feminist movement. Shafi's work calls our attention to the need to acknowledge and embrace the forms of activism that stand outside the mainstream feminist focus of institutional reforms.

The Split: Shafi as Activist and Artist

Sufism, considered a mystical tradition within Islam, comprises heterogeneous groups and multiple traditions with origins in different regions of the world. The themes of universal love, healing, inclusion, and diversity are central to most of the Sufi traditions. The Sufi themes that echo in Shafi's music have been deeply influential for local music and art forms in Pakistan and are often employed by the state and other institutions to present to the world a "softer" image of Pakistan as a Muslim country. In fact, it was Qawwali, a Sufi musical genre, that effectively introduced South Asian Sufism to the West (Gaind-Krishnan 2020). These frameworks, however, are confined to the world of art and culture, and are not employed in legal, political, feminist, or other activist discourses to engage with issues such as sexual harassment, women's rights, or other political projects.

Creating spaces for Sufi themes within feminist political thought and projects can open new ways to engage with empowerment, healing, and transformation. For example, the Sufi mystics from the South Asian region preached how transcending class, religious, gender, and other social hierarchies was central to finding the true meaning of life. These Sufi traditions presented artistic genres such as music as an expression of the sacred journey of finding the Divine through finding self. The *dargahs* in different parts of Pakistan hold regular musical gatherings where devotional music and dance become a path for the participants to experience a different sense of self. These Sufi themes and practices position individual identity as impactful as well as dynamic and fluid. In this narrative, individual healing is conceptualized as becoming more intrinsically aware of one's connection not only to a higher power but also to all forms of life that surround us.

The integration of these themes within feminist politics and thought can facilitate more inclusive and dynamic modes of self-expression and establish dialogic and relational conversations with modern institutions. Shafi embodies this feminist politics by fully embracing the multidimensionality of her identity. She lends her full-throated support to the issues of choice and consent, through embracing the slogan *Mera jism, meri marzi*, that ask for cultural and social change as well as institutional reform. On the other hand, she also speaks of her submission to *taqdeer*, fate, and destiny in the *Coke Studio* song "Na Tuttiya Ve" as her path to healing. Similarly, Shafi's 2018 song "Leela" engages with the same themes, asking, "In whom do you believe? And what do you doubt? You are a timeless tale yourself." Expanding on these lyrics in an interview,

Shafi talked about how these questions explored the nature of human connection with the universe. The song narrated her conversation with the moon, the divine feminine, to seek healing. She shared how this song was meant to speak to and embrace all shades of her existence, including the outbursts, breakdowns, and gushes of love that she experiences.

"Mein hoon" (I am) was Shafi's first song that went viral after she came forward with the sexual harassment allegations. She performed it live at the music show sponsored by Pepsi Cola, Inc. The song, choreographed in a dream-like sequence, included the lyrics:

> *Dil sang-o-khist*
> *Pighlay tau iss*
> *Gardish-e-ishq se*
> [Stone cold heart
> Can melt only
> With the circumambulations of this love.]

> *Dard-e-firaaq*
> *Ghul ke yahaan*
> *Ban jaaye aaj hawaa*
> [If only the pain of separation
> Would dissolve here
> And turn to air.]

> *Mein raasta hoon*
> *Har jaga hoon*
> *La pataa hoon*
> [I am the path
> Everywhere
> And lost.] (Shafi 2018a)

This song speaks to the journey of finding self through being lost, and of melting into nothingness as the way to become one with everyone. This oneness is spoken as power, but the power that requires the courage to embrace the vulnerability of following the path of love without knowing the destination. This song offers a nonsecular framing of a self that seeks to end separation with the beloved or a higher power in order to receive healing. The vulnerability, thus, offers the power to see different selves and to heal them. Similarly, the song "Na Tuttiya Ve" imagines these women as the modern-day Heers, Sassis, Sohnis, and Lailas, the popular folklore characters who defied patriarchal norms in pursuit of their hearts' desires. These "daughters of Eve" demand not only respect, but also love from their partners, families, and societies as their divine inheritance. Their desire to dream and love makes them vulnerable subjects of the customs that demand their submission. But for Heer, Sassi, and Sohni, their vulnerability becomes their strength as they submit to the divine higher power, *taqdeer*, rather than to the rules of the world. Their vulnerability becomes a living embodiment of the unbroken spirit of love connecting them to all the souls that dared to love and dream. "Na Tuttiya Ve" represents vulnerability as true power as these women seek love from those who do not extend them any kindness. For instance, the song states, "I welcome and accept your family as mine. But I am also your family, this you should remember." While challenging patrilineal cultural norms where a wife is relegated to secondary status in the family, the desire for love in the song is emblematic of the transformation that the women are seeking within their families. Through centering love and positioning themselves as active seekers of this love, they embody both vulnerability and power. This song thus depicts vulnerability and power as notions that are tightly woven together rather than in opposition to each other. The song tells the stories of empowered and vulnerable women who seek love as their divine inheritance in the same world that has wounded their hearts. The women with unbroken hearts and mountain-like power submit to *taqdeer*, fate and destiny, to carve their own path. The self in this discourse refuses to surrender to social institutions or norms and instead finds love and healing in submitting to the higher power that constitutes but is not limited to the material realm.

By declaring "I've come to your home, my love, to share all the joys and sorrows, oh don't eat your bread alone, invite me to share it too," the women in "Na Tuttiya Ve" refuse to accept their inferior status in their husbands' families. As is customary, women are supposed to live with their husbands' families after getting married. In order to secure respect, rights, and acceptance within their "new" families, women are expected to sacrifice their needs and desires for the good of the family. The lyrics refer to the practice where women are supposed to eat after serving food to their husbands and the family, But the protagonist asks to eat with her husband, and not wait for him to finish his food, as a sign that the family loves and respects her. Here, the rejection of the patriarchal norms does not imply rejection of the people who enforce these oppressive customs, as they seek love from within and outside the very same families who uphold patriarchal ideals of femininity. This same vulnerability, however, also becomes their strength as it connects them to a higher power. Their trust in and surrender to this higher power, rather than to any institution, empowers them to continue their journeys toward collective healing. The collective voice of the established and new women singers narrating the pain, struggles, and power of women, as well as the cruelty of patriarchal families and norms, made it a powerful introduction to the show.

Ironically, a song with the potential of becoming a "feminist anthem" has become a commercial hit but has yet to be associated with the #MeToo movement that seems to have inspired it. Despite receiving critical and commercial acclaim, mainstream public and feminist discourses do not associate Shafi's music with the #MeToo movement. This is particularly intriguing as her art is heavily imbued with symbolic references to her #MeToo journey. Shafi moves between different spaces, social media, judicial activism, and musical expression, without always articulating her choices or explicitly connecting these different spaces that she inhabits. Her lack of naming these spaces as connected could be interpreted as her not wanting to upset the corporate sponsors of her music by making explicit references to her #MeToo activism. However, I view her selection of music and poetry and even the presentation of her music as reflections of her feminist activist work. "Na Tuttiya Ve" was originally meant to be her only solo performance for the annual season of this most anticipated music show. However, her willingness to invite the voices of all the women singers shows a commitment to collective healing and empowerment.

Concluding Thoughts

Meesha Shafi has emerged as a leading figure in the #MeToo movement in Pakistan. Her #MeToo activism has highlighted the possibility of a feminist self that can simultaneously hold vulnerability and empowerment on her journey to healing. Her journey has also brought to light the splits from within which the #MeToo movement has been operating in the postcolonial context of Pakistan. In its efforts to combat the brutal Islamization process initiated by the Pakistani state, the conventional feminist movement has created an outwardly driven feminist self that seeks to reform patriarchal institutions, laws, and policies to achieve gender empowerment. The overlooking of Shafi's musical expression in this feminist self-making is loud and clear.

The notion of spiritual activism, in this context, is not an opposite of a rational, secular, and liberal framing of empowerment. It is also not about turning away from modern institutions in order to develop an inward-looking feminist self. Instead, it proposes an active engagement with these institutions while contemplating their connectedness to forms of power and self-making that secular politics and thought might not be able to access. The newness of the #MeToo movement as well as the shifting feminist landscape in Pakistan can become productive grounds to generate a more holistic feminist thought and politics. Such feminist thought and politics would entail a continuous contemplation and reflection on feminist faith in secular thought. For example, the response to the state- and institution-focused agenda of secular feminism makes unintelligible the kinds of spiritual activism that I argue we can locate in Shafi's musicality.

If we center Tarana Burke's (Daily Show 2018) version of the #MeToo movement and center collective healing, we need to seriously engage with nonsecular modes of being and healing. Talking about healing as a goal of feminist thought, Anzaldúa and Keating (2015) offer insights into a conception of healing that emerges through the merging of individual and collective selves. It is only the multidimensional and vulnerable, and not the fixed self, that can enter into and receive empowerment and healing in this fluid world. A feminist embrace and active engagement with these expressions of self, even as they exceed what is knowable within feminist thought and politics, can decolonize the notions of empowerment and healing.

REFERENCES

Abbas, Nadeem (@Nadu805). 2018. "As @AliZafarsays has never been scadalise through his Career, so u must be damm sure about wht u r saying about superstar of Pak, and if he's done so than he must have explanations and ready to be charged as he let down his fans and nation being Role model of our youth." Twitter, April 19, 2018, 7:08 a.m. https://twitter.com/Nadu805/status/986924571533168640.

Adil, Hafsa. "Pakistan Top Court Moves to Hear #MeToo Case Against Singer Zafar." *Al Jazeera*, January 15, 2021. https://www.aljazeera.com.

Ali (@umIamAli). 2018. "Feminism in Pakistan is not about equal rights, they want something else, their azadi to be vulgur, to call man dogs while not doing their job properly except abusing and blaming feminist like you are shame for the nation without any evidence how could you do blame a celebrity." Twitter, April 19, 2018, 7:09 a.m. https://twitter.com/umIamAli/status/986924724801425408.

Anzaldúa, Gloria. 2012. *Borderlands/La Frontera: The New Mestiza.* 4th ed. San Francisco: Aunt Lute Books.

Anzaldúa, Gloria. 2015. *Light in the Dark = Luz en lo Oscuro: Rewriting Identity, Spirituality, Reality.* Edited by AnaLouise Keating. Latin America: Duke University Press.

Arvin, Maile, Eve Tuck, and Angie Morrill. 2013. "Decolonizing Feminism: Challenging Connections Between Settler Colonialism and Heteropatriarchy." *Feminist Formation* 25 (1): 8–34.

The Daily Show. "Tarana Burke on What Me Too is Really About." YouTube video, 00:09:16, June 4, 2018. https://www.youtube.com/watch?v=GfJ3bIAQOKg.

Gaind-Krishnan, Sonia. 2020. "Qawwali Routes: Notes on a Sufi Music's Transformation in Diaspora" *Religions* 11 (12): 685.

Gilson, Erinn Cuniff. 2016. "Vulnerability and Victimization: Rethinking Key Concepts in Feminist Discourses on Sexual Violence." *Signs* 42 (1): 71–98. https://doi.org/10.1086/686753.

Haider, Shuja, and Asim Raza. 2020. "Na Tutteya Ve." Translated by LyricsRagg. http://lyricsraag.com.

Keating, AnaLouise. 2013. *Transformation Now! Toward a Post-Oppositional Politics of Change.* Urbana: University of Illinois Press.

Lorde, Audre. 2007. *Sister Outsider: Essays and Speeches.* Berkeley, CA: Crossing Press.

Mahmood, Saba. 2005. *Politics of Piety: The Islamic Revival and the Feminist Subject.* Princeton, NJ: Princeton University Press.

Mansoor, Maliha (@malihamansoor1). 2018. "There something not so right (read convincing) here. She s too bold a person to let it happen firstly; and do nothing to counter the act secondly. I think both of em must ve been doped outa their minds wen it happened. Nothing abnormal in their class, btw." Twitter, April 19, 2018, 7:19 a.m. https://twitter.com/malihamansoor1/status/986927326926725120.

Roshanravan, Shireen. 2021. "On the Limits of Globalizing Black Feminist Commitments: 'Me Too' and its White Detours." *Feminist Formations* 33 (3): 239–55.

Schaffer, Felicity. 2018. "Spirit Matters: Gloria Anzaldúa's Cosmic Becoming Across Human/Nonhuman Borderlands." *Signs: Journal of Women in Culture and Society* 43 (5): 1005–29.

Shafi, Meesha. 2018a. "Mein." Translated in "Meesha Shafi's 'Mein' Is More Than Just a Pop Song," by Hasan Zaidi, *Dawn*, September 6, 2018. http://images.dawn.com.

———— (@itsmeeshashafi). 2018b. "Sharing this because I believe that by speaking out about my own experience of sexual harassment, I will . . ." Twitter, April 19, 2018, 6:45 a.m. https://twitter.com/itsmeeshashafi/status/986918710991519744.

———— (@itsmeeshashafi). 2019. "With a Sprinkle of Stardust, Meesha's 'Leela' is Ethereal Experience of a Timeless Tale." Interview by Haseem uz Zaman. *Geo TV News*, August 26, 2019. www.geo.tv.

———— (@itsmeeshashafi). 2020. "Beshak izzat denay wali zaat sirf Allah kee hai #RohailHyatt and I about to spin some musical magic together after a decade of #Jugni #ChoriChori #DashteTanhai and #IshqAapBhiAwalla on the platform that changed my life forever." Twitter, November 24, 2020, 12:30 a.m. https://twitter.com/itsmeeshashafi/status/1331107931883008000.

Shaheed, Farida. 2019 "Maintaining Momentum in Changing Circumstances: Challenges of the Women's Movement in Pakistan." *Journal of International Affairs* 72 (2): 159–172.

ACKNOWLEDGMENTS

CHAITANYA LAKKIMSETTI AND VANITA REDDY

This anthology began as a three-year seminar titled #MeToo and the Transnational Politics of Social Media Feminisms in 2019 at our home institution of Texas A&M University. Funded by the Melbern G. Glasscock Center for the Humanities, the seminar gathered feminist scholars from across the United States and Canada to read, discuss, and present works-in-progress on the political possibilities and limitations of #MeToo as a transnational feminist social movement and its role in addressing gender justice from a transnational feminist perspective. We would like to thank participants in this seminar—Landon Sadler, Vrushali Patil, Paulomi Roychowdhary, Sudeshna Chatterjee, Gloria Gonzalez-Lopez, Caitlin Carroll, Seon-Myung Yoo, Shireen Roshanravan, Ashley Currier, Emily Finbow, Jyotsna Vaid, and Victoria Millen—for reading and discussing critical feminist work that was instrumental in developing the framework for this anthology. We could not have embarked on this five-year journey without the support of the Glasscock Center, which not only offered us financial support but also provided physical space for us to have these conversations. We give special thanks to Dr. Emily Brady, Dr. Jessica Howell, and Amanda Dusek for their support of and excitement around the seminar and our project.

In addition to the three-year seminar, the Glasscock Center also provided each of us the opportunity to teach the Undergraduate Summer Scholars Program (Vanita in Summer 2020; Chaitanya in Summer 2021) on the topic of *MeToo and Transnational Gender Justice*. This intense summer seminar helped us to delve deeper into existing literature that engages this topic and some of its central concepts. We would like to thank our undergraduate students from this seminar—Megha Viswanath, Zoe Simmons, Nydia Gomez, Tanvi Deshpande, Marla Guerra, and Abigail Jablon—for engaging with the assigned readings, designing impactful public humanities projects addressing gender-based violence, and doing the hard work of writing honors theses.

Patti Duncan, editor-in-more than chief of *Feminist Formations*, enthusiastically supported our proposal for a special coedited dossier (Winter 2021) on the Transnational Feminist Politics of #MeToo. Patti's team, who included Miranda Findlay, Carina Tipton Buzo, and others, made the process of curating and editing the dossier as smooth and efficient as possible. We would also like to thank the contributors to the dossier: Ashley Currier, Hae Yeon Choo, Ayesha Khurshid, Shireen Roshanravan, Gloria González-López, Lydia Cordero Cabrera, Caitlin Carrol, Sudeshna Chatterjee, Erin Winchester, and Emily Chien. Ashwini Tambe offered encouragement and wrote an insightful afterword for the dossier. Without the intellectual labor of these feminist scholars, the dossier would not have been possible. We are also grateful to garima thakur for providing the cover art for the journal, and South Korean poet laureate Choi Young-Mi for allowing us to publish her poems as part of the dossier.

The #MeToo and Transnational Gender Justice symposium that we organized in February 2022 to celebrate the publication of the dossier further energized us to expand this work into a book. We are grateful to the participants in this symposium for their support and intellectual insights and to ramesh kathanadhi for designing the symposium flier. We would also like to thank Hae Yeon Choo for inviting us to participate in the #MeToo Asia seminar at the University of Toronto. This seminar helped us establish networks outside our own.

Our NYU Press editor Clara Platter was very enthusiastic when we pitched the idea of the anthology to her, and we thank her and the two anonymous reviewers who made this anthology a reality. Of course, this anthology would not have materialized without the work of our contributors: Ratna Kapur, Brenda Cossman, Ashwini Tambe, Barbara Sutton, Nadeen Shaker, Zeina Dowidar, Dinah Hannaford, Landon Sadler, Ayesha Khurshid, Hae Yeon Choo, and Sudeshna Chatterjee. Macy Dunklin provided important support during the final phase of submission by taking on the tedious labor of copyediting and formatting so that we could finalize the writing of our introduction. Other scholars who wanted to be part of the anthology but couldn't because of extenuating circumstances also provided initial enthusiasm and support. Special thanks to Manisha Desai for offering feedback on the introduction to the anthology.

We would also like to thank our colleagues and friends at Texas A&M University in Women's and Gender Studies and in the Departments of Sociology and English who have supported us throughout this journey: Kevin Barge, Jyotsna Vaid, Mary Campbell, Nancy Plankey-Videla, Theresa Morris, Maura Ives, and Emily Johansen.

The intellectual journey of this book overlaps with the height of the COVID-19 pandemic and the uncertainties and precarities that came with it, both personally and professionally. If not for the support of our loving families and friends we would not have been able to embark on this journey. Graham Stewart, Matt Daniel, Kylan Reddy, and Keanu Daniel provided unwavering love and support, and our nonhuman children, Kenzie and Wes, showered us with much-needed distraction, play, and silliness.

Vanita offers immeasurable thanks to Chaitanya for filling the multiple roles of feminist sister, colleague, and soulmate. Chaitanya not only took the lead in imagining this project, but also in its organization and logistics, which took shape over the course of my two pregnancies and the birth of my two children. Her patience, understanding, and quiet support—in the form of loving my children, encouraging us to stay on top of our deadlines, pushing me to think more precisely, and carrying the heavier load of intellectual and logistical labor when I simply could not provide my fair share—have been critical in seeing this book through to publication. I cannot think of anyone else whose sharpness, kindness, and joy matches hers—she brought all of these to this project. Her sisterhood means everything to me.

Chaitanya wants to thank Vanita for being her intellectual comrade and soul sister throughout this process. Vanita has humored me whenever I came up with ambitious ideas such as pitching the idea for an anthology in the midst of a pandemic and childbirth. She was a comrade in this long journey despite going through birthing and parenting during the challenging time of the COVID-19 pandemic; personal and family health challenges; and the everyday grind of childcare responsibilities. She never compromised on contributing to her share of work despite these time-consuming responsibilities. Without her intellectual sharpness, unwavering commitment, and feminist camaraderie none of this would have come to fruition. She is not only the most intellectually sharp person I have ever known but also the most humorous and adventurous. This collaboration not only is intellectually meaningful but also personally rewarding as I have established a forever bond with Vanita. I have also been given the honor of being *pedamma* to Kylan, Keanu, and Kenzie, who add immeasurable joy and spark to my life.

ABOUT THE CONTRIBUTORS

SUDESHNA CHATTERJEE is a scholar-practitioner in inclusive governance, human rights, and social justice. She currently serves as Director of Diversity, Equity, Inclusion & Justice (DEIJ) at Manomet, an environmental services nonprofit organization where she leads the development and implementation of organization-wide equity strategies that align with the organization's mission and vision. With over seven years of experience in the fields of higher education, community engagement, and change management, she serves on several racial justice networks in the Boston area such as YW Boston's Advocacy Committee and the Massachusetts Human Rights Coalition. Prior to joining Manomet in August 2023, she served as the inaugural Director of Equity and Social Justice for the Town of Reading in Massachusetts, where she established and coordinated the town's efforts to promote equity, diversity, inclusion, and justice across all municipal departments and community sectors. She holds a PhD in Global Governance & Human Security from the University of Massachusetts Boston and continues to be active in several academic organizations such as National Women's Studies Association and the International Studies Association. Some of Sudeshna's publications include "Consent Wars? Towards a Critical-Governmentality Approach to Consent in Post-Roe America," "Non-immigrant Precarity and the Corporate University: Rethinking Limitations of Critical Research and Reimagining Decolonial Possibilities," and "Gendering Precarity in Postcolonial Sites: Health Securitization and Sexual Labor in India's Commercial Sex Trade Industry."

HAE YEON CHOO is Associate Professor of Sociology at the University of Toronto. She is the author of *Decentering Citizenship: Gender, Labor, and Migrant Rights in South Korea*. Her research on gender, intersectionality, citizenship, and urban sociology has appeared in *Gender & Society*, *Sociological Theory*, *positions: asia critique*, *Urban Studies*, and *Sexualities*. Her current book project examines social activism in contemporary

South Korea as a site of emergent critical social theory and new political imagination. She has translated Audre Lorde's *Sister Outsider*, Patricia Hill Collins's *Black Feminist Thought*, and Grace Cho's *Tastes Like War* into Korean.

BRENDA COSSMAN is Goodman-Schipper Chair, Associate Dean of Research, and Professor of Law at the University of Toronto. She is a Fellow of the Royal Society of Canada. Her teaching and scholarly interests focus on the legal regulation of gender, sexuality and family. Her most recent book was *The New Sex Wars: Sexual Harm in the Age of #MeToo*. She is also the coeditor of *Enticements: Queer Legal Studies* with Joseph Fischel.

ZEINA DOWIDAR is an award-winning audio producer and the founder of Hekayyatna, an organization producing experiential story-telling podcasts and events. She has an MPhil in Development Studies from the University of Cambridge and works in the development sector. Her research interests include gender-based violence and postcolonial studies.

DINAH HANNAFORD is Associate Professor of Anthropology at the University of Houston. She is the author of *Aid and the Help: International Development and the Transnational Extraction of Care* and *Marriage Without Borders: Transnational Spouses in Neoliberal Senegal*. She is coeditor, with Joanna Davidson, of *Opting Out: Women Messing with Marriage Around the World*.

RATNA KAPUR is Global Law Chair, Queen Mary University of London; Faculty, Institute of Global Law and Policy, Harvard Law School; and Distinguished Visiting Faculty, Symbiosis School of Law, Pune. She teaches and publishes extensively on postcolonial and feminist legal theory, international law, and human rights, focusing on gender, sexual, and religious minorities. Her latest book is *Gender, Alterity and Human Rights: Freedom in a Fishbowl*.

AYESHA KHURSHID is Associate Professor of International and Comparative Education at Florida State University. She focuses on the issues of gender, culture, and education in Muslim communities. Her current ethnographic research examines gendered identity formation and performance in a Mayan Muslim community in Chiapas, Mexico, and in a rural Punjabi Muslim community in Pakistan.

CHAITANYA LAKKIMSETTI is Associate Professor of Sociology at Texas A&M University. She is the author of *Legalizing Sex: Sexual Minorities, AIDS, and Citizenship in India*. Her research and teaching interests are at the intersection of gender, sexuality, law, and social movements. She is the coeditor of the dossier *#MeToo and Transnational Gender Justice*. Her work at the intersections of gender, sexuality, law, and social movements also appeared in *Feminist Formations, Sexualities, Signs: Journal of Women in Culture and Society, positions: asia critique,* and *Qualitative Sociology.*

VANITA REDDY is Associate Professor of English at Texas A&M University, with a faculty affiliation in Women's and Gender Studies. She is the author of *Fashioning Diaspora: Beauty, Femininity, and South Asian American Culture*. Her research examines practices of cultural identity, belonging, and political community within the South Asian American and the global South Asian diaspora. She is the coeditor of a special issue of the *Scholar and Feminist Online*, "Queer and Feminist Afro-Asian Formations," and of a dossier *#MeToo and Transnational Gender Justice*. Her work at the intersections of race, gender, and diasporic cultural production has appeared in *Verge: Studies in Global Asias*, the *minnesota review*, the *Scholar and Feminist Online, Journal of Asian American Studies, meridians: feminism, race, transnationalism,* and *Contemporary Literature.*

LANDON SADLER (he/any pronouns) is Lecturer in English at Texas A&M University. He is in the process of adapting his dissertation "Time Will Tell: Dystopian Cultural Production and Queer Ethics of Care" into an academic monograph. His article "'If You Can't Love Yourself, How in the Hell You Gonna Love Somebody Else?': Care and Neoliberalism on *Queer Eye, RuPaul's Drag Race, and Pose*" is published in the *Journal of Popular Culture.*

NADEEN SHAKER is an award-winning journalist and podcast producer. Her areas of interest include regional and global policy, gender and feminist movements, and Middle Eastern histories.

BARBARA SUTTON is Professor and Chair of the Department of Women's, Gender, and Sexuality Studies at the University at Albany, SUNY. She is interested in body politics, multiple forms of violence, and intersecting inequalities, among other sociological issues. Her book *Bodies in Crisis: Culture, Violence, and Women's Resistance in Neoliberal Argentina* received the Gloria E. Anzaldúa Book Prize from the National Women's Studies Association. She is also the author of *Surviving State Terror: Women's Testimonies of Repression and Resistance in Argentina*, which received Honorable Mentions for the Distinguished Book Award by the American Sociological Association Sex & Gender Section and for the Marysa Navarro Book Prize by the New England Council of Latin American Studies. She coedited the book *Security Disarmed: Critical Perspectives on Gender, Race, and Militarization* with Sandra Morgen and Julie Novkov and *Abortion and Democracy: Contentious Body Politics in Argentina, Chile, and Uruguay* with Nayla Luz Vacarezza. Her most recent book is *Bulletproof Fashion: Security, Emotions, and the Fortress Body*.

ASHWINI TAMBE is Director of Women's, Gender, and Sexuality Studies (WGSS) and Professor of History and WGSS at George Washington University. She is a scholar of transnational South Asian history focused on the relationship between law, gender, and sexuality. She is also Editorial Director of *Feminist Studies*, the oldest journal of interdisciplinary feminist scholarship in the United States. Over the past two decades, she has written about how South Asian societies regulate sexual practices. Her book *Codes of Misconduct: Regulating Prostitution in Late Colonial Bombay* traces how law-making and law-enforcement practices shaped the rise of the city's red-light district. Her book *Defining Girlhood in India: A Transnational Approach to Sexual Maturity Laws* explores how the expectation of sexual innocence is distributed in uneven ways for girls across class and caste groups. Her book *Transnational Feminist Itineraries* (coedited with Millie Thayer) features essays by leading gender studies scholars confronting authoritarianism and religious and economic fundamentalism.

INDEX

Page numbers in italics indicate Figures.

www.ingramcontent.com/pod-product-compliance
Lightning Source LLC
Chambersburg PA
CBHW031534260326
41914CB00032B/1809/J